Strategic
Co-Teaching in Your School

Strategic
Co-Teaching in Your School
Using the Co-Design Model

by

Richael Barger-Anderson, Ed.D.

Robert S. Isherwood, Ed.D.

and

Joseph Merhaut, Ed.D.

Slippery Rock University
Slippery Rock, Pennsylvania

·P·A·U·L·H·
BROOKES
PUBLISHING CO.®

Baltimore • London • Sydney

Paul H. Brookes Publishing Co.
Post Office Box 10624
Baltimore, Maryland 21285-0624

www.brookespublishing.com

Typeset by Network Publishing Partners, Inc., Glenview, Illinois.
Manufactured in the United States of America by
Sheridan Books, Inc., Chelsea, Michigan.

Cover image © iStockphoto/mangostock. Clip art in Figures 3.1 and 14.1 © Jupiterimages Corporation.

The individuals described in this book are composites or real people whose situations are based on the authors' experiences. Real names and details are used by permission. In some instances, names and identifying details have been changed for confidentiality.

Library of Congress Cataloging-in-Publication Data

Barger-Anderson, Richael.
  Strategic co-teaching in your school : using the co-design model / by Richael Barger-Anderson, Ed.D.,
Robert S. Isherwood, Ed.D., and Joseph Merhaut, Ed.D., Slippery Rock University, Slippery Rock, Pennsylvania.
    pages   cm
  Includes bibliographical references and index.
  ISBN-13: 978-1-59857-166-0 (pbk.)
  ISBN-10: 1-59857-166-4 (pbk.)
  1. Teaching teams. 2. Classroom management. I. Title.

LB1029.T4B37 2013
371.14'8—dc23   2012042725

British Library Cataloguing in Publication data are available from the British Library.

2016   2015   2014   2013   2012

10   9   8   7   6   5   4   3   2   1

Contents

About the Authors

From left to right: Robert Isherwood, Richael Barger-Anderson, and Joseph Merhaut.

Richael Barger-Anderson, Ed.D., is an associate professor of special education at Slippery Rock University. She served as a special education teacher in the Moniteau and Union school districts in Pennsylvania for 7 years. She also served as adjunct faculty for Butler Community and Mt. Aloysius colleges in the psychology and early childhood departments. During her time in the public schools and currently at Slippery Rock University, she has written and executed several grants in the areas of inclusion and collaboration. She is the recipient of the 2009 Red Apple Award for Butler County, Pennsylvania. This award is presented annually by the United Way of Butler County to recognize one professor from Slippery Rock University for outstanding teacher quality and community involvement. Dr. Barger-Anderson lives in East Brady, Pennsylvania, with her husband, Philip, and two sons, Luke and Levi Anderson.

Robert S. Isherwood, Ed.D., is an associate professor of special education at Slippery Rock University. He also teaches in the Special Education Supervisory Program at Slippery Rock University and holds the position of Graduate Coordinator. He was a special education teacher in the Elizabeth Forward and Highlands school districts in Pennsylvania for 8 years and an elementary school principal in the Leechburg Area and Plum Borough school districts, also in Pennsylvania, for 6 years. Dr. Isherwood has served as a member of the Butler Area School District Board of Directors in Pennsylvania. He is the recipient of the 2008 Red Apple Award for Butler County, Pennsylvania. He lives in Butler, Pennsylvania, with his wife, Kelly, and daughter Teddi.

Joseph Merhaut, Ed.D., is an associate professor of special education at Slippery Rock University and Chairman of the Department of Special Education. He was a special education teacher in public schools in Pennsylvania for 8 years and a high school assistant principal and principal in the Mars and Hampton Township School Districts in Pennsylvania for 8 years. Dr. Merhaut served as a hearing officer for the Office for Dispute Resolution in the Pennsylvania Department of Education. He also served as a school board member in the Pine Richland School District in Pennsylvania and as President of the Pine Richland School Board for 1 year during the 4-year term. Dr. Merhaut was the 2009 recipient of the President's Award for Excellence in Teaching for Slippery Rock University. He and his wife, Rhonda, are the parents of three teenage daughters: Madison, Molly, and Myah. He and his family reside in Gibsonia, Pennsylvania.

Foreword

Public education in America has evolved rapidly since 2001, the year that marked the passage of the No Child Left Behind (NCLB) Act of 2001 (PL 107-110). This legislation has transformed public education faster than any other reform movement, and its impact has been far reaching. From increased assessments, to mastery learning for proficiency, to requirements for highly qualified teachers and staff, NCLB has changed the landscape of teaching and learning. In many schools, the students most affected by NCLB are those identified to receive special education services.

In the 1970s and 1980s, self-contained classrooms for special education were thought to meet the needs of many students identified as exceptional. Students identified with special needs would participate in homeroom or the classroom opening exercises and then be whisked away for their instruction. Until this set of students had lunch or recess or packed their book bags for the day, they were nearly invisible to other students or teachers.

Many schools currently have self-contained classrooms, but the atmosphere is one characterized by flexibility and inclusiveness. The door to these types of classrooms is no longer shut but revolving, allowing students with special needs to participate, to the maximum extent appropriate, in general education programs and classes.

Parents, teachers, and administrators still struggle with defining what each child needs and which general education classes will be beneficial. As an administrator who has attended hundreds of individualized education program meetings, I have asked teams of teachers, parents, and advocates to reflect on a plethora of questions: Is this course appropriate? Will the adaptations be enough? Will the student feel awkward if he or she is not able to do the same activities as the other students? I honestly thought that I facilitated these conversations well until my nephew was diagnosed with a disability. My outlook and approach to serving children with special needs completely changed.

Through proficiency requirements from NCLB, co-teaching, inclusive education, and a belief that every child can benefit in some way from the general classroom, my nephew is growing and developing as a learner and young boy. There is no magical classroom titled learning support that has made the difference. His success at school can be attributed to access to the general education curriculum, appropriate supports, a collaborative team approach, and specific pull-out classes that address his language and socialization needs.

Collaboration and communication among school personnel are positive outcomes of NCLB and are critical to successful co-teaching practices. In addition, our students identified with special needs are now included in general classrooms with the supports necessary to allow them to be successful. The result for my nephew and for the thousands of students my districts have served is greater mastery of learning, increased socialization, and greater acceptance by others. Unlike businesses, which can be selective about their raw materials, public education in America accepts *all* students.

These successes in public education would not have been possible without professional development for staff and a commitment from school leaders who have agreed to serve students with special needs in an inclusive setting. This book can guide educators in how they can provide an appropriate education for the diverse learners that are in their classrooms.

The authors, Bob, Richael, and Joe, have worked in my district and have helped transform our program, staff, and classrooms into an inclusive, welcoming educational setting that supports success for all students. Implementing collaborative practices via the Co-Design Model works. It takes time to make it appear easy and seamless, but by following the recommendations found in this book and addressing proactively the concerns that accompany co-teaching and other collaborative challenges, your classroom or school can become an inclusive setting that embraces all children at all ability levels.

Our children have one opportunity to get the best education that meets their needs. Most students can achieve and thrive in a variety of settings. But for students with special needs, each instructional moment is precious. The Co-Design Model provides maximum supports for student growth and development. I encourage the reader to embrace this book, collaborative practices that go beyond the Co-Teaching Model, and the students who benefit from these recommended practices.

Michelle Miller, Ed.D.
Superintendent
Blackhawk School District
Beaver Falls, Pennsylvania

Preface

If you have been told to this read this manual (by either your professor or your administrator), you may be asking yourself, "Why do I need *another* training guide?"

We, the authors, hope that you have chosen to read this manual of your own accord because you think it will enhance the teaching methodology you currently embrace. However, we know that free time for teachers is scarce, and the reason you are reading this book doesn't matter; *the important thing is that you are reading it!* So, whether you are a beginning or veteran teacher; an early childhood, middle, secondary, general, or special educator; or a paraprofessional or administrator, the purpose of this manual is to promote collaborative, research-based practices via the Co-Design Model. The Co-Design Model may be implemented in your classroom, grade level, building, and district through preservice teacher training and professional development. Continuous and ongoing support for faculty is endorsed. The Co-Design Model promotes collaborative education in inclusive learning environments for all levels of learners. We hope you find this book exciting, motivating, practical, and most of all *successful* for *all* of your students!

When we started providing professional development for school districts on the implementation of co-teaching, we had no idea that our program would continue to evolve and become of interest to such a wide audience. The three of us serve as professors in the Department of Special Education at Slippery Rock University. This book is the product of our work and research conducted in school systems over several years in the areas of inclusion, co-teaching, collaboration, and compliance. The collaborative approach to education that is promoted in this manual is the *Co-Design Model,* a term we coined. The Co-Design Model has been presented at various international, national, state, and local conferences. Several journal publications that showcase our work are in circulation as well. Because of the wide acceptance and implementation of the model, we wanted to formally document the model's elements and pathways.

This book is intended for use by teachers at all grade levels and with any level of experience, content specialists in all curriculum areas, and many other professionals in the educational system, such as instructional coaches, reading specialists, physical and occupational therapists, nurses, and speech and language therapists. The book is also of interest to paraprofessionals and administrators, both at building and district levels.

Section I of this book includes two chapters. Chapter 1 serves as a foundation that briefly highlights the history of special education. This is information that all readers of this book should be familiar with. For some, it will be an introduction to the material; to others, it might be a refresher. Chapter 1 also includes information on specific disabilities, prevalence rates, and instructional considerations that may be beneficial for partners in a collaborative environment. Chapter 2 provides a look at inclusion, important court cases, and other issues that affect classrooms and influence practices within a school system.

Section II introduces and explains the Co-Design Model. This model comprises nine essential elements for promoting a collaborative approach to education. Along with these nine elements, there are four pathways for instructional implementation.

These pathways for instruction are techniques that have been proven in the classroom and are presented as recommended practices.

The nine essential elements are 1) leadership; 2) assembly of site; 3) curriculum knowledge; 4) co-instruction; 5) classroom management; 6) adaptations, accommodations, and modifications; 7) assessment; 8) personality types; and 9) co-design time. Specific examples are provided to help you implement the Co-Design Model in your own classroom or building. These chapters reference a series of forms that were devised specifically to support implementation of the Co-Design Model. Completed example forms are given in the chapters as models, and blank, reproducible versions are given in the appendix for use in the classroom.

The remainder of Section II discusses the four pathways for instruction: co-teaching, differentiated instruction, technology, and scaffolding. These four strategies have been shown to be effective again and again in the professional literature. The chapters on the pathways for implementation offer specific examples to help you execute the Co-Design Model to promote collaborative practices, no matter what the grade level, content area, or experience of the collaborative partners. As with the elements, forms have been developed to correspond to the pathways, and both completed examples and blank reproducible copies are provided.

Section III of the manual includes two chapters. Chapter 17 considers training and professional development opportunities for faculty, staff, administration, and preservice teachers. It examines the ongoing need for these services, as well as cost concerns for the district. The final chapter of the book addresses measuring a school's success with the implementation of the Co-Design Model. As with any school initiative, it is necessary to ensure the quality and commitment of the program.

As noted previously, an appendix with reproducible forms is included. An annotated bibliography also is provided to help you locate more information in areas of specific disabilities and topics.

You have probably noticed that preservice teachers are included in the audience for this book. We promote the model in both our undergraduate and graduate classes in the College of Education. In fact, Slippery Rock University hosts a workshop, open to all education majors, that promotes the student teacher and host teacher as co-teachers. This approach dovetails with our message and complements our in-district training. So, our training on collaborative education is not limited to special education majors; all education majors at our university and their host teachers have an opportunity to learn from our approach and research.

To explain the evolution of our work, we will tell our story from the beginning. Our initial efforts began in 2003 with a $10,000 grant through Temple University and the Inclusion Initiative for Higher Education. We approached the Karns City Area School District (a small, rural school district in western Pennsylvania) about serving as the host school for the professional development. The average graduating class is approximately 119. The rate for free and reduced-price lunches in the 2012–2013 school year is more than 40%.

The teachers and administrators of Karns City graciously agreed to allow the stipulations of the grant to be implemented at the Junior Senior High School. The grant provided for a research study that included seven special education and seven general education teachers at the high school level. We provided a total of 4 hours of training for these teachers on co-teaching in an inclusive setting. Focus-group interviews were also conducted with the teachers before and after the training.

The response by the teachers to the training on co-teaching and inclusion was overwhelmingly positive. The consensus of the participants was that more teachers in the district needed this training. During the following summer, the school district offered the training to teachers on a voluntary basis. About 30 faculty members attended this summer training. These teachers felt the training should be received by all faculty members in the district. We were asked to provide additional professional development to the entire district during the 2004–2005 school year. This district has received two national awards: Sugarcreek Elementary was named a U.S. Department of Education Blue Ribbon School in 2009–2010, and the high school first won a bronze rating in 2009–2010 in *U.S. News and World Report*'s Best High Schools rankings.

Over time, we have elaborated and expanded our training topics and sessions. For example, with the assistance of Dr. Monique Mawhinney, Director of Pupil Services for Hampton Township School District (HTSD), we began classroom observations with preobservation and postobservation debriefing sessions in this district. We have completed these visits at the elementary, middle, and high school levels. HTSD is located in western Pennsylvania, approximately 20 miles north of Pittsburgh. Although HTSD is a relatively small school district, with graduating classes of roughly 150 students, it has a larger-than-life reputation in Pennsylvania. With state assessment scores that routinely place it as one of the top five school districts in Pennsylvania, HTSD also has earned national recognition as an outstanding school district. The administration and school board of this district has a deep commitment to professional development.

We also value the collaborative relationship we have established with the Blackhawk School District. Shortly after we began our work with Hampton Township, we met a Blackhawk teacher in one of our graduate courses at Slippery Rock University. She mentioned our work with Hampton Township and Karns City to the Blackhawk administration. Since then, we have provided professional development and consultations to the co-teachers of the district for more than 5 years. Because of the progressive attitude of the teachers and administrators there, the Blackhawk School District is making great strides with efforts to increase levels of inclusive education.

Through word of mouth and presentations at state and national conferences, our involvement with other districts continued to grow. In an evolutionary process, we arrived at the qualities and concepts of education highlighted in this book. At an early point in our work to deliver training, we began to conceptualize the Co-Design Model for promoting collaborative and inclusive education. It is a flexible model that can meet the individual needs of teachers and students in each district and at every building and grade level.

In January 2007, we formalized our consulting efforts and established Keystone Educational Consulting Group, LLC (KECG). The group comprises more than 30 education and legal professionals dedicated to providing professional development and related services to school districts and other educational entities. KECG has trained and provided support to more than 60 such clients in Pennsylvania, Texas, Iowa, and the U.S. Virgin Islands, including public and parochial schools, correctional facilities, alternative educational placements, and an Intermediate Unit (Allegheny Intermediate Unit 3 of Pennsylvania). The consultants present their work at conferences and in journal articles, and a web site (http://www.keystone-educational.com) provides resource materials, contact information, and more for teachers, preservice teachers, and administrators.

Many school districts that use this training model credit the initiative for augmenting levels of inclusiveness in classrooms and raising achievement scores, as reflected in the following comments we have received in personal communications to KECG. One special education director wrote,

Last year we were placed on tier 2, which placed us in approximately the bottom 10% of school districts in the state on the LRE [Least Restrictive Environment] Index. The LRE Index results for 2009–2010 have been released. I am pleased to announce that we have progressed from tier 2 to tier 3!

A specialist of Intermediate Unit (IU) 28 in Pennsylvania writes,

I was at a Procedural Safeguards meeting at ARIN [ARmstrong and INdiana] counties IU 28 this morning and it sounded like every school district represented was working with your consulting group! They were all raving about how well the program is received and how it has helped teachers and instructional assistants.

Paul Kasunich, superintendent of Trinity School District in Washington, Pennsylvania, and former superintendent of the Blackhawk School District of Pennsylvania wrote,

The Blackhawk School District has been in partnership with the Keystone Educational Consulting Group for 4 years. These professionals have been involved in training, consulting, and observing teaching staff and paraprofessionals at all grade levels. They have provided numerous resources, technological assistance and instructional strategies which proved invaluable. These strategies have had a positive impact on student engagement, a decrease in behavior issues as well as enhanced teacher performance in implementing differentiated instruction and co-teaching models. As a result, students have demonstrated an increase in class participation, work completion, personal confidence and the district has observed a gradual improvement in PSSA [Pennsylvania System of School Assessment] scores.

Christopher Stone, former principal of David E. Williams Middle School of the Montour School District located in Coraopolis, Pennsylvania, attested,

Because of the training and professional development provided by this group, nearly 90% of our children with special needs are receiving their instruction in the general education classrooms. Without reservations, I would highly recommend the Keystone consultants to any school district that is interested in providing "realistic" training for teachers in the area of inclusionary practices.

Success for students in the classroom is our ultimate goal. Testimonials from teachers and administrators that attribute our training to help achieving results are quite a compliment. It gives us the motivation and inspiration to continue our research and work in the field. We take pride in our efforts with districts and try not to forget how hard it is to be in the classroom and meet all of the pressures felt by school administrators and faculty members.

We hope you enjoy reading this book. Whatever your role or grade level or content expertise, we hope the ideas presented here inspire you to promote successful, inclusive, and collaborative education that benefits all learners.

Acknowledgments

The authors would like to recognize the Blackhawk, Hampton Township, and Karns City Area school districts in Pennsylvania. It was in these three districts that the Co-Design Model got its start. Also, we extend special thanks to several of our Slippery Rock University students: Kaleigh Hoover, Laura Kepple, Jessica Nichols, and Alyssa Williams. Finally, the authors would like to recognize the support and dedication offered by Steve Plocher and Rebecca Lazo of Paul H. Brookes Publishing Co.

To our children:

Luke and Levi Anderson

Teddi Isherwood

Madison, Molly, and Myah Merhaut

SECTION I

Foundation

CHAPTER 1

Brief Overview of Special Education

When I first walked through the imposing doors of the large brick building known as the nursery, my senses were assailed by the brilliant white of the nurses' stiff uniforms, the echoing sounds of distressful voices, and the odor of antiseptic cleaners, all of which intensified my awareness of the overwhelming task ahead. Seeking employment at a state school and hospital for people with disabilities in the early part of the 1970s began as a means to finance my college education, but it was to be the beginning of a lifelong journey in the field of special education.

Totally ignorant as to what constituted a disability, I simply began my soon-to-be career by performing needed and sometimes life-sustaining tasks for individuals with intensive and pervasive needs who were engaged in a behavior modification program. My work consisted of arriving at 4:30 a.m. to awaken the residents of Ward E, and then assisting another employee in the bathing, dressing, feeding, and toileting of all individuals included in the program. The afternoon consisted of providing lunch, additional bathroom assistance, and toothbrushing, with the residents' day ending at 6:00 p.m., when they were placed in dormitory beds for the night.

A few of the residents were provided with individual attention by the permanent employees, but the majority of the residents—approximately 60–80 per ward—spent their days in one large common area of the building. In retrospect, I remember that only a few objects or toys were shared by these residents, with most of their days being spent in repetitive behaviors such as perseverating with string, twirling in circles, or rocking in place while repeating their haunting mantras. There was no music, television, or other stimulation except on days when some residents were permitted to spend time in the enclosed area outside. I vividly remember the blank looks on their faces as they stood for hours holding on to the wrought iron fence that defined the parameters of their narrow world.

The school and hospital were situated on many acres of land that included facilities that made the institution virtually self-sufficient, providing all of the foods and milk products needed to keep it functioning. Many of the adult residents spent their days working inside the many dormitories and wards, the cafeterias, and the laundry, as well as outside assisting in the fields and barn areas. The residents who assisted us in the nursery were proud of the work they did and the sense of purpose it gave them. I realize now that some parts of the residents' institutional lives were purposeful and fulfilling; however, for the majority, life was lived in limbo. Sadly, even the grave markers of many of the deceased residents contained only a number on a small circle of metal to mark the area in which they were buried.

It was only after I left this summer employment that I began to understand the need for change in these institutions and the need to respect every human life by offering individuals with disabilities the opportunity for a life of quality as opposed to endless days and nights blurred into an aimless period of time. Nevertheless, because the residents' transition away from this confinement was filled with difficulties and mistakes, the professionals of this new era wrestled with the rights and wrongs of their decisions regarding the residents' needs. Hence, as professionals in the 21st century continue to work in the field of disabilities, many of these past failures persist, but sentencing others to a life in limbo does not appear to be one of them.

By M. Rebecca Badgett, Associate Professor of Special Education
at Slippery Rock University

Understanding the past, present, and future of special education begins with realizing the depths from which the field has developed. Through examination of the former treatment of people with disabilities, it is clear that progress has been made. Yet, as educators in the early 21st century face the challenges of standardized testing, inclusion, mandatory state and federal standards, and more, it is clear that the journey toward the improvement of education for individuals with disabilities is far from over. It is also evident from the prevalence rates of disabilities in inclusive classrooms that the nation's schools are heterogeneously comprised as never before (Friend, 2011). Bryant, Smith, and Bryant (2008) report that the number of students with disabilities receiving instruction in pull-out programs, such as a resource room, is dwindling. In the past, the majority of students who received special education were serviced primarily in a pull-out setting. The most recent statistics from the U.S. Department of Education, National Center for Education Statistics (2011) show that 95% of all students served under the Individuals with Disabilities Education Improvement Act (IDEA) of 2004 (PL 108-446) attend their regular school district, with 58% of the population in the general education classroom for some instruction during the day and 13% of students with multiple disabilities spending more than 50% of their day in the general education classroom.

HISTORY OF SPECIAL EDUCATION: 16TH–19TH CENTURIES

Before and during the 19th century, the care of individuals with disabilities was often cruel (Taylor, Smiley, & Richards, 2009). Rosenberg, Westling, and McLeskey (2008) state that during this time period individuals with disabilities were believed to be a lost cause. In other words, society believed that they could not be helped through any type of intervention. Many people during this time felt that a person with a disability, and possibly even his or her family, was somehow being punished. Murdick, Gartin, and Crabtree (2006, as cited in Heward, 2009) note that children with disabilities were frequently excluded from public education programs. In fact, this practice continued well into the 20th century: Before the 1970s, many states even enforced laws to prohibit enrollment of some students with disabilities in public education.

However, one of the first documented positive attempts to educate people with disabilities occurred near the end of the 16th century in Spain (Winzer, 1998, as cited in Rosenberg et al., 2008). Pedro Ponce de Leon, a Benedictine monk, taught affluent boys who were deaf the letters of the alphabet with some success. Since that time, despite many setbacks, there have been more success stories and advantageous strides toward the treatment and education of individuals with many types of disabilities. These positive events and reforms that were centered in the best interests of educating students with disabilities are momentous and need to be celebrated, because they have helped pave the way for the gains made thus far in education (Rosenberg et al., 2008).

Reformers who made great achievements in the education of people with disabilities in the 19th and early 20th centuries include Samuel Howe, Dorothea Dix, Horace Mann, and Elizabeth Farrell. Their accomplishments are outlined in Table 1.1. These reformers and many others throughout history have contributed to the progress made in the area of improving education for individuals with disabilities.

SPECIAL EDUCATION IN THE 20TH CENTURY

At the beginning of the 20th century, more and more advances were being made for improving the education and treatment of people with disabilities; however, there were some obstructions as well. One of the major accomplishments during this period was the release of Helen Keller's autobiography, entitled *The Story of My Life*, in 1905. Helen Keller was the first person who was both deaf and blind to be admitted to college.

Unfortunately, not every landmark event in that period was as positive. The publication in 1912 of *The Kallikak Family: A Study in the Heredity of Feeble-mindedness*

Table 1.1. Contributions of Samuel Howe, Dorothea Dix, Horace Mann, and Elizabeth Farrell to the field of educating people with disabilities

Samuel Howe

Graduate of Harvard Medical School (1824)

Created the Perkins Institution and Massachusetts School for the Blind (now known as Perkins School for the Blind) in 1832

Hired Laura Bridgman (the first deafblind person to be educated) as a teacher at the institute

Dorothea Dix

Opened "a little dame school" (a school for girls only) in 1816; at this time, girls were not permitted to attend public schools

Played a major role in the creation of 32 mental hospitals

Best known for her work with people who were incarcerated or living in poorhouses in the United States

Helped establish libraries in prisons and mental hospitals

Was influential in European care for people with mental illness in 1854–1856

Served as Superintendent of Union Army nurses in the Civil War

Horace Mann

Known as the "Father of the Common School"

As Secretary of the Massachusetts Board of Education in 1837, ensured that local taxes would provide a basic education for every child

Was instrumental in establishing the first Normal Schools in Massachusetts for teacher training (1838)

Fought for the recruitment of women teachers

Elizabeth Farrell

Started the first classes in public schools for students with disabilities in New York City (1900)

Had insightful ideas in the areas of referral processes for special education and inclusion of students with disabilities in general education classrooms

Taught the first university-level courses for special education teacher preparation at the University of Pennsylvania (1912)

Advocated for the creation of professional organizations for special education teachers

Was a founder and first President of the Council for Exceptional Children

Sources: "Dorothea Dix" (2005); "Elizabeth E. Farrell" (1981); Encyclopædia Britannica (2010); Pinto and Levin (2000); Rosenberg, Westling, and McLeskey (2008); Smith and Tyler (2010); and Viney and Zorich (1982).

by H.H. Goddard was a negative incident that contributed to the exploitation of individuals with disabilities. In this book, the author claimed that heredity was the origin of intellectual disabilities and criminality. The scientific facts for this conclusion were based on a case study that he conducted. Goddard, along with other eugenicists, promoted sterilization of criminals and of adults with intellectual capacities of less than 12 years old (Rosenberg et al., 2008; Smith & Tyler, 2010).

A triumph in the history of special education was the establishment of the Council for Exceptional Children (CEC) in 1922 (Rosenberg et al., 2008). Since its inception, CEC has expanded to become the largest international membership organization for professionals dedicated to promoting improvements in the education of students with disabilities and/or giftedness. CEC actively participates in providing professional development services for special educators, setting professional standards, and serving as an advocate for government policies that are fair and appropriate for students with disabilities (CEC, 2010).

The creation of United Cerebral Palsy (UCP) was another landmark event for the promotion of people with disabilities in the 20th century (Rosenberg et al., 2008). This national organization was founded in 1949 and has grown to be one of the leading health-related charities in America. UCP strives to promote independence and participation in the community, work force, and school settings. More than 170,000 children and adults with disabilities and their families receive services from UCP. These services include help with employment, housing assistance, early intervention, and more (UCP, 2010).

Civil Rights and Special Education

The Civil Rights movement for racial equality in the 1950s and 1960s had a positive impact on the field of special education (Fleischer & Zames, 2001, as cited in Friend & Bursuck, 2008). The U.S. Supreme Court's *Brown v. Board of Education* (1954) decision established that it is unlawful under the 14th Amendment to discriminate arbitrarily against any group of people. By the 1960s, parents and advocates started using this court decision to ensure that the rights of students with disabilities were protected (Friend & Bursuck, 2008; Smith & Tyler, 2010).

The Education for All Handicapped Children Act of 1975 (PL 94-142) was signed into law in November 1975. Provisions for improved education of all children were the purpose of this legislation. The six major mandates of the original law—zero reject, least restrictive environment, nondiscriminatory identification and evaluation, individualized education program, due process, and parental participation—have remained consistent throughout the amendments made since its initial passage and continue to have an impact on education. The Individuals with Disabilities Education Improvement Act (IDEA) of 2004 (PL 108-446) is the most recent amendment (Friend & Bursuck, 2008; Salend, 2008). Understanding how the courts have influenced and helped to shape special education is essential. Influential court cases, federal legislation, and the reauthorization of IDEA are discussed in more detail in Chapter 2.

DISABILITIES AND PREVALENCE RATES IN THE EARLY 21ST CENTURY

People with disabilities once were prevented from partaking in and fully participating in educational services provided to their peers who were without disabilities. Derogatory terms were applied to individuals with intellectual, physical, and behavioral disabilities. As of the beginning of the 21st century, individuals with disabilities continue to be labeled and classified but with different, more positive designations. The intent of these revised labels is to identify individuals for eligibility to receive special education and related services (Heward, 2009). Because of the increased inclusion of students with disabilities in general education classrooms, it is important for educators to have an understanding of various types of disabilities, their prevalence rates in schools, and implications for the instruction of students with these disabilities.

It is not the purpose of this book to describe all disabilities. However, during professional development programs for the Co-Design Model (see Chapter 3), audiences have asked for information on the disabilities most commonly seen in inclusive classrooms. The professional development audiences include preservice teachers, beginning and veteran teachers, general and special educators, speech and language therapists, physical and occupational therapists, physical education teachers, technology specialists, art and music teachers, paraprofessionals, early childhood to secondary teachers, and administrators at every level.

The disabilities we have chosen to describe were selected on the basis of the most frequent requests from the Co-Design Model audiences. It is not our intention to exclude any type of disability, whether it be categorized as a high-incidence, low-incidence, physical, or intellectual disability. The annotated bibliography at the end of the book provides lists of sources with more information about a wide range of disabilities, their prevalence rates, and instructional considerations.

Some of the most commonly seen disabilities include specific learning disabilities (SLDs), attention-deficit/hyperactivity disorder (ADHD), autism spectrum disorders (ASDs), mild intellectual disabilities, and emotional or behavior disorders. Smith and Tyler define the term *disability* as "result of conditions or impairments" (2010, p. 5). Section 504 of the Rehabilitation Act of 1973 (PL 93-112) provides a more general definition of the term as "a physical or mental impairment which substantially limits one or more major life activities" (as cited in Office for Civil Rights [OCR], 2006, p. 1). These activities include walking, seeing, hearing, and learning (OCR, 2006).

It is likely that most teachers have encountered or will encounter a student with at least one of these disabilities. Therefore, understanding these disabilities is imperative if teachers are to provide an appropriate education to these students as well as to all of the students in the class (Barger-Anderson, Isherwood, Merhaut, & Hoover, 2010). Table 1.2 presents a concise overview of information on these disabilities, including descriptions, examples of instructional suggestions, and prevalence rates.

Specific Learning Disabilities

A child who is identified as having an SLD is recognized as having one of the most commonly labeled disabilities in schools. Statistics indicate that an average of 4% of the school-age population is identified as having a learning disability. A 2007 report from the Office of Special Education and Rehabilitative Services showed that 45.3% of students with disabilities between the ages of 6 and 21 had a diagnosed learning disability—that is, about 4% of school children (as cited in Heward, 2009). SLDs include any disorder that impedes a person's ability to understand or process language. The definition for SLD was redefined in IDEA 2004, which states,

> The term specific learning disability means a disorder in one or more of the basic psychological processes involved in understanding or in using language, spoken or written, which disorder may manifest itself in the imperfect ability to listen, think, speak, read, write, spell, or do mathematical calculations. (20 U.S.C. § 1401 [30])

The term *SLD* is meant to include conditions such as dyslexia and perceptual disorders. However, it is not meant to include an impairment that is the result of

Table 1.2. Overview of commonly seen disabilities in inclusive classrooms, with instructional suggestions

Disability	Description	Instructional suggestions	Prevalence rate
Specific learning disability (SLD)	Defined in the Individuals with Disabilities Education Improvement Act (IDEA) of 2004 as a disorder characterized by an impaired ability to listen, think, speak, read, write, spell, or do mathematical calculations	Clear, concise instruction Visual support during lessons Presentation of information in various ways Graphic organizers Differentiated instruction Guided notes Mnemonics	Approximately 4% of school-age children
Attention-deficit/hyperactivity disorder (ADHD)	A condition in which a child exhibits developmentally inappropriate inattention, impulsivity, and hyperactivity	Implementation of a behavior plan Consistency between home and school Seating assignment with minimal distractions Longer or frequent breaks Object or toy provided to release stress or energy Have students record assignments in an organizer	Approximately 8.4% of children ages 3–17
Autism spectrum disorders (ASDs)	Developmental disorders characterized by impairments in social relationships and communication and by repetitive behaviors	Highly structured environment Themed lessons involving child's interests Data-based programs, such as Precision Teaching Transition time between activities	Less than 1% of school-age children but has been increasing
Mild intellectual disabilities	Developmental disabilities characterized by impairments in intellectual functioning and adaptive skills	Explicit, systematic instruction Model and encourage communication Reinforce appropriate behaviors Focus on functional academics Cooperative learning strategies Peer tutoring	Of the approximately 1% of school-age children who are identified as having intellectual disabilities, approximately 60% are considered to have mild intellectual disabilities
Emotional or behavior disorders	Disorders with identified characteristics that occur over an extended period of time, to a marked degree, and that negatively affect a child's educational experience; this category of disabilities includes three types: externalizing, internalizing, and low incidence	Social skills training Behavior self-management programs Explicit instruction Promotion of peer collaboration	Accurate prevalence rates are difficult to determine; reported rates vary, ranging from just below 1% of school-age children to between 3% and 10%

Sources: American Psychological Association (2000); Bryant, Smith, and Bryant (2008); Centers for Disease Control and Prevention (2010); Friend (2011); Hardman, Drew, and Egan (2008); Heward (2009); Individuals with Disabilities Education Improvement Act (IDEA) of 2004 (PL 108-446); Kluth (2010); Mercer and Mercer (2008); and Smith and Tyler (2010).

an intellectual disability, hearing or vision loss, or environmental factors such as socioeconomic situation (Heward, 2009). Rosenberg et al. state that when identifying an SLD, "The most widely used criterion is a severe discrepancy between how well the student is achieving in an academic area and how well the student is expected to achieve based on ability" (2008, p. 143). This discrepancy model, based on a student's IQ test results, is the most commonly used criterion, but the law does not require a discrepancy within the IQ findings to exist for identification. The reauthorization of IDEA in 2004 introduced an early intervention and prevention model to identify students with learning disabilities. This new model differs from the discrepancy model in that it no longer requires a child to fail before being identified as having an SLD. In the new model, a response to intervention (RTI) considers a child's ability to respond to research-based practices (Heward, 2009). More information about RTI is available from the National Center on Response to Intervention web site (http://www.rti4success.org).

An example of how the IDEA model changed some of the identification criteria is that a school must prove that a child's impairments are not the result of poor education or limited English proficiency and that the child needs services to help him or her succeed (Rosenberg et al., 2008). The process for implementation of RTI includes four principles. The first tenet is to conduct schoolwide screening (commonly referred to as universal screening). This means that all students in the school are part of this initiative. The second step is progress monitoring of students. All students are monitored for determination of behavior indicating the potential to fall behind peers academically. Opportunity for a tiered service delivery model is the third stage of the RTI process. This means that students who demonstrate, via progress monitoring, a need for more intense assistance to achieve success move upward on the tiered system to receive additional adaptations to promote achievement. The fourth and final principle is ensuring fidelity of implementation. This is necessary to ensure consistency in the realization of services provided by the teachers (Johnson, Mellard, Fuchs, & McKnight, 2006).

In Pennsylvania, the RTI model has been revised to the Response to Instruction and Intervention (RtII) model. The Pennsylvania Training and Technical Assistance Network (PaTTAN) defines the RtII model as a "complex, multi-year process that requires the realignment and reengineering of the school infrastructure" (PaTTAN, 2010, p. 1). It contains standard-aligned strategies with multiple tiers. The goal is to ensure early identification of students who require academic or behavioral interventions. RtII is intended to provide a standard for teachers to follow that assists with the identification of students with SLDs and with providing these students with assistance for both academic and behavioral challenges before the student experiences failure. As with the RTI model, the RtII model also supplies data for decision-making purposes to determine a child's possible eligibility for special education services due to an SLD or other disability (PaTTAN, 2010).

Although more boys than girls have been identified as having SLDs (Friend, 2011; Lieberman, Kantrowitz, & Flannery, 2005; Mercer & Mercer, 2008), students with SLDs are a heterogeneous group. Friend reports an interesting trend in the diagnosis of students with SLDs—namely, that the previous trend of SLDs being the fastest-growing category of disabilities is reversing itself. Even though SLD remains the largest identified disability category, the number of students who are diagnosed as having SLDs is actually decreasing. Smith and Tyler (2010) concur that this number is on the decline. In fact, the number of students who are identified as having learning disabilities has been steadily decreasing since 2000–2001.

Rosenberg et al. (2008) report that the main impairment of a child with an SLD involves processing language, but this is not the only impairment that may be present. Other characteristics of SLDs include low achievement and low motivation as well as inattention (Mercer & Mercer, 2008; Rosenberg et al., 2008).

Although well defined, the term *SLD* includes variant types of conditions that have different educational implications. Students with SLDs present differently, and not all of them have difficulty in the same academic areas. Heward states that students who are identified as having learning disabilities may encounter one or more of the following challenges: "reading problems, deficits in written language, underachievement in math, poor social skills, attention deficits and hyperactivity, behavior problems, and low self-esteem/self-efficacy" (2009, p. 179). Learning disabilities in the area of reading are the largest identified group of SLDs (Heward, 2009). An estimated 90% of students identified as having learning disabilities have reading-related SLDs (Kavale & Forness, 2000). Jenkins and O'Connor (2001) report that students with a specific learning disability in the area of reading often lack phonemic awareness. If this is the impairment area, teachers should focus instruction on the decoding skills necessary for comprehension of text. When teaching students who are identified as having SLDs in any classification, it is important to keep directions clear and concise. It is also beneficial to provide visual support whenever possible, including the use of charts, diagrams, and body language. This encourages consideration of numerous ways to present information to the class (Mercer & Mercer, 2008). Other instructional considerations include use of differentiated instruction, explicit instruction, universal design for learning, graphic organizers, guided notes, and mnemonics (Heward, 2009; Mercer & Mercer, 2008).

Attention-Deficit/Hyperactivity Disorder

The number of diagnosed cases of ADHD is on the rise in the United States, with prevalence rates of 8.4% among children ages 3–17 (Centers for Disease Control and Prevention [CDC], 2010). Heward (2009) states that one reason why diagnosed cases of ADHD are increasing is because students with this disability are now eligible to receive services under the "other health impairments (OHI)" category as designated in IDEA. The U.S. Department of Education (2007) estimates that this category has increased approximately 3% per year from 1997 to 2006. Friend (2011) and Smith and Tyler (2010) believe the prevalence rate is estimated at 7%. The increase in the number of children being diagnosed with ADHD may also be due to the fact that there are now medical guidelines to assist in the identification of the disorder. These guidelines are found in the *Diagnostic and Statistical Manual of Mental Disorders, Fourth Edition, Text Revision* (*DSM-IV-TR;* American Psychiatric Association, 2000).

ADHD is described as frequent hyperactivity, impulsivity, and/or inattention as compared with peers or with what is expected from adults in certain settings; often, these behaviors copresent themselves (American Psychiatric Association, 2000; Heward, 2009). Symptoms are primarily observed before the age of 7. Children can have one of three types of ADHD: predominantly inattentive, predominantly hyperactive-impulsive, or a combination (Smith & Tyler, 2010).

These three types of ADHD have common characteristics of impairment associated with them. Barkley (2007) describes these characteristics as 1) limited attention or persistence to tasks; 2) reduced impulse control, such as speaking out of turn or being unable to avoid distractions; and 3) excessive activity. This type of activity is not related to the task at hand and may be displayed in such behavior as playing with a pencil or moving frequently.

Children who are diagnosed with ADHD may be treated with medication and may possibly follow a behavior plan. If a behavior plan is in place, or if one is to be established, it is vital that the plan be followed at home *and* at school. Some children with ADHD qualify for special services under IDEA if the disorder has a negative impact on their learning. Even if the child does not qualify for special services because of lack of evidence that his or her learning is affected by ADHD, there are several tactics that are effective in educating a child with ADHD. A few strategies that are recommended practice for all students include ensuring that clear instructions are provided, consistent routines are maintained, and self-monitoring techniques are taught and implemented (Heward, 2009).

An educator must remember that many students with ADHD are easily distracted; therefore, the classroom environment should be taken into account and managed appropriately. When setting up the classroom, the teacher should consider seating and possible disturbances and then attempt to place a student with ADHD in an appropriate seat with limited distractions. The teacher should next consider the child's attention span and plan activities accordingly. If a longer activity is planned, a break should be allowed (Smith & Tyler, 2010). According to Heward (2009), another strategy is to let the student have a toy or object to manipulate to release energy. This toy can be used during a break or at a time when it will not interfere with the learning environment. It is important to keep children with ADHD organized and on a schedule. Encourage the child to record assignments and information in an organizer and stress the importance of being responsible.

Autism Spectrum Disorders

With the diagnosis of ASDs increasing since the early 1990s, educators have been faced with new challenges in learning about these disorders and their educational implications to help students succeed. The *DSM-IV-TR* characterizes ASDs as a type of pervasive developmental disorder (PDD; American Psychiatric Association, 2000). Common characteristics associated with ASDs are impairments in social interactions, impairments in communication skills, and repetitive behavior patterns. These disorders include Asperger syndrome, autism, and pervasive developmental disorder-not otherwise specified (PPD-NOS; Friend, 2011; Heward, 2009). Although there are other categories of ASDs as well, this section focuses on autism and Asperger syndrome.

The prevalence of ASDs is growing at an astounding rate. The number of students who are identified as having ASDs is increasing more than for any other disability group (Heward, 2009). The CDC has conducted two surveys to establish the prevalence rates of autism (2010, 2012). The study published in 2010 reports prevalence rates as one in 110 children in 2006. The 2012 report shows an increase to one in 88 children in 2008. Boys are more likely to be diagnosed with ASDs than girls. The 2012 CDC study found that one in 54 boys is likely to be identified as having an ASD, compared with one in 252 girls (2012). Smith and Tyler (2010) report that even though the number of students identified as having ASDs accounts for less than 1% of all students between the ages of 6 and 21, this category of disabilities is receiving attention from family members, education professionals, and the popular media because of the rapid growth of prevalence rates and the heterogeneity of these disorders.

Pennsylvania was the first state to release data in a study conducted to establish prevalence rates and projected prevalence rates of ASDs in adults (Pennsylvania Office of the Governor, 2009). The study estimated that of the total number of people who were identified as having ASDs in Pennsylvania in 2005, slightly more than 7%

were adults. The study also projected a 179% increase in the number of adults living with ASDs from 2005 to 2010, and that this rate would more than double by 2015.

It is essential for children to be screened for ASDs at an early age (typically before the age of 3), at the onset of symptoms, so that they can begin to receive early intervention. Educational implications are very similar for children with autism and children with Asperger syndrome. First and foremost, typical intelligence should be presumed. It may be easy to presuppose that when speech and communication skills are impaired, the child has an intellectual disability (Smith, Polloway, Patton, & Dowdy, 2006). This, however, is not always the case for children with ASDs, and assumptions should be avoided, with this and any diagnosis. Education planning, of course, depends on individual students' needs, but there are some specific strategies that may be effective. The educational environment should be highly structured, with schedules and routines in place. Always provide adequate transition time between activities (Kluth, 2010). Another strategy is to find what the child is passionate about (e.g., trains, cars, dinosaurs) and try to relate lessons to that theme whenever possible. There are also several programs associated with the instruction of students with autism. These include the Treatment and Education of Autistic and related Communication Handicapped Children (TEACCH) program and the Pyramid Approach to Education in Autism (National Autism Center, 2011; Smith & Tyler, 2010; Taylor & Fisher, 2010).

Still other suggestions for instruction in the areas of behavior and academics include the use of data-based programs such as Precision Teaching (Mercer & Mercer, 2008). Keep in mind, however, that "no single method is effective with all children with autism, partly because these children display widely variable characteristics" (Heflin & Simpson, 1998, as cited in Smith et al., 2006, p. 292).

Autism   As restated by Rosenberg et al. (adapted from Towbin, Mauk, & Batshaw, 2002), autism is a "severe developmental disability characterized by an early age of onset, poor social development, impairments in language development, and rigidity in behavior" (2008, p. 264). Kirk, Gallagher, and Anastasiow state that "autism is more common among boys, with about four times as many boys as girls identified" (2003, p. 339). Every child with autism is unique, and although there are typical characteristics associated with the disorder, each child presents differently.

Differences in development associated with autism can be found in three specific areas. These characteristics can be identified in most children with autism and include "impairments in social reciprocity, deficiencies in communication skills, and repetitive, stereotypical, and ritualistic behaviors" (Rosenberg et al., 2008, p. 266). Social reciprocity refers to the social cues and interactions that are not necessarily written but are accepted in society. These include, but are not limited to, the use of eye contact, body language, and speech. The impairments in social cues are related to the impairments in communication skills. Children with ASDs often have difficulty understanding the perspectives of others. This hinders their ability to relate well to peers and adults. Ritualistic behaviors can include behaviors such as rocking and hand flapping or a fascination with certain objects or subjects. These behaviors can range from being extreme and interfering with the function of other activities to being milder and controllable.

Asperger Syndrome   Asperger syndrome (called Asperger's Disorder in *DSM-IV-TR;* American Psychiatric Association, 2000) is frequently described as being similar to high-functioning autism. Children with either of these disorders often display similar characteristics. Rosenberg et al. clarify that "the presenting behaviors of Asperger's disorder are similar to high-functioning autism, except that people with Asperger's do not have the same intensity of impairment in language, cognition, and self-help skills" (2008, p. 265).

Children with Asperger syndrome may have some impairment in social communication. They frequently attempt to interact socially with peers, but the communications are often awkward and of poor quality (Smith et al., 2006). Promoting positive interactions, providing role models, and teaching coping skills are all ways to help children with Asperger syndrome develop appropriate relationships.

Summary   Although this section on ASDs provides descriptions and educational implications, it is important to repeat that every child with an ASD is different. For example, if specific instructional strategies have been successful with one child with autism, this does not necessarily mean that those same strategies will be effective with another child with autism. As the term *autism spectrum disorder* implies, there is a spectrum that covers a range of disabilities and abilities. Some children might be verbal but not aware of social cues, whereas others are nonverbal and need assistive technology to communicate their basic needs. Every child is unique and the successful educator must grow to know the child and try different techniques until the child thrives (Friend, 2011).

Mild Intellectual Disabilities

This category of disabilities has continued to have a high incidence since the early 1900s (Polloway, 2006). In areas such as intellectual functioning and adaptive behavior, children with mild intellectual disabilities share similarities with children who have moderate or severe intellectual disabilities; the difference lies in the severity to which each child is affected. A traditional way of describing the degree of intellectual impairment in children with intellectual disabilities is by an IQ measurement; children with mild intellectual disabilities have IQs of approximately 55–70 (Heward, 2009; Smith & Tyler, 2010). IQ is not the only classification criterion; intellectual functioning and adaptive skills, such as social and self-help skills, must be taken into account. Hardman, Drew, and Egan (2008) discuss how adaptive behaviors are gauged in children with mild intellectual disabilities. They state that adaptive behavior scales measure a person's capacity for personal care skills as well as social skills for various environments.

Prevalence rates for mild intellectual disabilities have dropped since the early 2000s. However, of the approximately 1% of all school-age children who are identified as having intellectual disabilities, it is estimated that more than half (approximately 60%) are considered to have mild intellectual disabilities (Smith et al., 2006). Heward (2009) concurs but also asserts that prevalence rates differ greatly from state to state.

Many studies have been conducted to determine the causes of intellectual disabilities. Although in some cases causes have been identified, it is not always possible to identify a reason for the disability. In fact, often the cause is unknown (Harris, 2006). Intellectual disabilities can sometimes be traced to biomedical factors such as chromosomal abnormalities (e.g., Down syndrome), behavioral factors such as prenatal use of drugs or alcohol, or a combination of biological and/or environmental contributors (Hardman et al., 2008; Heward, 2009).

Heward (2009) states that students with mild intellectual disabilities respond well to explicit instruction, instruction that is systematic, and techniques that have been proven as recommended practice through research. Lessons should be well planned and should focus on functional academics. One way this can be accomplished is by focusing on language development (Mercer & Mercer, 2008). Some language development activities include providing appropriate language models and encouraging students to speak and actively participate. Students with mild intellectual disabilities may also have goals in the areas of behavior and communication. Educators should always serve as models for appropriate behavior. To encourage these students to communicate with peers, teachers should "employ cooperative learning strategies wherever possible to promote effective learning by all students" (Hardman et al., 2008, p. 292). Research also suggests that teachers use peers without disabilities to help support students with intellectual disabilities both academically and socially (Carter & Hughes, 2005; Hardman et al., 2008).

Emotional or Behavior Disorders

Emotional or behavior disorders (categorized as emotional disturbance under IDEA) include three types: externalizing, internalizing, and low-incidence. Characteristics of a person exhibiting an externalizing type include acting out, perseveration, and aggression. Depression, anxiety, anorexia, and/or bulimia are distinguishing behaviors of the internalizing type. The low-incidence type, rarely diagnosed, may include schizophrenia. For all three types, the common attribute among students with emotional or behavior disorders is a lack of social skills. Often, this is the reason why the students are referred for testing (Bryant et al., 2008).

Prevalence rates for these disorders vary considerably from one source to the next. Bryant et al. (2008) report the prevalence rate as just below 1% of the school-age population but go on to state that this number may not be accurate, due to the fear of stigma attached to the label of this category. Heward (2009) reports that the occurrence rates may be between 3% and 10%. Heward also states that another problem with determining an accurate occurrence of this disability is the variance of criteria used to determine eligibility for this category of special education. Approximately 74% of students who are identified as having emotional or behavior disorders are male (Bryant et al., 2008).

Instructional concerns for students with these disabilities include skills not only in academics but also in personal and social areas. These students typically perform well when they are given explicit instruction. They also respond positively to teacher praise, clear directions, concise expectations, promotion of peer collaboration, and high levels of engagement in the learning process (Heward, 2009; Mercer & Mercer, 2008). Mercer and Mercer also suggest that self-management skills be taught as part of the curriculum.

SPECIAL EDUCATION IN THE EARLY 21ST CENTURY

Inclusion and collaboration are two irrefutable ingredients for classrooms in the early 21st century. Pivik, McComas, and LaFlamme (2002) liken inclusion to a puzzle: There are many pieces essential to completing the picture. However, some pieces may be missing; others are very complex, making it difficult to determine where they fit. Inclusion of students with disabilities in general education classrooms is undeniably an element or piece of the puzzle (Friend & Bursuck, 2008; Heward, 2009; Salend, 2008; Smith & Tyler, 2010). It is virtually impossible to be an expert in every factor affecting education, but having an understanding of certain disabilities can assuredly be beneficial for educators. Comprehending the characteristics and strengths of students can help any type of educator to prepare meaningful lessons. It is also important for professionals to realize that increasing emphasis is being placed on use of recommended practices that are supported by research, as opposed to following instructional fads or implementing instruction simply because that is the way it has been done in the past (Friend, 2011). This book focuses on recommended practices that are evidence based.

Because of the changing roles of special educators over the years and the different experience and expertise various professionals may have with certain types of disabilities, there is a strong need to promote collaboration between education professionals. Smith and Tyler (2010) report that collaboration is one of the key components for finding success in education. Educators should feel comfortable approaching other colleagues for support when presented with a situation with which they are unfamiliar or to share ideas about what works for a given student. Recognizing the strengths of other educators is an important step in collaboration. By promoting inclusive practices, collaboration, and use of proven best practices, the Co-Design Model helps teachers create classrooms that are responsive to the diverse student population. The Co-Design Model promotes strategies and practices that enable teachers and administrators to better meet the needs of the inclusive school environment.

CONCLUSION

Implementation of services for students with disabilities varies greatly from one school setting to the next. However, because of educational and legal strides made since the 1990s, schools are experiencing a more inclusive approach to education (Friend, 2011; Smith & Tyler, 2010). This is not to say that there are no roadblocks and hurdles to overcome, but through collaborative efforts implemented by professionals in the field of education, inclusive practices will continue to improve.

REFERENCES

American Psychiatric Association. (2000). *Diagnostic and statistical manual of mental disorders* (4th ed., text rev.). Washington, DC: Author.

Barger-Anderson, R., Isherwood, R., Merhaut, J., & Hoover, K. (2010, April). The Co-Design Model: A collaborative approach to inclusive education. In P. Tramdak (Chair), *Slippery Rock University of Pennsylvania research symposium.* Symposium conducted at Slippery Rock University, Slippery Rock, PA.

Barkley, R.A. (2007). School-based interventions for ADHD: Where to from here? *School Psychology Review, 36,* 276–289.

Bondy, A.S., & Sulzer-Azaroff, B. (2002). *The pyramid approach to education in autism.* Newark, DE: Pyramid Educational Products.

Brown v. Board of Educ., 347 U.S. 483 (1954).

Bryant, D.P., Smith, D.D., & Bryant, B.R. (2008). *Teaching students with special needs in inclusive classrooms.* Boston, MA: Allyn & Bacon.

Carter, E.W., & Hughes, C. (2005). Increasing social interaction among adolescents with intellectual disabilities and their general education peers: Effective interventions. *Research and Practice for Persons with Severe Disabilities, 30*(4), 179–193.

Centers for Disease Control and Prevention. (2010). *Autism spectrum disorders.* Retrieved from http://www.cdc.gov/ncbddd/autism/index.html

Centers for Disease Control and Prevention. (2012). *Autism spectrum disorders (ASDs): Data and statistics.* Retrieved from http://www.cdc.gov/ncbddd/autism/index.html

Council for Exceptional Children. (2010). *Council for Exceptional Children web site.* Retrieved from http://www.cec.sped.org/AM/Template.cfm?section=about_CEC

Dorothea Dix. (2005). Retrieved from http://www.civilwarhome.com/dixbio.htm

Education for All Handicapped Children Act of 1975, PL 94-142, 20 U.S.C. §§ 1400 *et seq.*

Elizabeth E. Farrell (1870–1932): A biographical sketch. (1981). *Journal of Special Education, 15*, 322–323.

Encyclopædia Britannica. (2010). *Samuel Gridley Howe.* Retrieved from http://www.britannica.com/EBchecked/topic/273525/Samuel-Gridley-Howe

Fleisher, D.Z., & Zames, F. (2001). *The disability rights movement: From charity to confrontation.* Philadelphia, PA: Temple University Press.

Friend, M. (2011). *Special education: Contemporary perspectives for school professionals* (3rd ed.). Boston, MA: Pearson.

Friend, M., & Bursuck, W.D. (2008). *Including students with special needs: A practical guide for classroom teachers* (5th ed.). Boston, MA: Allyn & Bacon.

Goddard, H.H. (1912). *The Kallikak family: A study in the heredity of feeble-mindedness.* New York: Macmillan Co.

Hardman, M.L., Drew, C.J., & Egan, M.W. (2008). *Human exceptionality: School, community, and family* (9th ed.). Boston, MA: Houghton Mifflin.

Harris, J.C. (2006). *Intellectual disability: Understanding its development, causes, classification, evaluation, and treatment.* New York, NY: Oxford University Press.

Heflin, L.J., & Simpson, R. (1998). Interventions for children and youth with autism: Prudent choices in a world of exaggerated claims and empty promises. Part II: Legal/policy analysis and recommendations for selecting interventions and treatments. *Focus on Autism and Other Developmental Disabilities, 13,* 212–220.

Heward, W.L. (2009). *Exceptional children: An introduction to special education* (9th ed.). Upper Saddle River, NJ: Pearson Merrill Prentice Hall.

Individuals with Disabilities Education Improvement Act (IDEA) of 2004, PL 108-446, 20 U.S.C. §§ 1400 *et seq.*

Jenkins, J.R., & O'Connor, R.E. (2001). *Early identification and intervention for young children with reading/learning disabilities.* White paper from Learning Disabilities Summit: Building a Foundation for the Future, National Research Center on Learning Disabilities. Retrieved from http://www.nrcld.org/resources/ldsummit/jenkins.html

Johnson, E., Mellard, D.F., Fuchs, D., & McKnight, M.A. (2006). *Responsiveness to intervention (RTI): How to do it.* Lawrence, KS: National Research Center on Learning Disabilities.

Kavale, K.A., & Forness, S.R. (2000). History, rhetoric, and reality: Analysis of the inclusion debate. *Remedial and Special Education, 21*(5), 279–296.

Keller, H. (1905). *The story of my life.* J.A. Macy (Ed.). New York: Doubleday, Page & Company. Retrieved from http://digital.library.upenn.edu/women/keller/life/life.html

Kirk, S.A., Gallagher, J.J., & Anastasiow, N.J. (2003). *Educating exceptional children* (10th ed.). Boston, MA: Houghton Mifflin.

Kluth, P. (2010). *"You're going to love this kid!" Teaching students with autism in the inclusive classroom* (2nd ed.). Baltimore, MD: Paul H. Brookes Publishing Co.

Lieberman, J., Kantrowitz, L., & Flannery, K. (2005). Male vulnerability to reading disability is not likely to be a myth: A call for new data. *Journal of Learning Disabilities, 38,* 109–129.

Mercer, C.D., & Mercer, A.R. (2008). *Teaching students with learning problems* (8th ed.). Upper Saddle River, NJ: Prentice Hall.

Murdick, N.L., Gartin, B.C., & Crabtree, T. (2006). *Special education law* (2nd ed.). Upper Saddle River, NJ: Merrill/Prentice Hall.

National Autism Center. (2011). *Practitioner education.* Retrieved from http://www.nationalautismcenter.org/learning/practitioner.php

Office for Civil Rights. (2006). *Fact sheet: Your rights under section 504 of the Rehabilitation Act.* Washington, DC: U.S. Department of Health and Human Services.

Office of Special Education and Rehabilitative Services. (2007). *California's part B FFY 2005 SPP/APR response table.* Retrieved from http://www.cde.ca.gov/sp/se/qa/documents/sppa-prtbl.doc

Pennsylvania Office of the Governor. (2009). *PA Governor Rendell: New report shows demand for autism services will continue to rise* [Press release]. Retrieved from http://www.prnewswire.com/news-releases/pa-governor-rendell-new-report-shows-demand-for-autism-services-will-continue-to-rise-70380767.html

Pennsylvania Training and Technical Assistance Network. (2010). *The RtII implementation process.* Retrieved from http://pattan.net-website.s3.amazonaws.com/files/materials/publications/docs/RtII-Implement.pdf

Pinto, M. (Associate Producer/Scriptwriter), & Levin, C. (Producer/Director). (2000). Schoolhouse pioneers [Television series episode]. In *Only a teacher.* Arlington, VA: Public Broadcasting Service. Retrieved from http://www.pbs.org/onlyateacher/horace.html

Pivik, J., McComas, J., & LaFlamme, M. (2002). Barriers and facilitators to inclusive education. *Exceptional Children, 69,* 97–107.

Polloway, E.A. (2006). *Mild mental retardation.* Mahwah, NJ: Lawrence Erlbaum Associates.

Rehabilitation Act of 1973, PL 93-112, 29 U.S.C. §§ 701 *et seq.*

Rosenberg, M.S., Westling, D.L., & McLeskey, J. (2008). *Special education for today's teachers: An introduction.* Upper Saddle River, NJ: Prentice Hall.

Salend, S.J. (2008). *Creating inclusive classrooms: Effective and reflective practices* (6th ed.). Upper Saddle River, NJ: Prentice Hall.

Smith, D.D., & Tyler, N.C. (2010). *Introduction to special education: Making a difference* (7th ed.). Upper Saddle River, NJ: Merrill.

Smith, T.E.C., Polloway, E.A., Patton, J.R., & Dowdy, C.A. (2006). *Teaching students with special needs in inclusive settings* (Rev. IDEA ed.). Boston, MA: Allyn & Bacon.

Taylor, B.A., & Fisher, J. (2010). Three important things to consider when starting intervention for a child diagnosed with autism. *Behavior Analysis in Practice, 3,* 52–53.

Taylor, R.L., Smiley, L.R., & Richards, S.B. (2009). *Exceptional students: Preparing teachers for the 21st century.* New York, NY: McGraw-Hill.

Towbin, K., Mauk, J., & Batshaw, M. (2002). Pervasive developmental disorders. In M. Batshaw (Ed.), *Children and disabilities* (5th ed). Baltimore, MD: Paul H. Brookes Publishing Co.

United Cerebral Palsy. (2010). *United Cerebral Palsy web site.* Retrieved from http://www.ucp.org/ucp_general.cfm/1/3

U.S. Department of Education. (2007). *Attention-deficit/hyperactivity disorder (ADHD): Data and statistics in the United States.* Retrieved from http://www.cdc.gov/ncbddd/adhd/data.html/

U.S. Department of Education. (2011). *The condition of education: Children and youth with disabilities.* National Center for Education Statistics. Retrieved from http://nces.ed.gov/programs/coe/indicator_cwd.asp [now available from http://nces.ed.gov/pubsearch/pubsinfo.asp?pubid=2011033]

The University of North Carolina TEACCH Autism Program. (2012). Retrieved from http://teacch.com

Viney, W., & Zorich, S. (1982). Contributions to the history of psychology XXIX: Dorothea Dix. *Psychological Reports, 50,* 211–218.

Winzer, M.A. (1998). A tale often told: The early progression of special education. *Remedial and Special Education, 19*(4), 212–218.

CHAPTER 2

The Legal System's Impact on Inclusion

The foundation of special education law in the late 20th and early 21st centuries began with the landmark school desegregation case *Brown v. Board of Educ.* (1954), in which the U.S. Supreme Court ruled that African American students should be educated in the same schools as European American children. In the early 1970s, special education lawyers used *Brown* in their arguments for inclusion of students with disabilities in general education classrooms. These lawyers reasoned that African American students were members of a minority group, as were students with disabilities. One notable decision from this period is *PARC v. Commonwealth of Pennsylvania* (1971), in which the Pennsylvania Department of Education (PDE) settled a case by agreeing that all students with intellectual disabilities should be identified, evaluated, and placed in an appropriate program of public education. That case, along with *Mills v. Board of Educ. of the District of Columbia* (1972), was instrumental in the passage of the Education for All Handicapped Children Act of 1975.

This law did more in one fell swoop for students with disabilities than all previous pieces of special education legislation combined. It has been reauthorized several times, but the most current iteration, the Individuals with Disabilities Education Improvement Act (IDEA) of 2004 signed into law on December 4, 2004, by President George W. Bush, still holds that students with disabilities must be educated in the least restrictive environment (LRE) to the maximum extent appropriate with the use of supplementary aids and services (SaS).

In the early 21st century, the field of education has seen litigation on issues ranging from whether e-mails are educational records (*S.A. v. Tulare County Office of Educ.* [2009]) to whether service animals should be allowed in public schools (*Kalbfleisch v. Columbia Community Unit Sch. Dist. Unit No. 4*). Litigation has also occurred over whether a student with disabilities can receive a free appropriate public education (FAPE) even if his or her standardized test scores diminish (*Jaccari J. v. Board of Educ. of the City of Chicago, Dist. No. 299* [2010]) and whether individualized education program (IEP) team meetings should be held if the parent does not attend (*T.S. v. Weast* [2010]).

Litigation is clearly driving special education legislation, and it will be interesting to see what future challenges are brought through the legal system.

By Dennis T. Fair, Ph.D., Professor and Chairperson of the
Special Education Department at Slippery Rock University and former
Hearing Officer for the Office of Dispute and Resolution for the Commonwealth of Pennsylvania

The legal process has led to significant changes in how children with disabilities are educated. Table 2.1 summarizes some of the federal legislation and court cases that have had a major impact on special education and inclusion.

Legal issues in special education truly began in 1954 with *Brown v. Board of Educ.* (Wisneski, 2010). Later, in the *PARC v. Commonwealth of Pennsylvania* case in 1971, the plaintiffs, Pennsylvania Association for Retarded Children (PARC), alleged that students with intellectual disabilities were not receiving the FAPE that students without disabilities received. PARC alleged that Pennsylvania was violating the 14th Amendment. The case was resolved with a consent agreement in which the PDE agreed that the students with disabilities had to be provided with an FAPE ("Pennsylvania Assn.," 1971).

On November 29, 1975, President Gerald Ford signed the Education for All Handicapped Children Act of 1975. Since its original passage, the law has had several reauthorizations and amendments, such as the Individuals with Disabilities Education Act (IDEA) of 1990 (PL 101-476), the Individuals with Disabilities Education Act Amendments (IDEA) of 1997 (PL 105-17), and its most recent reauthorization, the Individuals with Disabilities Education Improvement Act (IDEA) of 2004, (PL 108-446). As a result of this legislation, schools are required to 1) provide nondiscriminatory evaluation for all students who are thought to be exceptional, 2) educate students who are identified as having disabilities in the LRE to the maximum extent appropriate, 3) make due process procedures available for parents who allege that the school district is not providing their child with an FAPE, 4) develop an IEP for every child identified as having a disability, and 5) provide an FAPE for every child who is receiving special education services (Howard, 2004).

IS INCLUSION REQUIRED BY LAW?

There are two federal laws that mandate education for all students with disabilities. Neither law requires inclusion, but they both require schools to educate students with disabilities with their peers without disabilities to the maximum extent appropriate while providing appropriate SaS (Gordon, 2006). These two laws are Section 504 of the Rehabilitation Act of 1973 and IDEA. IDEA mandates that all students with one or more of the 13 recognized disability categories under the law must be provided with a free public education that must be driven by an IEP with all of the services necessary to assist students in the LRE.

Both laws shape special education in significant ways. Section 504 is sometimes referred to as a nondiscrimination law. This means that no person with a disability can be discriminated against in any public context, including school. Because the definition of disability is more expansive in Section 504 than in IDEA, more students qualify for services under Section 504 than under IDEA. There are some disabilities that do not qualify as one of the disability categories recognized under IDEA; therefore, students with these disabilities who do not qualify for special education services under IDEA are protected under the Rehabilitation Act of 1973. A Section 504 service agreement can be developed for these students that would require the school staff to accommodate the children's disabilities. For example, a student with a field of vision impairment may need seating in the classroom that would accommodate his or her needs, such as sitting closer to the front of the room, sitting away from the natural light of the windows, or having preferential seating on one side of the room.

Affleck, Madge, Adams, and Lowenbraun (1988) explained that IDEA recognizes that sometimes it is not appropriate to include students with disabilities in general education classrooms with their peers without disabilities; however, it is equally

Table 2.1. Examples of court cases and federal legislation that have influenced special education and inclusion

Action	Influence
Brown v. Board of Educ. (1954)	This landmark decision by the U.S. Supreme Court established that racial segregation in schools denies equal opportunity for African American students. In the 1970s, this case also helped ensure equal rights for students with disabilities.
Diana v. State Board of Educ. (1970)	This ruling established that students who do not speak English as their first language must be assessed in their native language. The plaintiff in this case was a Spanish-speaking student who was placed in a classroom for students with intellectual disabilities based on the results of an intelligence test given in English.
Mills v. Board of Educ. of the District of Columbia (1972)	This decision found that schools' financial limitations were not a valid argument for denying educational services to students with disabilities. The case is important because it established that schools must provide services based on the needs of students, not the schools' ability to pay for the services.
PARC v. Commonwealth of Pennsylvania (1971)	This ruling was significant because it established that all children, with or without disabilities, were entitled to receive a free appropriate public education (FAPE). The decision also determined that a state law denying public school education to students with disabilities who were considered to have received no benefits from attending the public school violated the 14th Amendment. Another important result of this ruling is that parents must be notified of any pending changes in their child's educational program.
Larry P. v. Riles (1984)	In this case, a U.S. district court in California found that an African American student could not be identified as having an intellectual disability based on the results of an intelligence test that was determined to be both culturally and racially biased. In 1986, the ruling was expanded to extend the same protection to students with any type of disability.
Board of Educ. of the Hendrick Hudson Sch. Dist., Westchester County v. Rowley (1982)	This decision by the U.S. Supreme Court established that appropriate services for students identified for receiving special education services was not optimum. In this case, the parents of a student with a hearing impairment sued the school district because it had refused their request for a sign language interpreter to assist their child in the classroom. The district argued that it had denied the request because the child was achieving at grade level without the interpreter.
Oberti v. Board of Educ. of the Borough of Clementon Sch. Dist. (1993)	This U.S. Court of Appeals decision upheld a district court's ruling that school districts must provide students with disabilities with reasonable accommodations, including a full range of services and supports, within the general education environment to the maximum extent appropriate. The case also established that students with disabilities cannot be excluded from general education classes simply because of differences in learning needs.
Section 504 of the Rehabilitation Act of 1973 (PL 93-112)	The Rehabilitation Act, along with its subsequent amendments, protects people with disabilities from discrimination in education, employment, access to public facilities, and housing. In terms of education, Section 504 ensures that students with disabilities have the right to receive the same educational opportunities as their peers without disabilities.
Americans with Disabilities Act (ADA) of 1990 (PL 101-336)	This sweeping legislation protects individuals with disabilities from discrimination in the workplace, transportation, state and local government services, telecommunications, and public accommodations, including some types of private schools. However, ADA does not apply to public school education. IDEA protects students with disabilities who require special education services within the public school system. The ADA protects students with disabilities who do not qualify for special education under section 504 of the Rehabilitation Act by requiring reasonable accommodations for students with disabilities.

(continued)

Table 2.1.   *(continued)*

Education for All Handicapped Children Act of 1975 (PL 94-142)	This historic legislation established the foundation for special education practice. The law requires schools to provide all students with an FAPE in the least restrictive environment (LRE) and to develop an individualized education program (IEP) for every student with a disability. It also established the process for identifying and evaluating students with disabilities, defines specific categories of disabilities that entitle a student to receive special education services, ensures zero reject, provides due process rights for parents who are not satisfied with their child's special education placement, and ensures family and student involvement in the decision-making process. Amendments and reauthorizations of the original 1975 law include • Education of the Handicapped Act Amendments of 1986 (PL 99-457) • Individuals with Disabilities Education Act (IDEA) of 1990 (PL 101-476) • Individuals with Disabilities Education Act Amendments (IDEA) of 1997 (PL 105-17) • Individuals with Disabilities Education Improvement Act (IDEA) of 2004 (PL 108-446)
No Child Left Behind Act of 2001 (PL 107-110)	This influential legislation, signed into law by President George W. Bush in 2002, was designed to create higher academic standards and raise student achievement levels. It also contains provisions that give students with disabilities access to more inclusive educational environments. Components of No Child Left Behind that address the needs of students with disabilities include • Budget suppleness to allow more flexible spending by school administrators • Student choices for schooling if the neighborhood school fails to increase achievement levels • Emphasis on the use of research-based instructional strategies in the Reading First portion of the law • A requirement that schools must provide highly qualified teachers for all students • Provisions for meeting the needs of students who are English language learners • More recently, President Obama supported the idea of testing as an essential way to measure achievement. He proposed reform to NCLB by having more flexibility regarding school evaluation and how students progress over time, not just in math and science but in other academic areas as well. He also wanted to make sure that graduating seniors are prepared for college.

Sources: Ellsworth, 1999; Friend and Bursuck, 2008; and Salend, 2008.

important to provide students with disabilities and their parents with a continuum of placement options that meet the individual needs of these students. The LRE for each student in special education is individualized and should be based on that particular student's needs. For example, some students are placed in approved private schools (APSs) because of the severity of their needs, based on the IEP team's determination that the child's needs could not be met in the general education program. In this case, the APS placement would be the LRE for this child. Although the APS placement would seem to be very restrictive, the IEP team determined that this is the LRE for this student because that is where he or she would be best served.

Another example would be a student with a mild learning disability. The IEP may indicate that this student needs learning support for one period a day. This placement does not seem restrictive at all. For this student, one period a day in the learning support classroom would be the LRE.

COURT DECISIONS THAT HAD AN IMPACT ON INCLUSION

The following are court decisions that have had an impact on inclusion.

Greer v. Rome City Sch. Dist. (1992)

In this case, the parents of a student who had been placed in a self-contained special education classroom sued the school district because they objected to their daughter's exclusion from the general education classroom. The court ruled in favor of the plaintiffs, stating, "Before the school district may conclude that a handicapped child should be educated outside of the regular classroom it must consider whether supplemental aids and services would permit satisfactory education in the regular classroom." SaS create systems of support that enable many students with disabilities to learn and participate alongside peers without disabilities, regardless of their unique instructional needs and differences. Consistent with IDEA's LRE principle, IEP teams must thoughtfully consider a full array of SaS that make it possible for students with disabilities to be included in general education classrooms, as well as nonacademic and extracurricular activities. These SaS must then be provided before a student with a disability can be removed from the general education environment.

The court in *Greer* found that the school district had failed to consider the full range of options that might have enabled the student to remain in the general education classroom. In fact, the district had offered only three options: the special education classroom, the general education classroom with no SaS provided, and the general education classroom with only some speech therapy provided.

The court also struck down the defendants' argument that the costs of providing SaS to this student in the general education classroom would be prohibitively expensive. Instead, the court ruled that the district could not deny services to a child because of additional cost (although the ruling did not provide clear guidelines in regard to what constitutes reasonable versus excessive costs). However, the court also ruled that a school district is not required under IDEA to provide a student who has a disability with his or her own full-time teacher.

Oberti v. Board of Educ. of the Borough of Clementon Sch. Dist. (1993)

This case, brought by the parents of a student with Down syndrome, resulted in a ruling that school districts must provide students with disabilities with reasonable accommodations, including a full range of SaS, within the general education environment. As in the *Greer* case, the parents in *Oberti* objected to their child being excluded from the general education classroom and placed in a self-contained special education classroom. The court ruled in favor of the parents and a more inclusive placement, stating that students with disabilities could not be removed from general education classrooms simply because of differences in learning needs.

This decision also resulted in guidelines for courts to follow in determining whether or not a more restrictive placement of a student with a disability is warranted. The court in *Oberti* stated that courts should consider three factors:

- Has the school district made reasonable efforts to accommodate the child in the general education environment and considered the full range of SaS?

- How would the educational benefits the student would receive in a general education classroom with SaS compare with the benefits he or she would receive in a special education classroom?

- What effect would the inclusion of the child with a disability have on the education of other children in the general education classroom?

Finally, if a court determines that the student cannot be educated successfully in a general education classroom, a fourth factor must be considered: Has the school included the child in school programs to the maximum extent appropriate?

Sacramento City Unified Sch. Dist. v. Rachel H. (1994)

The decision in this case, like *Oberti,* was precedent setting in that it established specific guidelines for courts to consider in determining what would be the most appropriate placement for a child with a disability. In this case, the parents sued the school district over its decision to place their child half time in a special education classroom and half time in a general education classroom; they wanted their daughter to be educated in the general classroom 100% of the time. When the court ruled in favor of the Holland family, the district filed an appeal with the circuit court, which upheld the lower court's decision.

The court based its ruling on a Texas case, *Daniel R.R. v. State Board of Educ.* (1989), which determined that the general education classroom is an appropriate LRE if a student with a disability can receive a satisfactory education there, even if it is not the best academic setting for the child. In other words, the district must also take into account the nonacademic benefits of including the child in the general classroom and consider a range of SaS to meet the child's needs in nonacademic courses such as fine arts, as well as extracurricular activities.

The circuit court established that courts must consider four factors in determining whether or not a placement is an appropriate LRE as mandated by IDEA and whether or not the child can be successful in that placement:

- The educational benefits of placing the child in a general education classroom full time

- The nonacademic benefits

- The effect that inclusion of the student with a disability would have on the teacher and other students in the general classroom

- The costs associated with the placement

The *Gaskin* Settlement

In Pennsylvania, many pressing legal issues in special education have arisen as a result of the historic case *Gaskin v. Pennsylvania Dept. of Educ.* (2005). *Gaskin* was a class action lawsuit brought on behalf of Pennsylvania public school students with physical, behavioral, and developmental disabilities (PDE, n.d.). The plaintiff class representatives were 12 students with significant disabilities. Other plaintiffs included the students' parents and 11 national and state organizations that advocated for the rights of people with disabilities. The defendants included the PDE, various PDE officials, and members of the Pennsylvania State Board of Education.

The *Gaskin* action alleged that students with disabilities had been denied their federal statutory rights to an FAPE in general education classrooms with provision of necessary SaS. In particular, the plaintiffs claimed that the PDE had systematically failed to enforce the provisions in federal law that require local schools and school districts to offer a full continuum of support services to enable children with disabilities to be educated in general education classrooms (PDE, n.d.).

In 2004, more than 10 years after the lawsuit was originally filed, a settlement agreement was finally reached. As a result of the settlement, PDE agreed to make many changes designed to increase opportunities for students with disabilities to be included in general education classrooms (PDE, n.d.). These changes included, among others,

- Developing materials to be displayed in all public schools to make it clear that all children are welcome

- Ensuring the development of IEP goals that can be implemented in general education classrooms with the help of SaS

- Implementing a single combined plan for students with disabilities who are also eligible for gifted support

- Implementing LRE monitoring—term borrowed from IDEA—to ensure that districts comply with federal and state laws that protect the rights of students with disabilities

- Establishing an LRE advisory panel, made up of parents, advocates, and educators, to review systemwide progress in the delivery of instruction to students with disabilities in general education schools and classrooms

In response to the mandates of the *Gaskin* settlement, the PDE has made a significant effort over the years to ensure that public schools in Pennsylvania are in compliance with the settlement agreement.

Poolaw III v. Bishop (1995) and *Sch. Dist. of Wisconsin Dells v. Z.S.* (2002)

Not all of the significant special education court cases in the 1990s and early 21st century resulted in decisions that favored inclusion. In the *Poolaw* case, in which the school district's offer of a residential placement was challenged by the child's family, the court ruled in favor of removing the child from the general education classroom. The court noted that the district had already made attempts to place the student in a general education environment with SaS, but these placements had been only minimally successful. Therefore, the court concluded, the residential placement was the most appropriate LRE for meeting the child's educational needs.

Similarly, in the *Sch. Dist. of Wisconsin Dells* case, the court decided in favor of a more restrictive placement for a student with autism who had a history of violent, disruptive behavior in school. This behavior included biting and kicking people and damaging school property. The school district had attempted to educate this child in various placements, including a general education public school, a residential facility (where his behavior improved), and a specialized school. However, when the district tried to return the child to the general education classroom, his behavior became unmanageable again. When the district finally decided to place the boy in a homebound education program, his guardian sued to keep him in the public school. In siding with the district, the court held that the homebound placement did not violate the student's rights under IDEA, because his history showed that there was no basis for believing that he could be educated successfully in an inclusive environment.

Summary

These court decisions and others have helped mold special education practice in the late 20th and early 21st centuries. Some of these rulings were successes for parents who fought against placements that would have excluded their children from general education classrooms; in other cases, the courts ruled in favor of school districts' decisions to place a child with a disability in a more restrictive setting. The significance of cases such as *Greer, Oberti,* and *Gaskin* is that they forced schools to exhaust the use of SaS options before placing a child in a more restrictive environment. Arriving at legal decisions such as these is not always easy; the *Gaskin* case required 10 years of fact finding before a settlement agreement could be reached.

The lesson learned from these cases is that there is a process that must be followed in determining the most appropriate placement for a student with special needs. Federal law requires IEP teams to look carefully at each child's specific needs, determine what SaS are necessary to meet those needs, and make a well-considered decision as to what would be the LRE for that particular student. When schools follow the appropriate procedures and parents are involved in the decision making, the process is more likely to run smoothly and there is less potential for disagreement.

CONCLUSION

Since the passage of the Education for All Handicapped Children Act of 1975, the basic premise of the law has not changed. Yet in many cases, for a variety of reasons, it has taken more than 35 years for America's schools to come into full compliance with the law. Fortunately, parents, advocacy groups, lobbyists, and professional organizations dedicated to protecting the rights of people with disabilities have changed the face of special education by working hard to make sure that school districts and state departments of education were held accountable for meeting the mandates of the law. This is why it is so important for parents and advocates to continue the work of educating the public about special education law. The need for this work has not ended; perhaps it never will.

REFERENCES

Affleck, J.Q., Madge, S., Adams, A., & Lowenbraun, S. (1988). Integrated classroom versus resource model: Academic viability and effectiveness. *Exceptional Children, 54*(4), 339–348. Retrieved from http://www.cec.sped.org/content/NavigationMenu/Publications2/exceptionalchildren/

Americans with Disabilities Act (ADA) of 1990, PL 101-336, 42 U.S.C. §§ 12101 *et seq.*

Board of Educ. of the Hendrick Hudson Central Sch. Dist., Westchester County v. Rowley, 458 U.S. 176 (1982).

Brown v. Board of Educ., 347 U.S. 483 (1954).

Daniel R.R. v. State Board of Educ., 53 Ed. Law Rep. 824 (5th Cir. 1989).

Diana v. State Board of Education, 793 F.2d 969 (9th Cir. 1970).

Education for All Handicapped Children Act of 1975, PL 94-142, 20 U.S.C. §§ 1400 *et seq.*

Ellsworth, J. (1999). Important court cases in special education. *ESE 504: Methods and Materials in Special Education.* Retrieved from http://jan.ucc.nau.edu/~jde7/ese504/class/advanced/courtcases.html

Friend, M., & Bursuck, W.D. (2008). *Including students with special needs: A practical guide for classroom teachers* (5th ed.). Boston, MA: Allyn & Bacon.

Gaskin v. Pennsylvania Dept. of Educ., Gaskin v. Pennsylvania, No. Civ. A. 94-4048, 1995 WL 355346, at (E.D. Pa. June 12, 1995).

Gordon, S. (2006). Making sense of the inclusion debate under IDEA. *Brigham Young University Education and Law Journal, 2006*(1), 189–225.

Greer v. Rome City School District, 967 F.2d 470 (11th Cir. 1992).

Howard, P. (2004). The least restrictive environment: How to tell? *Journal of Law and Education, 33,* 167.

Individuals with Disabilities Education Act (IDEA) of 1990, PL 101-476, 20 U.S.C. §§ 1400 *et seq.*

Individuals with Disabilities Education Act Amendments (IDEA) of 1997, PL 105-17, 20 U.S.C. §§ 1400 *et seq.*

Individuals with Disabilities Education Improvement Act (IDEA) of 2004, PL 108-446, 20 U.S.C. §§ 1400 *et seq.*

Jaccari J. v. Board of Educ. of the City of Chicago, Dist. No. 299, 54 IDELR 53 (N.D. Ill. 2010).

Kalbfleisch v. Columbia Community Unit Sch. Dist. Unit No. 4, No. 5-09-0447 (Ill. App. Ct. 5th December 16, 2009).

Larry P. v. Riles, 793 F.2d 969 (9th Cir. 1984).

Mills v. Board of Educ. of the District of Columbia, 348 F. Supp 866 (D. D.C. 1972).

No Child Left Behind Act of 2001, PL 107-110, 115 Stat. 1425, 20 U.S.C. §§ 6301 *et seq.*

Oberti v. Board of Educ. of Borough of Clementon Sch. Dist., 83 Ed. Law Rep. 1009, 2 A.D.D. 64 (3rd Cir. 1993).

PARC v. Commonwealth of Pennsylvaniva, 334 F. Supp. 1257 (E.D. Pa. 1971).

Pennsylvania Assn. for Retarded Children v. Commonwealth of Pennsylvania: Order, injunction consent agreement, and appendix. (1971). Retrieved from http://tlc-patch.tourolaw.edu/patch/Parc/

Pennsylvania Department of Education. (n.d.). *Fact sheet: Gaskin settlement agreement overview.* Retrieved from http://www.pealcenter.org/images/Gaskin_Fact_Sheet.pdf

Poolaw III v. Bishop, No. 94–15324 (9th Cir. October 4, 1995).

Rehabilitation Act of 1973, 29 U.S.C. §§ 701 *et seq.*

S.A. v. Tulare County Office of Educ., 12 FAB 38 (E.D. Cal. 2009).

Sacramento City Unified Sch. Dist. v. Rachel H., 14 F.3d 1398 (9th Cir. 1994).

Salend, S.J. (2008). *Creating inclusive classrooms: Effective and reflective practices* (6th ed.). Upper Saddle River, NJ: Prentice Hall.

Sch. Dist. of Wisconsin Dells v. Z.S., 295 F.3d 671 (7th Cir. 2002).

T.S. v. Weast, 54 IDELR 249 (D. Md. 2010).

Wisneski, M. (2010). *In pursuit of freedom and equality: Brown v. Board of Education of Topeka.* Retrieved from http://www.nps.gov/brvb/planyourvisit/in_pursuit_of_freedom_and_equality.htm

The Co-Design Model for Collaborative Instruction

CHAPTER 3

Explanation of the Model

Collaboration is a term that is often mentioned as a positive initiative within schools. Many education professionals speak of the favorable impact that collaboration has on the planning and delivery of instruction. If educators want schools to improve and students to reap the greatest benefits from instruction, it is essential that they seek input from fellow teachers from whom they can learn. Collaboration involves creating communities of professionals who work together to share ideas, solve problems, and promote positive changes that benefit students. Although there is no one right way to collaborate, effective collaboration requires mutual respect and trust, open communication, and the sharing of work to achieve a common goal.

When I was working as a building principal, I attempted to create an atmosphere in which teacher collaboration would drive the planning and instruction of school programs. Lesson planning, data analysis, and co-teaching were all addressed in a collaborative environment. Like many other administrators, I firmly believed the old adage that many heads are better than one. I felt that I was on solid ground in my effort to promote collaboration among the staff, even though the benefits were primarily of the "feel-good" variety. The staff enjoyed the opportunity to share ideas and materials, and the mutual planning time made the teachers happy. However, it was not until I began my doctoral work that I truly realized the impact that collaboration can have on teaching and learning.

I conducted a qualitative study of a school that had implemented a collaborative structure in 2003. After years of working in isolation in three separate buildings, the teachers were brought together in one building where their grade level could meet daily. This meeting time was used to establish program goals, plan instructional activities, share resources, and discuss student progress. The results of this research revealed six indisputable benefits from the efforts of collaboration:

1. One hundred percent of the study participants stated that their teaching had improved since the collaboration model was established. The teachers felt that the model gave them more support to try new ideas and fine-tune their activities to meet the students' needs.

2. Teachers agreed that the collaborative atmosphere expanded their repertoire of resources and promoted the use of recommended practices for instruction.

3. Continuity improved within the curriculum and instruction. The staff commented that they were all on the same page with regard to instructional planning and delivery.

4. The instructional focus shifted from the teachers to the children. The teachers acknowledged that their conversations began to focus more on student learning and on teaching to the students' learning styles.

5. Academic rigor increased dramatically as the teachers developed core competencies that they expected their students to achieve, as well as formative and summative assessments to evaluate student achievement.

6. The collaborative structure gave the teachers a greater sense of accountability. They felt more responsible for ensuring student success and more accountable to their peers for meeting school goals.

Clearly, the concept of collaborative instruction is not merely a simple, feel-good school initiative. In fact, an effective collaborative environment can reap benefits for both students and teachers that far exceed expectations.

By Wesley Shipley, Ed.D., Superintendent, Shaler Area School District
serving Shaler Township, Millvale, Etna, and Reserve Township, Pennsylvania

Collaborative instruction is an undeniable ingredient for successful education (Friend, 2011; Villa, Thousand, & Nevin, 2004; Werts, Culatta, & Tompkins, 2007). Gargiulo (2006) reports that the use of collaborative practices in schools is increasing. At some point in their teaching careers, it is likely that most educators will be expected to collaborate and co-instruct with other professionals. The Co-Design Model for collaborative instruction (Barger-Anderson, Isherwood, & Merhaut, 2010; Hoover, Barger-Anderson, Isherwood, & Merhaut, 2010) provides a means for support and professional development, along with strategies for implementation, to ensure that collaborative and inclusive efforts meet success.

Shade and Stewart (2001) stated that general educators in inclusive classrooms often find it difficult to select proper instructional strategies for students with disabilities. These researchers also found that lack of administrative support and planning time is a common problem. Often, schools implement inclusive practices expeditiously without providing proper training and support to the general education teachers (Hammond & Ingalls, 2003). The goal of collaboration in the educational setting is to achieve shared accountability for all students in an inclusive environment. Using the Co-Design Model as a framework for developing and implementing collaborative and inclusive initiatives can assist educators and administrators in accomplishing this goal.

The Co-Design Model is composed of nine elements. These elements are essential for realizing the model's maximum potential. The model also endorses four pathways that educators can use on a day-to-day basis to implement strategies and tactics within the collaborative environment. These pathways are research-based recommended practices that have proven successful in promoting achievement for all levels of learners. There are two analogies that are helpful to understanding how the elements and the pathways work together. The first is to think of the model as a brick building. The elements serve as the bricks and the pathways are the mortar used to hold the bricks together. In other words, the pathways are used to support the structure. The other analogy is that of a vehicle, as illustrated in Figure 3.1. The automobile represents the elements, and the pathways act as the gasoline that enables the car to get from Point A (i.e., the students' initial level of knowledge) to Point B (meeting new learning goals and objectives). In either example, the key to success is understanding how to combine the implementation of the elements and pathways to work synergistically as one model.

These nine elements may appear separately in many classrooms. But when all of the elements are implemented simultaneously, they form the Co-Design Model. It is difficult to say whether one element is more important than another. Therefore, the

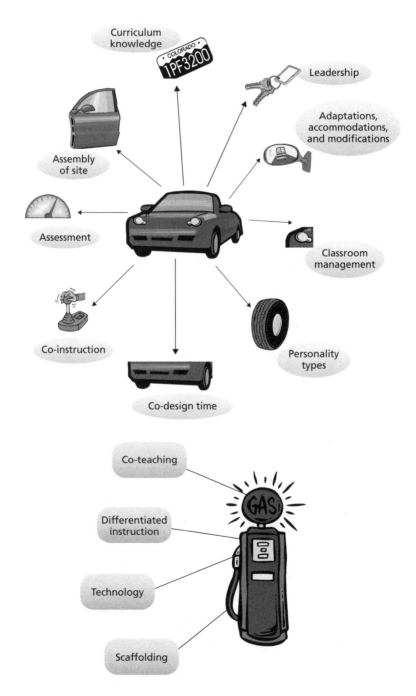

Figure 3.1. A visual analogy of the nine elements and four pathways of the Co-Design Model. (*Source:* Barger-Anderson, Isherwood, Merhaut, and Hoover, 2010.)

Co-Design Model stresses that all nine elements must be implemented and addressed; if one or more elements are left out, the participants risk compromising their ability to reach the highest level of collaborative success.

The *Co-Design Model* is defined as the interaction of professionals engaged in collaborative efforts who share in the obligatory responsibilities for the administration of instructional and noninstructional duties and tasks within an educational setting (Barger-Anderson et al., 2010). This means that the model takes the concept of collaboration in inclusive classrooms beyond just the implementation of common co-teaching models by promoting collaboration that extends beyond the instructional aspects of planning and executing lessons. The model emphasizes the need for reliable and effective collaborative approaches to classroom management, parental contacts, grading of homework, assessments, adaptations, and other components necessary to successfully operate a classroom (Barger-Anderson et al., 2010).

ELEMENTS OF THE CO-DESIGN MODEL

The nine elements of the Co-Design Model are

1. Leadership

2. Assembly of site

3. Curriculum knowledge

4. Co-instruction

5. Classroom management

6. Adaptations, accommodations, and modifications

7. Assessment

8. Personality types

9. Co-design time

Leadership

The element of leadership (discussed in more detail in Chapter 4) encompasses several of the other elements of the Co-Design Model as well as some of the pathways for implementation. For this reason, it is positioned as the first of the nine elements. Some advocates of the Co-Design Model argue that no educational initiative of any kind can succeed without the support of effective leadership by school and district administrators. The leadership element emphasizes the crucial need for administration to ensure sustainability, continued reinforcement, and a long-term commitment throughout the collaborative initiative.

In the Co-Design Model, the leadership element addresses issues such as providing the collaborative partners with common planning time and opportunities for professional development. It also addresses teacher evaluations. Specifically, the leadership element advocates enhancing teachers' professional growth via classroom observations by administrators and outside consultants, peer observations, and feedback on specific lessons. This support includes providing time for the administrators and consultants to conduct preobservation and postobservation conferences with the teachers, both individually and with their collaborative partners.

Gargiulo (2006) found that few general educators believe they have the basic foundation of knowledge needed to address the increasingly diverse needs of all learners in inclusive classrooms. Santoli, Sachs, Romey, and McClung (2008) accentuate that administrative support is necessary for the success of inclusive and collaborative education. Their research demonstrates that even though most teachers at the middle level feel that they receive sufficient support in most other areas, they do not feel that the administrative team allots enough planning time between the general educator and the collaborative partner(s).

Assembly of Site

Assembly of site (discussed in Chapter 5) refers to the organization of physical components within a shared educational venue, along with the promotion of collaborative practices via site management (Barger-Anderson et al., 2010). This element of the Co-Design Model addresses issues such as location of the teaching site, the arrangement of furniture and other items within the shared space, and promoting communication between the collaborative partners to help them plan these logistics. The physical setting for collaborative instruction may be a classroom, an auditorium, two classrooms split between two groups of students, or any other configuration. Even though no two schools are physically the same, lack of adequate space seems to be a common problem.

Gately and Gately (2001) and Villa et al. (2004) agree that the physical arrangement of a shared teaching site needs to be discussed between the collaborative partners. The assembly of site element also helps ensure that the physical setup creates a truly collaborative environment that promotes parity between the partners. Parity is achieved when all partners in a collaborative relationship feel a sense of value and contribution to the educational experience. Parity does not mean that all responsibilities are divided equally; rather, it recognizes that education professionals have individual strengths and differing areas of expertise (Friend, 2011; Villa et al., 2004).

The physical assembly of the classroom or site of instruction should send a clear message that the setting is a shared environment. For example, this may include providing two teacher desks and displaying the names and pictures of both teachers in the room.

Curriculum Knowledge

Curriculum knowledge (see Chapter 6) refers to the different backgrounds, knowledge, and skill sets that each teacher brings to the collaborative classroom. The general education teachers are trained and certified within their own content disciplines. The special educators are experts who are trained and certified in the discipline of special education. In many cases, the special educators may be certified or deemed highly qualified to teach in at least one additional content area. The Co-Design Model's curriculum knowledge element addresses issues such as resolving concerns about one co-teacher's possible lack of curriculum knowledge, providing the time required for teachers to learn curriculum, and ensuring that co-teachers respect each other's strengths, disciplines, and skills. The success of a collaborative teaching relationship may hinge on the level of content and subject area assigned. The content knowledge and skill sets of each partner may differ greatly depending on the class assignment (Friend & Hurley-Chamberlain, n.d.; Gately & Gately, 2001).

Because, according to the U.S. Department of Education, National Center for Education Statistics (2011), the number of students with disabilities who receive their education in inclusive environments is increasing, curriculum knowledge is an important element within the Co-Design Model. The Individuals with Disabilities Education Improvement Act (IDEA) of 2004 (PL 108-446) has given students with disabilities greater access to general education classrooms and to standardized assessments that evaluate acquisition of knowledge in the general education curriculum. IDEA also resulted in the implementation of teacher preparation guidelines to help ensure that students with disabilities receive an appropriate education in general education classrooms. The passage of the No Child Left Behind Act of 2001 (PL 107-110) provided opportunities for students with disabilities to have access to more inclusive environments because of assessment procedures. Required assessments of all students led to more access to the curriculum in the general education classrooms. It also addressed the need for teachers to be highly qualified in their content areas. When IDEA was reauthorized in 2004, it aligned with No Child Left Behind (Kight, 2008).

Like assembly of site, the curriculum knowledge element stresses the importance of parity between the collaborative partners. Respect for each other's skill sets is essential to helping the partners determine strengths within a curriculum. Also, the longer collaborative partners remain consistent with each other and with the same content, the more confident both partners become in all aspects of sharing a class assignment.

Co-instruction

Co-instruction (see Chapter 7) is defined as professionals engaged in consistent and routine collaborative efforts for the implementation of instructional practices within an educational setting (Barger-Anderson et al., 2010). The collaborative partners must not only allocate instructional time but also be committed to the initiative on a consistent basis. In other words, this element of the Co-Design Model goes beyond co-teaching to include dependable sharing of all classroom responsibilities. Co-instruction encompasses two processes: Not only does it include lesson execution but also addresses the realm of professionalism. Collaborative partners must be committed to both the success of the relationship and the overall success of the initiative. This commitment can be fostered through open communication of educational philosophies and beliefs. It is not necessary for all collaborative partners to agree on all issues. It is, however, important to promote open dialogue, understanding, and openness to compromise. Also, maintaining consistency of partners from year to year typically helps to strengthen a collaborative relationship. Building trust and comfort levels between the partners is another key consideration. The longer the collaborative pairs remain together, the more the relationships can grow.

Of course, there may sometimes be situations when partnerships need to be terminated. This does not necessarily mean that one (or both) of the teachers is incompetent or lacking skills as an instructor. Rather, the failure of the relationship may be the result of factors such as differences in personality types, educational philosophies, teaching styles, and approaches to behavior management and classroom management. Therefore, it is crucial to promote dialogue between co-instructors on issues that may create tension if not discussed in advance. Some of the most common co-instruction issues that are encountered during assistance to schools with implementation of the Co-Design Model include establishing common principles in areas such as classroom routines for transition times and homework policies. This area also encompasses professionalism between the two teachers. Items that may need to be discussed include cell phone use in class and the importance of coming to class on time—that is, cell phone use and prompt arrival *by the teachers*. Finally, co-instruction includes sharing of instructional time. Teaching styles and philosophies should be communicated between partners at the start of the school year as well as throughout the year.

Classroom Management

The element of classroom management comprises two distinct areas: creating the collaborative environment and managing teacher–student relationships within that environment (see Chapter 8). The Co-Design Model emphasizes the importance of dialogue between co-instructors to agree upon rules, roles, responsibilities, and other important issues necessary for managing a shared classroom effectively. Some examples of potential problem areas collaborative partners may encounter include whether or not to allow food and drink in the classroom and managing noise levels. Research supports the importance of establishing common rules and routines. By agreeing on rules prior to the start of the school year, some difficulties may be averted. For example, it is important to agree upon the restroom pass policy and when it is appropriate to sharpen a pencil (Gately & Gately, 2001; Mercer, Mercer, & Pullen, 2010). This agreement helps the co-instructors manage the room more effectively and creates a sense of community.

It is essential for the collaborative partners to discuss their classroom management preferences with each other as soon as possible. If there is an opportunity for this to occur before the first day of class, that is recommended. However, in many cases teachers do not know their new class assignments until the first day of school.

Some students with disabilities may have individualized education program (IEP) situations that require a specific behavior plan. When this is the case, having two professionals in the classroom can be helpful in fulfilling the IEP requirements. Other times, a teacher may choose to implement individual or classwide behavior systems even if this is not required in a specific IEP. If a special education teacher is one of the collaborative partners, his or her expertise can be beneficial to the general education teacher in establishing these systems.

Communication is a significant and common component throughout the Co-Design Model, yet it seems to be especially important in this area. The classroom management element provides strategies to help co-instructors continue to maintain open discourse about the needs of all learners in the shared classroom environment.

Adaptations, Accommodations, and Modifications

There are many differing definitions for these terms in the educational arena (see Chapter 9). For purposes of the Co-Design Model, an *adaptation* is an umbrella term that refers to any type of change from the typical means in which a teacher would execute instruction or assessment. The actual way to realize the change is through either a *modification* or an *accommodation* (Algozzine, Ysseldyke, & Elliott, 1997; Smith, Polloway, Patton, & Dowdy, 2006; Thurlow, 2002). Whether the adaptation is a modification or an accommodation depends on the type of change being made.

Modifications involve the change of content and/or change in goals deemed appropriate for individual students (National Dissemination Center for Children with Disabilities, 2010; Smith et al., 2006). Accommodations, on the other hand, are changes that give students with disabilities equal access to the same curriculum and assessments as their peers without disabilities (Thurlow, 2002). In other words, accommodations enable students to demonstrate their acquisition of knowledge by working around the barriers presented by their disabilities (National Dissemination Center for Children with Disabilities, 2010). For example, providing a student with supplementary aids and services, as stipulated within an IEP or response to intervention (RTI) plan, can be accomplished via accommodations and/or modifications.

As with the other elements of the Co-Design Model, the adaptations, accommodations, and modifications element stresses the need for open dialogue between the collaborative partners about educational philosophies and beliefs. This benefits the partners in the division of labor for completing and implementing the adaptations. It is also important for co-instructors to present adaptations to the students throughout the instructional process, not just at assessment time.

Assessment

The element of assessment (discussed in Chapter 10) as it relates to the Co-Design Model includes two types: formative assessments and summative assessments. Formative assessment consists of continuous evaluation, observations, and reviews that are used daily to provide teacher information and student feedback (Fisher & Frey, 2007). Summative assessment is conducted at the conclusion of a unit to determine the amount of learning that has occurred (Dodge, 2009). Mercer et al. (2010) state that both formative and summative data results should be used frequently to make data-driven decisions.

Assessment in the collaborative environment requires dialogue and agreement between the partners in terms of types and frequency of assessments. It is important to remember the reason for assessment: to gather data on student progress that will enable educators to make well-informed instructional decisions (Badgett & Christman, 2009; Salvia & Ysseldyke, 2004; Salvia, Ysseldyke, & Bolt, 2007). This element of the model helps ensure that appropriate preassessment and postassessment techniques are used to drive instructional planning, as well as to implement various assessment techniques for progress reporting.

Personality Types

This element of the Co-Design Model (see Chapter 11) focuses on understanding one's own personality type as well as a partner's type. Four types of personalities are presented. Both different and similar personality types, when paired together in a shared teaching environment, can be successful. The better teachers understand personality types and characteristics, the better they will be at understanding why people do certain things or act in various ways. Understanding personality types may also improve communication between partners, which is important because a collaborative teaching relationship is much like a marriage. Furthermore, a co-instructor in an inclusive classroom often has to work with more than one collaborative partner. Rohm (2004, 2008) found that understanding each other's personality types can make it easier for collaborative partners to work in tandem. Of course, for the professional with multiple collaborative partners, the task is more difficult. It takes effort and time to collaborate, communicate, and stay informed with all partners.

Co-design Time

The co-design time element (Chapter 12) stresses the importance of ensuring that collaborative partners have time for common planning. Unfortunately, this essential element is often lacking in collaborative education environments. In particular, research shows that common lesson-design time is needed (Gately & Gately, 2001; Hawbaker, Balong, Buckwalter, & Runyon, 2001; Santoli et al., 2008). The most difficult part of this element is finding the time for the collaborative partners to meet (Zigmond & Magiera, 2001). Ashton (2003) states that many co-teaching initiatives give only minimal concern to ensuring meeting time between teachers for planning purposes. Therefore, the Co-Design Model encourages education professionals to be creative and think outside the box for ways to identify and find opportunities for common planning time.

THE PATHWAYS FOR IMPLEMENTATION OF THE CO-DESIGN MODEL

Once the nine elements of the Co-Design Model have been put in place to assist in establishing an environment for collaborative instruction, the four research-based pathways can be used to promote successful learning for all students in the inclusive classroom setting. These pathways are

1. Co-teaching

2. Differentiated instruction

3. Technology

4. Scaffolding

Co-teaching

The purpose of the Co-Design Model is to assist schools and school districts in meeting both collaborative and inclusive needs (Barger-Anderson et al., 2010). Because collaboration is a necessary ingredient in inclusive education (Friend & Bursuck, 2008), co-teaching is a logical and practical strategy to employ. Co-teaching models, when used appropriately, can move all students, with and without disabilities, toward academic achievement (Rice & Zigmond, 2000).

Co-teaching between general education and special education teachers is a frequently used model for delivering instruction in inclusive classrooms (Friend, 2011; Villa et al., 2004). However, Friend (2011) states that co-teaching occurs when education professionals share planning, instructional, and assessment duties for all students in the inclusive classroom. Under this broader definition, the co-teachers may be any two or more professionals who share responsibilities for meeting the educational and behavioral needs of the students assigned to their class roster. Thus, co-teachers can include not only general education and special education teachers but also specialists such as librarians, physical education teachers, computer teachers, art teachers, and therapists (e.g., speech-language, physical, and occupational).

The Co-Design Model promotes the use of five co-teaching models, based on the research of Marilyn Friend (2005, 2007, 2011). These models (discussed in detail in Chapter 13) are 1) team teaching, 2) one teach/one assist, 3) the parallel model, 4) the stations model, and 5) the alternative model. One model of co-teaching is not superior to the others. However, this pathway also encourages collaborative partners to avoid getting into a routine of only using one model.

Differentiated Instruction

This pathway (see Chapter 14) focuses on collaborative strategies for successfully presenting instruction to both students with disabilities and students without disabilities in the inclusive classroom environment. It can include differentiation in content, process, and teaching tools in order to meet the learning needs of all students. Tomlinson (1999) describes differentiated instruction as a means for teachers to help individual students learn as much as possible and as deeply as possible by recognizing that learning styles differ from one student to the next.

Differentiating instruction to accommodate a range of learning styles is a time-consuming process. However, the reward is worth the effort. High levels of student learning are possible via differentiation. It is important for the collaborative partners to start small when implementing this component of the Co-Design Model so as not to feel overwhelmed. Choosing one lesson to differentiate is a good way to start. The more co-instructors become familiar with the practice of differentiated instruction, the more effectively they are able to use it.

Because differentiated instruction is recognized as a recommended practice, many teachers have already been trained or provided with professional development opportunities to learn more about this technique. However, even if each of the co-teachers has a good individual understanding of differentiation, both must still learn how to use it successfully in a collaborative environment.

Technology

Prensky (2001) uses the term *digital natives* to describe the generation of students who are being educated in the early 21st century. Technology is a beneficial means of acquiring new skills for this generation of learners. Because these students respond to a multimodal approach to education, this pathway in the Co-Design Model focuses on strategies for using technology to provide differentiated instruction and make inclusive adaptations for students with disabilities (see Chapter 15).

Examples of ways to make technology useful for student learning in a collaborative environment include the use of WebQuests, live streaming, or even web-based game templates. Of course, some school districts have more technological resources than others. Nevertheless, use of technology with a collaborative partner can make it easier for teachers to amalgamate these resources into daily lessons.

Scaffolding

Scaffolding, a concept popularized by the work of Vygotsky (1978) and others, is an instructional strategy that helps a learner obtain new skills or information (see Chapter 16). Throughout the scaffolding process, and with the presentation of all new skills, the student is provided with support as needed (Carter, Prater, & Dyches, 2009). At first, support is provided at the learner's initial level of comprehension. As the student begins the acquisition of new content, some of the support offered at the start is removed. This strategy is designed to promote independence at each level of new learning. The effectiveness of scaffolding has been proven through research in many content areas (Beers, 2003; Bodrova & Leong, 2007; Smith & Tyler, 2010). The Co-Design Model promotes scaffolding as a means of helping students in inclusive classrooms achieve success. Because scaffolding lends itself to learning via social constructs, it is easily incorporated into a collaborative environment.

CONCLUSION

Research indicates that many teachers have fears concerning some aspects of implementing inclusion practices in the general education environment. Some of these fears stem from factors such as lack of knowledge about how to manage students with severe disabilities, the belief that inclusion will have a negative impact on the general education students, and concern that more work will be added to teachers' already full plates (Kavale & Forness, 2000). Santoli et al. (2008) report that many teachers do not hold the belief that students who are receiving special education services can be successful in inclusive placements.

The Co-Design Model offers a research-based approach to achieving a successful, collaborative, and inclusive program that meets the needs of all students. Potential benefits of using the model include a less restrictive environment for students with disabilities, higher levels of achievement for all students, increased student engagement, and greater access to highly qualified teachers in the content areas. The elements and pathways of the Co-Design Model intertwine to equip schools with the tools they need to provide appropriate education for students with disabilities in the least restrictive environment.

REFERENCES

Algozzine, B., Ysseldyke, J., & Elliott, J. (1997). *Strategies and tactics for effective instruction.* Longmont, CO: Sopris West.

Ashton, T.M. (2003). What are teachers' greatest co-teaching concerns? *Academic Exchange Quarterly, 7*(3), 100–104.

Badgett, J.L., & Christman, E.P. (2009). *Designing elementary instruction and assessment using the cognitive domain.* Thousand Oaks, CA: Corwin.

Barger-Anderson, R., Isherwood, R., & Merhaut, J. (2010, February). *The Co-Design Model: A collaborative approach to inclusive education.* Paper presented at the 47th Annual International Conference of the Learning Disabilities Association of America, Baltimore, MD.

Barger-Anderson, R., Isherwood, R., Merhaut, J., & Hoover, K. (2010, April). The Co-Design Model: A collaborative approach to inclusive education. In P. Tramdak (Chair), *Slippery Rock University of Pennsylvania research symposium.* Symposium conducted at Slippery Rock University, Slippery Rock, PA.

Beers, K. (2003). *When kids can't read: What teachers can do—A guide for teachers 6–12.* Portsmouth, NH: Heinemann.

Bodrova, E., & Leong, D.J. (2007). *Tools of the mind: The Vygotskian approach to early childhood education* (2nd ed.). Upper Saddle River, NJ: Merrill.

Carter, N., Prater, M.A., & Dyches, T.T. (2009). *Making accommodations and adaptations for students with mild to moderate disabilities.* Upper Saddle River, NJ: Pearson.

Dodge, J. (2009). *25 quick formative assessments for a differentiated classroom.* New York, NY: Scholastic.

Fisher, D., & Frey, N. (2007). *Checking for understanding: Formative assessment techniques for your classroom.* Alexandria, VA: Association for Supervision and Curriculum Development.

Friend, M. (2005). *The power of 2* (2nd ed.). Port Chester, NY: National Professional Resources.

Friend, M. (2007). *Co-teaching.* Retrieved from http://www.marilynfriend.com/basics.htm

Friend, M. (2011). *Special education: Contemporary perspectives for school professionals* (3rd ed.). Boston, MA: Pearson.

Friend, M., & Bursuck, W.D. (2008). *Including students with special needs: A practical guide for classroom teachers* (5th ed.). Boston, MA: Allyn & Bacon.

Friend, M., & Hurley-Chamberlain, D. (n.d.). *Is co-teaching effective?* Retrieved from http://www.cec.sped.org/AM/Template.cfm?Section=Home&CONTENTID=7504&TEMPLATE=/CM/ContentDisplay.cfm

Gargiulo, R. (2006). *Special education in contemporary society* (2nd ed.). Belmont, CA: Wadsworth.

Gately, S.E., & Gately, F.J. (2001). Understanding co-teaching components. *Teaching Exceptional Children, 33*(4), 40–47.

Hammond, H., & Ingalls, L. (2003). Teachers' attitudes toward inclusion: Survey results from elementary school teachers in three southwestern rural school districts. *Rural Special Education Quarterly, 22,* 24–30.

Hawbaker, B.W., Balong, M., Buckwalter, S., & Runyon, S. (2001). Building a strong BASE of support for all students through co-planning. *Teaching Exceptional Children, 33*(4), 24–30.

Hoover, K., Barger-Anderson, R., Isherwood, R., & Merhaut, J. (2010). The Co-Design Model: A collaborative approach to inclusive education. *Journal of Scholarly Endeavor, X,* 54.

Individuals with Disabilities Education Improvement Act (IDEA) of 2004, PL 108-446, 20 U.S.C. §§ 1400 *et seq.*

Kavale, K.A., & Forness, S.R. (2000). History, rhetoric, and reality: Analysis of the inclusion debate. *Remedial and Special Education, 21*(5), 279–296.

Kight, J.S. (2008). *The relationship between training and experience and general educators' attitudes toward the inclusion of students with disabilities.* Available from ProQuest Dissertations and Theses database. (UMI No. 3376431)

Mercer, C., Mercer, A., & Pullen, P.C. (2010). *Teaching students with learning problems* (8th ed.). Upper Saddle River, NJ: Prentice Hall.

Merhaut, J., & Hoover, K. (2010, April). *The Co-Design Model: A collaborative approach to inclusive education.* In P. Tramdak (Chair), *Slippery Rock University of Pennsylvania research symposium.* Symposium conducted as Slippery Rock University, Slippery Rock, PA.

National Dissemination Center for Children with Disabilities. (2010, September). *Supports, modifications, and accommodations for students.* Retrieved from http://www.nichcy.org/EducateChildren/Supports/Pages/default.aspx

No Child Left Behind Act of 2001, PL 107-110, 115 Stat. 1425, 20 U.S.C. §§ 6301 *et seq.*

Prensky, M. (2001). Digital natives, digital immigrants. *On the Horizon, 9*(5), 1–6.

Rice, D., & Zigmond, N. (2000). Co-teaching in secondary schools: Teacher reports of developments in Australian and American classrooms. *Learning Disabilities Research and Practice, (15)*4, 190–197.

Rohm, R. (2004). *You've got style: Your personal guide for relating to others.* Marietta, GA: Personality Insights.

Rohm, R. (2008). *Positive personality profiles.* Marietta, GA: Personality Insights.

Salvia, J., & Ysseldyke, J.E. (2004). *Assessment* (9th ed.). Boston, MA: Houghton Mifflin.

Salvia, J., Ysseldyke, J.E., & Bolt, S. (2007). *Assessment in special and inclusive education* (10th ed.). Boston, MA: Houghton Mifflin.

Santoli, S.P., Sachs, J., Romey, E.A., & McClurg, S. (2008). A successful formula for middle school inclusion: Collaboration, time, and administrative support. *Research in Middle Level Education Online, 32*(2). Retrieved from http://www.amle.org/Publications/RMLEOnline/Articles/Vol32No2/tabid/1780/Default.aspx

Shade, R.A., & Stewart, R. (2001). General education and special education preservice teachers' attitudes toward inclusion. *Preventing School Failure, 46*(1), 37–41.

Smith, D.D., & Tyler, N.C. (2010). *Introduction to special education: Making a difference* (7th ed.). Upper Saddle River, NJ: Merrill.

Smith, T.E.C., Polloway, E.A., Patton, J.R., & Dowdy, C.A. (2006). *Teaching students with special needs in inclusive settings* (Rev. IDEA ed.). Boston, MA: Allyn & Bacon.

Thurlow, M. (2002). *Accommodations for students with disabilities in high school* (Issue Brief, Vol. 1, No. 1). Retrieved from National Center on Secondary Education and Transition web site: http://www.ncset.org/publications/viewdesc.asp?id=247

Tomlinson, C.A. (1999). *The differentiated classroom: Responding to the needs of all learners.* Alexandria, VA: Association for Supervision and Curriculum Development.

U.S. Department of Education. (2011). *The condition of education: Children and youth with disabilities.* National Center for Education Statistics. Retrieved from http://nces.ed.gov/programs/coe/indicator_cwd.asp [now available from http://nces.ed.gov/pubsearch/pubsinfo.asp?pubid=2011033]

Villa, R.A., Thousand, J.S., & Nevin, A.I. (2004). *A guide to co-teaching: Practical tips for facilitating student learning.* Thousand Oaks, CA: Sage Publications.

Vygotsky, L. (1978). Interaction between learning and development (M. Cole, Trans.). In M. Cole, V. John-Steiner, S. Scribner, & E. Soberman (Eds.), *Mind in society* (pp. 79–91). Cambridge, MA: Harvard University Press.

Werts, M.G., Culatta, R.A., & Tompkins, J.R. (2007). *Fundamentals of special education: What every teacher needs to know* (3rd ed.). Upper Saddle River, NJ: Pearson.

Zigmond, N., & Magiera, K. (2001). A focus on co-teaching: Use caution. *Current Practice Alerts from the Division for Learning Disabilities and Division for Research of the Council for Exceptional Children, 6,* 1–4. Retrieved from http://www.dldcec.org/alerts/

CHAPTER **4**

Leadership

As the old song goes, "You gotta have heart." In education, having "heart" is critical, but the heart of a servant leader is unique. Physiologically, servant leaders' hearts are the same as others' hearts: They are the size of a fist and weigh between 250 and 350 grams. A servant leader's heart appears to be no different than another person's heart until he or she steps into an inclusive classroom. Once it is surrounded by students with diverse needs, a servant leader's heart is remarkably different. It pulses with each breath his or her students take and it beats tirelessly as they journey through the learning process.

The term *servant leader* refers to someone who leads in order to serve others. When one leads with a servant leader's heart, the emphasis is on collaboration, trust, empathy, and communication. These attributes are key in creating effective co-teaching teams and supporting student achievement in inclusive classrooms. A servant leader's heart is a prerequisite for all leaders who support the concept of co-teaching, from superintendents to principals to teachers.

At Blackhawk School District, I am proud to be surrounded by administrators and faculty who are servant leaders. They place their colleagues' and students' needs above their own. At the heart of each inclusive classroom at Blackhawk are co-teachers who are servant leaders. They are leading quietly but in powerful and life-altering ways. The result is a culture of service, achievement, and collaboration led by the hearts of co-teachers.

By Michelle Miller, Ed.D., Superintendent of Blackhawk School District

Collaboration between specialists and general education teachers is commonplace in the early 21st century as schools attempt to meet the needs of diverse students, including students with disabilities as well as children who are identified as gifted or talented, all in one classroom. Although many educators would say that the progress made in the area of inclusive education since the passage of the Education for All Handicapped Children Act of 1975 (PL 94-142) has been nothing short of remarkable, there are still some school districts across the United States that practice business as usual by using antiquated service delivery models that reflect a bygone era of education dominated by pull-out classrooms for students with intellectual, behavioral, or physical disabilities. These pull-outs typically contain students with similar disabilities, and in many instances those students spend a majority of their school day receiving all or most of their core instruction from one teacher.

One glaring difference between the inclusive schools we visit in our work as consultants and the schools that struggle to embrace concepts such as inclusion, co-teaching, differentiated instruction, and the belief that all children have worth and can learn is that the latter schools lack leadership, vision, and planning from their administrations. What is often missing in these schools is a transformational leader with the courage and knowledge to change the culture, revoke the status quo, and force education professionals to reflect on their own practices. In our experience, many troubled school districts have high rates of turnover in important leadership positions, including the superintendent and other key administrators such as principals and central office personnel. This revolving door of leadership results in quick-fix ideas and initiatives that are never fully accepted, lack follow-through, and do little to improve student achievement and culture change. Visionary, creative, knowledgeable, principled, and inspirational leaders are vital to building and fostering the positive school environment that is necessary to help meet public education goals in the 21st century (Simonson, 2005). There is little doubt that behind every good school there is at least one good leader with vision and a passionate desire to make things better.

There is a specific type of leader who is particularly successful in creating school environments that accept concepts such as inclusion and differentiated instruction. These leaders are what Robert Greenleaf called "servant leaders" in his 1977 book, *Servant Leadership: A Journey into the Nature of Legitimate Power and Greatness.* Servant leaders differ from the typical leader in that they are more interested in serving others than in serving themselves. Belief in the tenets of servant leadership as a practical operational approach for school communities has gained momentum among scholars and practitioners since the 1980s (Sendjaya & Sarros, 2002). Studies have shown a relationship between implementing principles of servant leadership and achieving positive organizational climates (Ehrhart, 2004; Hunt, 2002; McCowan, 2004). Greenleaf emphasizes that true leadership "emerges from those whose primary motivation is a deep desire to help others" (1977, p. 2). In his second major essay, "The Institution as Servant," Greenleaf articulated the credo for servant leaders by stating,

> This is my thesis: caring for persons, the more able and the less able serving each other, it is the rock upon which a good society is built. Whereas, until recently, caring was largely person to person, now most of it is mediated through institutions—often large, complex, powerful, impersonal; not always competent; sometimes corrupt. If a better society is to be built, one that is more just, and more loving, one that provides greater creative opportunity for its people, then the most open course is to raise both the capacity to serve and the very performance as servant of existing major institutions by new regenerative forces operating within them. (1977, p. 5)

Servant leadership is a leadership style that attempts to move organizations toward a more meaningful leadership model that is based on teamwork, community, morals, involving others in decision making, and promoting the growth of individuals within the organization (Lubin, 2001; Spears & Lawrence, 2004; Yukl, 2002).

Patterson (2003) presents the theory of servant leadership as a logical extension of transformational leadership theory (see Figure 4.1). She suggests that servant leaders are guided by seven virtuous constructs that define their leadership. The servant leader 1) demonstrates *agapao* love, 2) acts with humility, 3) is altruistic, 4) is visionary, 5) is trusting, 6) empowers followers, and 7) is serving (Patterson, 2003). *Agapao* love is a moral love that includes doing the right thing at the right time for the right reason (Winston, 2002); it is the cornerstone of servant leadership (Patterson, 2003). This is the type of leadership that is needed to create an inclusive school culture.

LEADING AND ADMINISTERING THE INCLUSIVE SCHOOL

Acquiring the right servant leader who has a transformational vision is the first step in creating a culture of acceptance and inclusion in a school. However, this is not the only part of the equation. A leader who is attempting to transform a school's culture must also understand important practical aspects of managing and leading in an inclusive school (see Figure 4.2). Technical and educational subsystems must be handled correctly, including areas such as scheduling, classroom composition, handling the school's management information system to reflect the practice of co-teaching, providing common planning time, promoting the use of instructional technology, and training teachers in the five models of co-teaching.

The human subsystem must also be handled carefully. Developing a shared vision and building consensus, both inside the school and out in the community, are critical aspects of creating an inclusive school. An example of this occurred in 2010 when we were working in an affluent school district outside of the Pittsburgh area in which the mean household income was well above the mean income in the state. This school district could be characterized as one of the highest-achieving districts in Pennsylvania, and it includes a high school that *U.S. News & World Report* identified as one of the top 500 in the nation (Ramirez, 2008). Unfortunately, inclusion of students with disabilities was not a concept that was zealously accepted by the community. The school leaders and faculty did an outstanding job of creating an inclusive environment within the school walls through

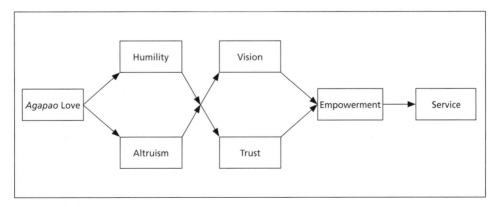

Figure 4.1. Patterson's theoretical model of servant leadership. (From Patterson, K. [2003]. Servant leadership: A theoretical model [Dissertation Abstracts International, 64 (02), p. 570.][(UMI No. 3082719], reprinted by permission.

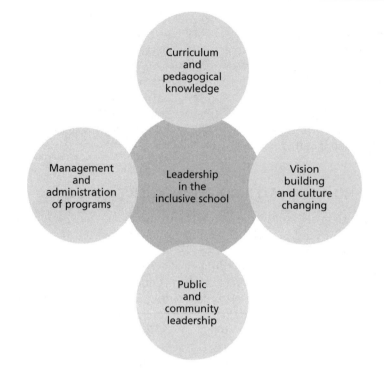

Figure 4.2. Elements of leading and administering an inclusive school.

vision building, professional development, and provision of support and resources. The community, on the other hand, did not embrace inclusion; small factions of parents wrote anonymous letters to parents of students with disabilities asking them to remove their children from the general education classrooms because they were distractions to the college-bound students without disabilities. The situation spilled over into the local newspaper, which published candid and painful letters to the editor from parents on both sides of the issue. It was a stark reminder that not everyone accepts inclusion and that school leaders must educate the public to promote better understanding of this issue; they must also be courageous and committed enough to the principles of servant leadership to withstand criticism and pressure.

In response to this situation, the school leaders quickly huddled together and developed a plan for educating parents and community members. The district's director of special education put together a public relations campaign that included information about the federal and state laws that mandate inclusion of students with disabilities, provided parents with data that supported the successful results of inclusion and co-teaching initiatives, and worked closely with the school board and community to construct policies and procedures that supported inclusion. All of this information was shared openly with parents and community members in an effort to gain support and build consensus. The school administrators did the right thing at the right time. They laid out a vision for the stakeholders, did not take the criticism personally, acted with humility, empowered community members by giving them an opportunity to participate in policy development, and most important, acted in a manner consistent with the principles of servant leadership. As of 2012, this school district has a model inclusion program.

Classroom Composition

Creating an inclusive school environment requires a principal or school leader who is willing to rethink the master schedule and make tough decisions that promote inclusion and support co-teaching. The first step is to develop a plan for classroom composition that includes a manageable ratio of students with IEPs to students without disabilities in any co-taught general education classroom. The literature on co-teaching supports a ratio of three students without disabilities to every one student with an IEP as an ideal class makeup and an optimal environment (Villa, Thousand, & Nevin, 2008; Zigmond & Magiera, 2001). Using this ratio can be challenging to schedule makers because there are usually a limited number of special education teachers available in any given school to establish co-taught classrooms. Therefore, some type of strategy for creating cluster groups of students with disabilities must be developed and used so that the students with the highest degree of need are scheduled in classrooms that have co-teachers. Cluster grouping is a concept that has its roots in gifted education but seems to be gaining momentum as a grouping strategy for students with disabilities included in general education classrooms. It is the process of placing four to eight students with similar needs in a classroom with a competent instructor or co-instructors trained in the use of co-teaching models and differentiated instruction. Cluster grouping should be more than just a random procedure completed by a computerized scheduling system; it must be a thoughtful decision that takes each student's individual needs into consideration and is based on analysis of student data. Principals and school leaders must play an active role in this process.

One helpful tool is the Scales for Predicting Successful Inclusion (SPSI) assessment (Gilliam & McConnell, 1997). This instrument is designed to assist teachers and school personnel in identifying which students with disabilities are likely to benefit from general education classes and which students are likely to need a more restrictive placement. The SPSI consists of four norm-referenced objective rating scales: Work Habits, Coping Skills, Peer Relations, and Emotional Maturity. These scales help quantify teachers' judgments about whether a student possesses the characteristics necessary for success in the general education environment. The SPSI can also be used to help school personnel plan appropriate interventions for students, provide evidence for the need for special education services, and evaluate the effectiveness of interventions that are already in place.

Ideally, students with disabilities who have the highest standard scores on the SPSI may be able to succeed in general education classrooms without the assistance of a special education teacher. A student with a moderate SPSI score might be successful in the general education environment with the help of co-instructors working in concert to meet the child's needs. Students with low scores might continue to need a more restrictive placement with intense direct instruction from a special education teacher. Once the scores are accumulated and analyzed, student cluster groups can begin to be developed with consideration given to individual students' needs, teacher availability, and manageable ratios. It is important for school leaders to promote and facilitate the use of assessment tools such as the

SPSI so that these data-driven approaches become accepted as part of the school culture.

Determining Collaborative Partnerships

Another important aspect of creating an inclusive school is determining who will work together as co-teachers. All too often, school administrators establish collaborative partnerships solely on the basis of logistics, such as the school schedule and teacher availability, without considering teachers' personalities and teaching styles during the matching and implementation process. This can result in the partnering of two teachers who are an incompatible match. Such incompatibility often encompasses multiple areas, such as classroom management, academic expectations, and the teachers' level of interest and ability in specific content areas (Isherwood & Barger-Anderson, 2008). To avoid such mismatches, administrators might consider permitting teachers to choose their collaborative partners. In addition, we have used personality inventories in our work with schools to determine which teachers might be the best fit when working together in a professional environment. See Chapter 11 for more information on using personality inventories to match compatible teachers.

To help schools establish a comprehensive action plan for developing and training effective co-teaching teams, we have created a group of tools that focus on the essential components of good collaborative relationships (see the appendix). These tools include checklists, planning forms, and discussion starters that can be used to promote dialogue between collaborative partners and help them establish common principles in essential areas such as teaching philosophy, assessment practices, and classroom management systems.

Scheduling Common Planning Time

The third key component of creating an inclusive school environment with effective co-teaching teams is ensuring that the collaborative partners are allotted enough common planning time to develop effective lessons that go beyond the one teach, one assist co-teaching model. Overwhelmingly, teachers report common planning time as the most important factor affecting the successful implementation of co-teaching. Yet over and over in our consulting work, we encounter schools in which administrators provide little to no common planning time in the master schedule. Jackson and Davis assert, "Time is perhaps the most important but least available resource in American education" (2000, p. 131). Dickinson and Erb (1997) and Wei, Darling-Hammond, Andree, Richardson, and Orphanos (2009) found that teachers in the United States taught more hours per year, yet were given significantly less planning time, than teachers working in schools abroad.

Effective leaders of inclusive schools communicate to their staff that they value collaboration. They recognize that successful co-teaching can only occur when the collaborative partners develop trust and respect for each other, and that co-teachers need to spend time together for such relationships to grow. They acknowledge that co-teachers require unencumbered time to plan collaborative classroom activities and coordinate instructional responsibilities in order to ensure the creation of classroom environments that meet the needs of all students.

Whenever possible, collaborative planning time should be scheduled at least once a week. Some administrators incorporate co-planning time into the master schedule; others are able to hire a floating substitute one day a week to give co-teachers time to plan.

Without a doubt, providing common planning time is absolutely critical in getting teachers to buy into co-teaching relationships and maximizing the use of a variety of co-teaching models. School leaders should ensure that this shared time is used in a manner that has a positive impact on the quality of instruction and that ultimately increases student achievement. Mertens and Flowers (2004) state that effective uses of common planning time include planning and coordinating activities (e.g., homework, tests, special assemblies), reviewing and assessing student work, and conferencing with students. Effective co-teaching teams also use common planning time to flexibly group and regroup students, collaborate and coordinate activities with exploratory or unified arts teachers, develop expectations for student behavior and academic achievement, plan and implement the use of community resources, and work to develop a team identity (Jackson & Davis, 2000). See Chapter 12 for more recommendations about how to find and use common planning time.

Promoting Effective Use of Co-Teaching Models

Friend and Cook (2003) state that co-teachers are partners with equal credentials who are working together for the benefit of all students. These researchers suggest that the power in co-teaching is the use of models that create small groups and increase the intensity of instruction. Yet, almost half of the observations of co-teaching teams we have conducted in our work as consultants is of two teachers stuck in the one teach/one assist model. We have nicknamed this model the "default model" because co-teachers naturally default to it when one of the teachers is unfamiliar with curriculum, there is no common planning time, or the teaching partners are struggling with philosophical or personal differences. Rice and Zigmond (2000) found that inconsistency in the use of co-teaching models, especially at the secondary school level, may be due to such factors as the intensity of the content, the tighter scheduling issues, and the pressure on secondary teachers to prepare students for high-stakes exams.

Although these are certainly legitimate issues, it is nevertheless important for principals and other school leaders to convey the message that collaborative teams are expected to use all of the effective co-teaching models—including those that decrease the student-to-teacher ratio. Bos and Vaughn (2002) confirm that students with the most intensive instructional needs require more of their instruction to be delivered in small groups. Small-group instruction increases students' opportunities to practice skills and receive feedback from teachers to enhance learning (Howell & Nolet, 2000). We see this frequently in the classroom observations we do almost on a daily basis. Co-teachers who use the stations model, the parallel model, and the alternative model tend to have students who are much more engaged in learning, participate more actively, and demonstrate less off-task behavior. School leaders can help ensure that these benefits are achieved by providing co-teachers with adequate training and professional development opportunities that focus on the use of all five co-teaching models.

Evaluating Co-Teaching Effectiveness

The final step in the process of creating and sustaining inclusive schools is evaluating teacher effectiveness. This includes setting clear expectations, validating collaborative efforts through frequent observation, providing co-teachers with regular feedback to help them grow professionally, and evaluating co-teaching teams in a fair and consistent manner (see Figure 4.3). To make these things happen, school leaders must make sure that the correct systems are in place to support teacher observation and evaluation in the collaborative environment.

In 2010, U.S. Secretary of Education Arne Duncan noted that schools use a system of teacher evaluation that "frustrates teachers who feel their good work goes unrecognized and ignores other teachers who would benefit from additional support" (2010, para. 64).

A study by Weisberg, Sexton, Mulhern, and Keeling (2009) reveals that most evaluation systems suffer from a series of design flaws, including infrequency, lack of focus, lack of differentiation, and lack of feedback. Their analysis of several evaluation systems studied in major school districts in America demonstrates that experienced teachers often go for several years without being observed and evaluated, student academic progress is not considered a factor in teacher evaluation, feedback almost never results in any meaningful instructional improvement, and nearly all teachers in the districts studied earned satisfactory ratings.

This list of design flaws can be substantiated in a 2008 study conducted by Isherwood and Barger-Anderson in a middle school in western Pennsylvania. In this study, too, teachers routinely cited infrequent classroom observations and the lack of quality feedback as roadblocks to the successful implementation of co-teaching.

If administrators expect their teachers to embrace co-teaching and inclusion, they must help them accept the redefining of the traditional roles to which they have

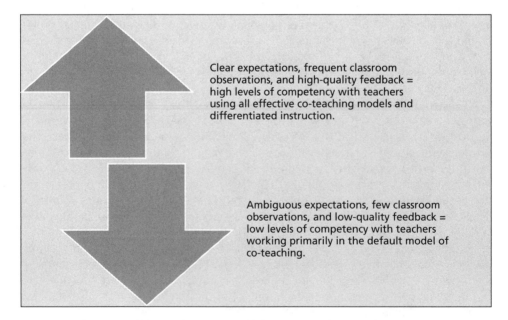

Clear expectations, frequent classroom observations, and high-quality feedback = high levels of competency with teachers using all effective co-teaching models and differentiated instruction.

Ambiguous expectations, few classroom observations, and low-quality feedback = low levels of competency with teachers working primarily in the default model of co-teaching.

Figure 4.3. Administrative behaviors that support and help sustain a quality co-teaching program.

become accustomed. This culture change begins with school leaders articulating a vision of co-teaching as an organizational and instructional strategy that is beneficial for all students, and then validating the importance of that strategy with frequent visits to co-taught classrooms. Finally, it is essential for school leaders to support successful co-teaching performance with praise and encouragement.

Most of the traditional observation forms and evaluation tools used in schools have been designed to observe and evaluate one teacher working in a classroom. These tools usually do not work very well for a co-taught classroom that involves two teachers working together. We did an extensive search for a co-teaching observation and evaluation tool and could find only one, the Magiera-Simmons Quality Indicator Model of Co-Teaching (Magiera & Simmons, 2007). This standardized evaluation tool is designed to

- Provide benchmarks for administrators, mentors, and co-teachers to follow in the implementation of co-teaching models

- Give teachers observation feedback to help improve the planning of co-teaching lessons

- Offer a structure that can help co-teachers examine their practice periodically with an administrator or mentor

- Allow observation of co-taught lessons directly or via video

- Allow co-teachers, administrators, and mentors to document growth in co-teaching practices

We initially tried to use a variation of this observation tool in our practice as consultants. However, we found that although this approach was ideal for evaluating co-instructors' use of co-teaching models, it did not accomplish our desire to focus on other, equally important elements that are indicative of a quality co-taught classroom, such as differentiated instruction and collaborative classroom management. As a result, we created our own observation tool that school leaders can employ to evaluate co-teachers' use of all of the essential elements and pathways that make up the Co-Design Model (see the Co-Teaching Observation Form in the appendix). It should be used with great frequency when first establishing a co-teaching relationship between two instructors. For a detailed example of how to use the observation form, see Chapter 17.

CONCLUSION

Beginning in 1975 with the passage of PL 94-142, the Education for All Handicapped Children Act, public schools have undergone significant transformation with regard to educational practice for students with disabilities. Today, many schools embrace the philosophy of inclusion as more and more parents, students, and school personnel advocate for the general education classroom as the first choice for students with exceptionalities. Although teachers are the ones responsible for instruction in the inclusive classroom, it is the school leader who will ultimately create a school climate that either supports inclusion or precludes it. School leaders are legally responsible for the specially designed instruction that students with exceptionalities receive, the use of appropriate supplementary aids and related services for students with exceptionalities, and ensuring the fidelity of the IEP across the school setting. Leadership in an inclusive school means understanding the tenets of inclusion and the LRE and working with teachers to ensure the execution of those tenets. This book provides a professional reference and tools that teachers and administrators can use to plan for and create a school culture to realize the full potential of inclusion.

REFERENCES

Bos, C.S., & Vaughn, S. (2002). *Strategies for teaching students with learning and behavior problems* (5th ed.). Boston, MA: Allyn & Bacon.

Dickinson, T., & Erb, T. (1997). *We gain more than we give: Teaming in middle schools.* Columbus, OH: National Middle School Association.

Duncan, A. (2010, July 27). *The quiet revolution.* Speech presented at the National Press Club, Washington, DC.

Education for All Handicapped Children Act of 1975, PL 94-142, 20 U.S.C. §§ 1400 *et seq.*

Ehrhart, M.G. (2004). Leadership and procedural justice climate as antecedents of unit-level organizational citizenship behavior. *Personnel Psychology, 57*(1), 61–94.

Friend, M., & Cook, L. (2003). *Interactions: Collaboration skills for professionals* (4th ed.). Boston, MA: Allyn & Bacon.

Gilliam, J.E., & McConnell, K.S. (1997). *Scales for predicting successful inclusion: Examiner's manual.* Austin, TX: PRO-ED.

Greenleaf, R.K. (1977). *Servant leadership: A journey into the nature of legitimate power and greatness.* New York, NY: Paulist Press.

Greenleaf, R.K. (2009). *The institution as servant.* Westfield, IN: Greenleaf Center for Servant Leadership.

Howell, K.W., & Nolet, V. (2000). *Curriculum-based evaluation: Teaching and decision making* (3rd ed.). Belmont, CA: Wadsworth.

Hunt, T.S. (2002). Servant leadership: Billy Graham. *Dissertation Abstracts International: 63*(07), 2615.

Isherwood, R., & Barger-Anderson, R. (2008). Factors affecting the adoption of co-teaching models in inclusive environments: One school's journey from mainstreaming to inclusion. *Journal of Ethnographic and Qualitative Research, 2,* 121–128.

Jackson, A., & Davis, G. (2000). *Turning points 2000: Educating adolescents in the 21st century.* New York, NY: Teachers College Press.

Lubin, K.A. (2001). Visionary leader behaviors and their congruency with servant leadership characteristics. *Dissertation Abstracts International: Section A, Humanities and Social Sciences, 62*(08), 2645.

Magiera, K., & Simmons, R.J. (2007). Evaluation of co-teaching in three high schools within one school district: How do you know when you are truly co-teaching? *Teaching Exceptional Children, 3*(3), 2–12.

McCowan, C.D. (2004). Leading before, during, and after a major organizational transition. *Dissertation Abstracts International: Section A, Humanities and Social Sciences, 65*(1), 53.

Mertens, S.B., & Flowers, N. (2004). *Research summary: Interdisciplinary teaming.* Retrieved from www.nmsa.org/ResearchSummaries/Summary21/tabid/250/Default.aspx

Patterson, K. (2003). Servant leadership: A theoretical model. *Dissertation Abstracts International, 64*(02), 570. (UMI No. 3082719)

Ramirez, E. (2008, December 15). America's best high schools. *U.S. News & World Report, 145*(13), 43–46.

Rice, D., & Zigmond, N. (2000). Co-teaching in secondary schools: Teacher reports of developments in Australian and American classrooms. *Learning Disabilities Research and Practice, 15*(4), 190–197.

Sendjaya, S., & Sarros, J.C. (2002). Servant leadership: Its origin, development, and application in organizations. *Journal of Leadership & Organizational Studies, 9*(2), 57–64.

Simonson, M. (2005). Distance education: Eight steps for transforming an organization. *The Quarterly Review of Distance Education, 6*(2), 7–8.

Spears, L.C., & Lawrence, M. (Eds.). (2004). *Practicing servant leadership: Succeeding through trust, bravery, and forgiveness.* San Francisco, CA: Jossey-Bass.

Villa, R., Thousand, J., & Nevin, A. (2008). *A guide to co-teaching: Practical tips for facilitating student learning* (2nd ed.). Thousand Oaks, CA: Corwin Press.

Wei, R.C., Darling-Hammond, L., Andree, A., Richardson, N., & Orphanos, S. (2009). *Professional learning in the learning profession: A status report on teacher development in the United States and abroad.* Dallas, TX: National Staff Development Council.

Weisberg, D., Sexton, S., Mulhern, J., & Keeling, D. (2009). *The widget effect: Our national failure to acknowledge and act on differences in teacher effectiveness* (2nd ed.). Washington, DC: The New Teacher Project.

Winston, B.E. (2002). *Agapao leadership: Inner resources for leaders.* Virginia Beach, VA: Regents University.

Yukl, G. (2002). *Leadership in organizations* (5th ed.). Upper Saddle River, NJ: Prentice Hall.

Zigmond, N., & Magiera, K. (2001). A focus on co-teaching: Use caution. *Current Practice Alerts from the Division for Learning Disabilities and Division for Research of the Council for Exceptional Children, 6,* 1–4. Retrieved from http://www.dldcec.org/alerts/

CHAPTER 5

Assembly of Site

As a parent of a child with physical disabilities who is confined to a 300-pound power wheelchair, I am very aware that the way a teacher sets up his or her classroom could have a dramatic effect on how well my daughter can access the classroom, along with the curriculum and instruction. Great teachers take into consideration the need for space for students who may need a little extra space to get around. This is important not only for Molly but for all of the other students in the classroom as well.

When my daughter was in elementary school, every August I would ask my husband to take a stroll over to the elementary school to see whether Molly's classroom was going to be accessible for her. Really what I was checking on was to see whether Molly's assigned classroom teacher(s) had the room set up to accommodate her. I must confess that each year I was relieved and pleased to see that her teachers truly assembled the classroom to make it an inviting place for her.

The reason why setting up the classroom to accommodate children in wheelchairs is so important is that safety can be a real concern if the assembly of the classroom site is not taken into consideration. These are some questions that I always ask myself after seeing the room: Can Molly and the other students in the room access all instructional materials? Are all students along with Molly able to see the teacher during large-group instruction? Is Molly in a position where she can easily exit the room in case of an emergency? Although these seem like simple questions, I feel they are very important.

By Rhonda Merhaut, parent of a child with physical disabilities

Because of laws and legislation at both the state and federal levels, as discussed in Chapter 2, contemporary classrooms are heterogeneous as never before (Friend, 2011). Inclusive classrooms encompass a diverse range of abilities and disabilities (Friend & Bursuck, 2008; Heward, 2009; Salend, 2008; Smith & Tyler, 2010). To ensure that all individuals are afforded opportunities to achieve at their highest potential, it is important to attend not only to the instructional and behavioral aspects of the classroom environment but also to the physical components (Gately & Gately, 2001). When the educational setting is a collaborative one, the physical setup in the classroom should send a clear message that the location for instruction is a shared environment (Barger-Anderson, Isherwood, & Merhaut, 2010). This chapter defines and explains the term *assembly of site,* which is specific to the Co-Design Model.

DEFINITION AND IMPORTANCE OF ASSEMBLY OF SITE

When co-teaching is being addressed, the area of physical arrangement of the learning environment should be discussed. This discussion should include physical arrangement of furniture and other items within the collaborative environment (Gately & Gately, 2001; Villa, Thousand, & Nevin, 2004). Within the Co-Design Model, the term *assembly of site* includes the physical arrangement of furniture and other items as well as a few additional components.

For purposes of the Co-Design Model, the assembly of site is defined as "organization of physical objects within a shared space along with promotion of collaborative practices via site management and communication" (Barger-Anderson et al., 2010, n.p.). The shared space may mean a classroom, science lab, or outdoor auditorium, to name a few possibilities. It may also mean the occasional sharing of two locations within the school. An example might be the use of the general education classroom and the library. This usage may be typical during the implementation of a station or parallel co-teaching model (these co-teaching models are discussed in Chapter 13).

The second half of this definition conveys the importance of taking collaboration beyond the sharing of workspace to include a clear development of agreed-upon practices for planning and instruction. Students should recognize that the two teachers sharing the room are both teachers and that it is not a case of one being "in charge" and the other being the "assistant." It should be evident that both teachers share not only governance but also instructional duties, housekeeping tasks, assigning and correcting of homework, parental communication, and dissemination of grades. Figure 5.1 provides a form that assists the collaborative partners in designing the assembly of site to send a clear message to students, other teachers, administrators, and parents that learning is a shared endeavor in that particular environment. (A reproducible version of the form is provided in the appendix.)

Let's take a closer look at the two parts of this definition for assembly of site: the physical components and the evidence for collaborative practices to promote parity, or sharing of responsibilities, within the environment. Figure 5.2 provides a flowchart showing how the pieces of the definition relate to one another.

PHYSICAL COMPONENTS

Consideration of the physical arrangement of the educational site requires deliberation between the two partners (Gately & Gately, 2001; Villa et al., 2004). Both teachers need to feel a part of the process of arranging the physical makeup of the site. This comprises not only student desks and teacher desks but also many other items and materials that will vary from site to site depending on the space and availability of resources. These may include

- Computers

- Tables for small-group instruction

- Seating arrangements

- Bookstands

- Location of pencil sharpener

- Listening centers

- Work centers

- Bulletin boards

The Co-Design Model stresses two important areas for consideration of the physical components: 1) teachers must ensure that the students' individual needs are met via the physical arrangement of the learning environment, and 2) the physical arrangement should transmit a clear message that it is a shared site (Barger-Anderson et al., 2010).

Regarding meeting individual student needs, collaborative partners should promote the heterogeneous grouping of students in terms of ability and take into consideration any special needs. Students with physical disabilities who use a wheelchair or braces may require a wider aisle for independent movement around the site. Students with sensory dysfunction disorder or sensory needs may require preferential seating. One cautious reminder: Preferential seating does *not* mean all of the students with an IEP sit in the same row or area of the room.

It is also important for collaborative partners to organize their shared workspace within the classroom or assembly of site to send a clear message that it is a shared environment. To determine the most appropriate approach to accomplish this goal, the collaborative partners must engage in dialogue and share their expectations and needs for the shared classroom setup. Collaborative pairs will find different ways

Checklist for Assembly of Site

Items to Discuss	Yes *Discussed together and decided it is needed at this time*	No *Discussed together and decided it is not needed at this time.*
Two teacher desks		√
Both teachers' names displayed in room	√	
Both teachers' pictures displayed in room		√
Both names listed on assignments	√	
Both names listed on communications sent to parents	√	
Table in room to provide small-group instruction	√	
Classroom rules posted and signed by both teachers	√	
Student desk arrangement (consideration of special needs; do not put all students with an individualized education program in one area)	√	
Additional area		
Additional area		

Figure 5.1. Copyright © 2013 by Keystone Educational Consulting Group. http://www.keystone-educational.com. Adapted by permission..

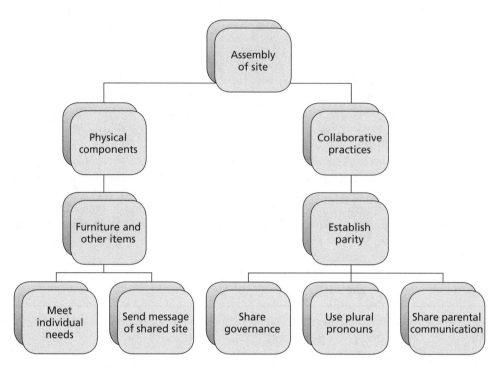

Figure 5.2.   Visual definition of assembly of site.

to accomplish this goal. The teachers may decide to post both names outside the instructional site as well as inside. The partners may decide to display their pictures within the classroom. They may want to each add a personal touch, such as hanging posters of favorite sport teams. The teachers may decide that there is or is not enough space at the site to include two teacher desks. What the issue boils down to is that the teachers must share their thoughts and feelings openly with their partners about sharing the classroom space. Communication is key! And finally, student desks must be arranged in a manner that allows both teachers to reach all students. The teachers must ask themselves: Can we support and instruct all students?

COLLABORATIVE PRACTICES TO PROMOTE PARITY

Parity happens when the partners who are engaged in a collaborative relationship feel that their thoughts are heard and they are valued for their presence and contributions (Friend, 2011; Villa et al., 2004). Friend and Cook (2003) emphasized the importance of co-teachers being viewed as colleagues in the classroom with equal credentials and equal status, serving as partners in the instructional process on behalf of all students in the classroom.

The assembly-of-site element goes beyond the physical arrangement of the site to address parity. Collaboration between the teachers is needed to establish equality of status within the site. Sending a message of parity will convey collaborative practices and shared responsibilities to other teachers in the building, administration, parents, and of course, the students (Barger-Anderson et al., 2010).

Parity may be accomplished in numerous ways within the Co-Design Model. One possible way is by establishing and enforcing classroom rules as a team—that is, by shared governance. Both teachers must demonstrate that they are united in enforcing compliance with rules (see Chapter 8). Another way of achieving parity is to speak as a team, saying "our classroom" instead of "my classroom" (Barger-Anderson et al., 2010). The use of plural pronouns sends a clear message of equality. It also suggests an alliance and a shared vision for the classroom. Another simple way to promote parity is to include both teachers' names on tests, guided notes, classroom handouts, and assignments.

Finally, a third method to promote parity within the element of assembly of site is shared communication with parents. The Co-Design Model encourages the collaborative partners to include both names on parental notes, homework assignments, and report cards. Likewise, it is important for both teachers to co-present themselves at school functions. These functions may include parent–teacher conferences, parent night, and other school events (Barger-Anderson et al., 2010). Parents will then have an opportunity to meet both teachers; perhaps then they will begin to view both individuals as teachers for their child, no matter whether their child has an IEP or not.

CONCLUSION

Assembly of site within the Co-Design Model goes beyond physical appearance. The goals for this element are to achieve sharing of physical components and to achieve collaborative practices by establishing parity. Many times the physical sharing is easy. Establishing collaborative practices—such as using "us" and "we" and sharing parental communication—takes time to develop.

The importance of demonstrating equality between teachers is heard in the following quote from a veteran elementary special education teacher:

> I started co-teaching with a general education teacher this year. I was nervous to get started but excited at the same time. During the initial setup of the classroom, we decided to post both of our names inside the classroom as well outside near the door. We also put a picture of ourselves outside the classroom to help welcome the students as they entered the room. We discussed and planned many ways to demonstrate from the start that we are both serving as the teachers for all of the students. On the first day of school, we did not mention that I was a special education teacher, just that they would have two teachers this year. The first day was off to a great start. As I was walking the students to lunch that day, one of the general education students congratulated me on my promotion. He said that he had seen me at school last year and was happy that I was finally a real teacher! (Anonymous, personal communication with Richael Barger-Anderson, September 15, 2009)

Sharing of classroom space, duties, instructional responsibilities, and management of behavioral concerns is challenging in today's inclusive and collaborative environment (Gately & Gately, 2001). It is difficult to say whether any one of these issues is more central than the others. As with a well-maintained vehicle, attention to all of the parts is necessary to keep it running smoothly. It takes the care and maintenance of all elements promoted within the Co-Design Model to keep the collaborative environment functioning well and to maintain productivity and success. Assembly of site is one of nine elements identified in the complex dynamics of supporting students, both with and without disabilities, to reach their maximum learning potential (Barger-Anderson et al., 2010).

REFERENCES

Barger-Anderson, R., Isherwood, R., & Merhaut, J. (2010, February). *The Co-Design Model: A collaborative approach to inclusive education*. Paper presented at the 47th Annual International Conference of the Learning Disabilities Association of America, Baltimore, MD.

Friend, M. (2011). *Special education: Contemporary perspectives for school professionals* (3rd ed.). Boston, MA: Pearson.

Friend, M., & Bursuck, W.D. (2008). *Including students with special needs: A practical guide for classroom teachers* (5th ed.). Boston, MA: Allyn & Bacon.

Friend, M., & Cook, L. (2003). *Interactions: Collaboration skills for school professionals* (4th ed.). Boston, MA: Allyn & Bacon.

Gately, S.E., & Gately, F.J. (2001). Understanding co-teaching components. *Teaching Exceptional Children, 33*, 40–47.

Heward, W.L. (2009). *Exceptional children: An introduction to special education* (9th ed.). Upper Saddle River, NJ: Pearson Merrill Prentice Hall.

Salend, S.J. (2008). *Creating inclusive classrooms: Effective and reflective practices* (6th ed.). Upper Saddle River, NJ: Prentice Hall.

Smith, D.D., & Tyler, N.C. (2010). *Introduction to special education: Making a difference* (7th ed.). Upper Saddle River, NJ: Merrill.

Villa, R.A., Thousand, J.S., & Nevin, A.I. (2004). *A guide to co-teaching: Practical tips for facilitating student learning.* Thousand Oaks, CA: Sage Publications.

CHAPTER **6**

Curriculum Knowledge

It is mid-August and, as has been the case for the past few years, Jeremy is waiting for his school schedule to arrive in the mail. When it does arrive, he anxiously opens the envelope to find some things he expected and other things that send his heart racing. The typical "classes" of study hall and lunch were expected. He sees that Language Arts is scheduled for Period 1 and is pleasantly surprised because he knows his friend is also in that class. In addition, he knows that he has had previous success with Language Arts and that gives him even more confidence about the start of his day. However, as his eyes move down the schedule, he soon reads Algebra II for Period 3 and Chemistry for Period 7. He starts to get nervous. Pejorative thoughts of previous experiences in math class and science class flood his head, and he thinks, "This can't be right. Do I have to go to school this year?" He is concerned about looking stupid in front of the class the first time he is asked a question for which he has no good answer. He thinks that in addition to his many other classes and responsibilities, he is now going to have to spend even more time just to keep his head above water in these two classes. He starts to bargain with himself, thinking that maybe there has been a mistake, or if not, maybe he can get his schedule changed if he is nice to the right person in the high school.

This reads like the typical story of a soon-to-be high school junior who has bitten off more than he can chew, but in reality, Jeremy is a special education teacher with 25 years of experience in a school district that has just implemented a co-teaching model. Jeremy's reaction is emblematic of a special education teacher who is asked to co-teach in a classroom with an unfamiliar curriculum. Most teachers have come to realize what Jeremy knows—namely, that effective teachers need both pedagogical knowledge and content knowledge. He realizes that if he is to effectively co-teach in Algebra II, he will need to know the difference between a function and a fraction, among other things. He thinks that over time, he will be just fine in the Algebra II classroom but is concerned, even as a veteran special education teacher, about his workload and his effectiveness during these initial years as a co-teacher in content-heavy courses. Jeremy's effectiveness as a co-teacher in Language Arts, Algebra II, or Chemistry will depend on several factors, such as common planning time, professional development, and collaboration with the general education faculty member.

By Dr. James Preston, Assistant Professor, Slippery Rock University

The term *curriculum knowledge* refers to the levels of familiarity and expertise that each professional possesses within the particular subject areas and grade levels they are assigned to teach.

Curriculum knowledge is recognized as an area essential for success in a collaborative classroom environment. This is because central components for success of collaborative efforts include the content being taught, the partners' knowledge of the content, and the skill set of each partner (Friend & Hurley-Chamberlain, n.d.; Gately & Gately, 2001). In a shared classroom, clear expectations, teacher training, and administrative support assist collaborative efforts and promote success, but knowledge of the content within the curriculum on the part of both co-teachers also plays an important role.

Although it is required that teaching partners have an understanding of the curriculum or content areas, both partners need not hold the same level of knowledge or expertise for each area. Quite frequently, one teacher in the co-teaching pair has a greater knowledge base regarding the curriculum. The other teacher may have a greater knowledge base in classroom management or creating differentiated assessments. Such differences are acceptable and should probably be expected in the start of the co-teaching relationship. Both teachers will benefit by learning from one another's strengths. The term to describe this situation is *parity*. Parity is realized when both teachers feel valued for the knowledge and skill sets they are able to share and use in the classroom. Co-teaching does not mean that both teachers need to have the same knowledge or understanding of all aspects of the classroom, and this is especially true for the element of curriculum knowledge within the Co-Design Model.

In collaborative efforts, the use of apparently interchangeable terminology such as *co-teaching*, *collaboration*, *teaming*, and *team teaching* is understandable. However, the aforementioned terms are not synonymous and can be a bit confusing unless clearly defined (Friend & Hurley-Chamberlain, n.d.). Confusion may arise when the terms *team* and *collaborate* are interpreted as meaning both teachers need to be equal. Other confusion arises when school district personnel have a muddied definition of the overall collaboration initiative. School district administrators need to be clear from the start that co-teaching relationships vary from pair to pair, that different pairs may work at different stages of collaboration, and that collaboration between professionals takes time to grow. To help alleviate this confusion and clear the "mud," it is crucial for co-design partners to understand that both partners do not need to possess the same level of curriculum knowledge within a collaborative initiative to achieve success.

SETTING THE STAGE

Prior to the amendments of IDEA, parents and advocates voiced concerns that students with disabilities needed access to the general curriculum (Bryant, Smith, & Bryant, 2008). These same parents and advocates also noted the need for these students to participate in standardized testing so that their progress in the general curriculum could be measured. With the reauthorization of the Individuals with Disabilities Education Act (IDEA) of 1990 (PL 101-476) as the Individuals with Disabilities Education Improvement Act (IDEA) of 2004 (PL 108-446), the law now provides students with disabilities greater access to the general education curriculum, requires more participation in standardized testing, and requires general education curriculum content to be taught by content experts (Bryant et al., 2008). IDEA 2004 also required states to address teacher preparation to help ensure an appropriate education in a general education classroom as much as possible. The No Child Left Behind Act of

2001 (PL 107–110) imposed higher expectations for students with disabilities and also required that teachers be highly qualified in content areas.

The result of the changes enforced by these laws is that more students with disabilities receive their education in the general education environment and the general education curriculum. The most recent statistics from the U.S. Department of Education, National Center for Education Statistics (2011) show that in 2000–2001, 47% of all students with a disability received less than 21% of their education outside of the general education classroom, whereas in 2009–2010, that portion had increased to 59%.

State litigation, in Pennsylvania and elsewhere, in combination with federal legislation, has had a significant impact on the numbers of students with disabilities receiving their education in the general education environment. Federal and state provisions to ensure education in the least restrictive environment, along with other conditions, are increasing levels of inclusiveness in the general education classrooms. For example, the Pennsylvania Department of Education (PDE), because of the *Gaskin* settlement decision, has developed guidelines to ensure access to the general education curriculum for students with disabilities. Of course, this access is accomplished with supplementary aides and services when necessary. Collaborative practices via co-teaching are one supplementary service option available to grant greater access for students with disabilities to the general education curriculum (PDE, 2006). More widespread use of collaborative practices within general education classroom is an increasing trend (Friend, 2011).

RECOMMENDATIONS FOR SUCCESS: PARITY AND COMMITMENT

When co-teaching partners feel valued for their skills, knowledge, and contributions to the collaborative classroom, parity is realized (Friend, 2011; Villa, Thousand, & Nevin, 2004). Friend and Cook (2003) emphasized the importance of co-teachers being viewed as colleagues in the classroom with equivalent credentials and equal status. An important factor for achieving success in co-teaching is having both partners serve in the instructional process on behalf of all students in the classroom.

Parity is important for both general and special educators. Often, when parity is not realized, the general educator will be reluctant to share instructional time with the special educator because of concerns about lack of curriculum knowledge and familiarity (Gately & Gately, 2001). Because of the intensity of high-stakes testing, general educators are pressured to cover a definite amount of content during the school year. Sharing the stage in the classroom with a nonexpert may generate feelings of resentment on the part of the general educator. These feelings of resentment may stem from the frustration of having limited time to prepare students for state assessments in addition to taking time with the co-teacher to share plans and content knowledge (Barger-Anderson, Isherwood, & Merhaut, 2010).

Special educators may be reluctant to take instructional responsibility for the same reasons. They may not feel confident with presenting the content in some curricular areas. Interview responses from a study conducted by Isherwood, Barger-Anderson, Merhaut, Badgett, and Katsafanas (2011) revealed that issues with curriculum familiarity tended to be more of a problem at the secondary than at the elementary level. Such concerns were especially present for math and the sciences. Special education teachers frequently reported not feeling competent in these areas and were hesitant to take on a significant role in delivering the instruction because of their lack of knowledge in the subject area. This concern can be heard in the voice of a special education teacher interviewed by Isherwood et al.:

I haven't had algebra since high school. I wasn't a very good math student then, so having me co-teach algebra wasn't a very good idea. Ed teaches the content and I watch, take notes, and ask him to explain something in a different manner when I think some of the students aren't getting it. I think things will get better next year. I need to learn the curriculum and do the problems with the students. After that, I think I will be able to contribute a little more. This takes time. Also, don't forget, I am co-teaching in other areas of the curriculum as well. Not only am I learning algebra I, but I am also learning biology.

Anonymous teacher (Isherwood et al., 2011, p. 117)

Comments such as this support the strategy of placing special education teachers in co-taught classrooms in which they already have a background in the subject area or feel at least competent enough to provide some instruction in the class. According to participants in the study by Isherwood et al., this approach may help minimize a learning curve that can reduce the role of the special education teacher to that of an assistant during most of the first year. Participants in the focus groups of this study also recommended allowing a few years for teachers to become competent in the curriculum. Yes, years. It may take as long as 3 years for the special education teacher to feel confident about providing instruction in some of the co-taught classrooms because of curriculum knowledge concerns. Thus, administrators must make a multiyear commitment to the co-teaching partners, a strategy every focus group recommended (Isherwood et al., 2011). When a district makes multiyear commitments to partners, it often signifies that the school district has a clear goal of creating a more inclusive and collaborative school.

CONCERNS BEYOND CONTENT KNOWLEDGE: COMMUNICATION

Even when the special educator does feel confident with the content, parity may not be present in the relationship. The general educator may not trust the special educator to teach the content with the same level of integrity. The special educator may also

Curriculum Discussion Starters

Curriculum area: _Math_

Unit	Topic/skills	Responsibility
Numbers, expressions, and equations	Order of operations Solve problems by applying PEMDAS Evaluating incorrect problems: Find errors and solve correctly	Ms. Chiapusie
Geometry	Angles: Define, label, and/or identify right, straight, acute, and obtuse angles	Ms. Wingerstahn

Figure 6.1.   Example of completed Curriculum Discussion Starters form. Example contributed by Melanie Wingertsahn and Stephanie Chiapusio. (Copyright © 2013 by Keystone Educational Consulting Group. http://www. keystone-educational.com. Reprinted by permission.)

have feelings of frustration for having more requirements put on his or her plate while having nothing removed.

Special educators often feel mounting pressure when they are expected to complete the necessary paperwork of IEPs and assume the added instructional responsibility for new content in the classroom without having any additional preparation time allotted (Isherwood & Barger-Anderson, 2007). Communication between partners to discuss upcoming lessons, units, and chapters is necessary. Planning and preparation time is an element of the Co-Design Model (Chapter 12).

The form shown in Figure 6.1 can support and promote dialogue between collaborative partners for identifying strengths and addressing responsibility. It is suggested that partners use this form prior to the start of the school year. This discussion will assist in planning, allowing the collaborative pairs to get to know each other and promoting an open relationship. By creating the form at the start of the year, the partners are then more likely to use it throughout the year on a consistent basis or at least as needed. If one or both of the collaborative partners feel a need to promote more dialogue or to broach an awkward topic, the form is available as a tool to help achieve this goal. (A reproducible version of this form is provided in the appendix.)

Figure 6.2 presents a graphic organizer of the element of curriculum knowledge. It includes the definition, along with some of the recommendations and concerns addressed in this chapter.

Curriculum knowledge
Levels of familiarity and expertise that each professional possesses within the particular subject areas and grade levels they are assigned to teach constitute curriculum knowledge.

Recommended for success

Parity is realized when both teachers feel valued for the knowledge and skill sets they are able to share and utilize in the classroom.

Multiyear commitments to keeping co-teachers together will help increase knowledge of curriculum and promote collaboration.

Clear definition of initiative by the district helps everyone understand the goals of collaboration, co-teaching, and creating a more inclusive school.

Communication between the co-teaching partners helps them to discuss curriculum content in upcoming units and chapters.

Concerns

The special education teacher may not feel confident in content he or she is assigned to co-teach.

The general education teacher may feel resentment toward the special education teacher for having to give up valuable teaching time in order to share.

The special education teacher may have multiple co-teaching partners and multiple content-area responsibilities. Learning multiple content areas may be difficult.

Special education teachers already have a full plate, and now new responsibilities are added but nothing is taken away (e.g., paperwork, individualized education programs).

Schedules may not allow enough time for communication between the co-teaching partners about curriculum content in upcoming units and chapters.

Figure 6.2. Graphic organizer of curriculum knowledge. (*Sources:* Barger-Anderson, Isherwood, and Merhaut, 2010; Friend, 2011; Gately and Gately, 2001; Isherwood and Barger-Anderson, 2007.)

CONCLUSION

With the increasing diversity of student populations, the need for parity, collaboration, and professional understanding cannot be overstated. Recognizing each other's knowledge and skill sets is an essential task of co-teaching teams in today's educational environments (Friend, 2011). In states such as Pennsylvania, as well as the rest of the country, larger numbers of students with disabilities are now having their IEPs implemented in the general education classroom. As a result, pull-out services and the number of resource rooms are decreasing (Moody, Vaughn, Hughes, & Fischer, 2000), and full-inclusion classrooms, in which teaching is shared between the general educator and special educator, are becoming the model of delivery for educational services of students with disabilities (Villa et al., 2004).

Furthermore, general educators share more responsibility for the education of students with disabilities than ever before and are expected to manage a greater spectrum of learning, behavioral, sensory, and physical differences among their students (Heward, 2009). For all students with disabilities to receive an appropriate education in the general education classroom environment, general educators must be prepared to meet the diverse learning needs of every student in the classroom.

This trend of including students with special needs in the general education classroom has caused many teachers to ask questions about appropriate instructional strategies. As a result, general classroom teachers are faced with new issues and concerns regarding instruction for students with special needs that may not have been previously addressed in professional development (Smith, Price, & Marsh, 1986). The Co-Design Model promotes parity and clearly defined expectations and goals for the inclusive initiative by the school district administration. The model also promotes the importance of keeping co-teaching partners together from year to year to allow partners to develop greater comfort with each other and with the curriculum and also greater respect for each other's skills and strengths. Communication between the co-teaching partners for planning purposes and to discuss content familiarity and knowledge is a must. As with all of the nine elements of the Co-Design Model, understanding this information about curriculum knowledge will help teachers meet the needs of all students, both with and without disabilities, in the collaborative and inclusive classroom.

REFERENCES

Barger-Anderson, R., Isherwood, R., & Merhaut, J. (2010, February). *The Co-Design Model: A collaborative approach to inclusive education.* Paper presented at the 47th Annual International Conference of the Learning Disabilities Association of America, Baltimore, MD.

Bryant, D.P., Smith, D.D., & Bryant, B.R. (2008). *Teaching students with special needs in inclusive classrooms.* Boston, MA: Allyn & Bacon.

Friend, M. (2011). *Special education: Contemporary perspectives for school professionals* (3rd ed.). Boston, MA: Pearson.

Friend, M., & Cook, L. (2003). *Interactions: Collaboration skills for school professionals* (4th ed.). Boston, MA: Allyn & Bacon.

Friend, M., & Hurley-Chamberlain, D. (n.d.). *Is co-teaching effective?* Retrieved from http://www.cec.sped.org/AM/Template.cfm?Section=Home&CONTENTID=7504&TEMPLATE=/CM/ContentDisplay.cfm

Gately, S.E., & Gately, F.J. (2001). Understanding co-teaching components. *Teaching Exceptional Children, 33*, 40–47.

Heward, W.L. (2009). *Exceptional children: An introduction to special education* (9th ed.). Upper Saddle River, NJ: Pearson Merrill Prentice Hall.

Individuals with Disabilities Education Act (IDEA) of 1990, PL 101-476, 20 U.S.C. §§ 1400 *et seq.*

Individuals with Disabilities Education Improvement Act (IDEA) of 2004, PL 108-446, 20 U.S.C. §§ 1400 *et seq.*

Isherwood, R.S., & Barger-Anderson, R. (2007). Factors affecting the adoption of co-teaching models in inclusive classrooms: One school's journey from mainstreaming to inclusion. *Journal of Ethnographic and Qualitative Research, 2*, 121–128.

Isherwood, R., Barger-Anderson, R., Merhaut, J., Badgett, R., & Katsafanas, J. (2011). First year co-teaching: Disclosed through focus group and individual interviews. *Learning Disabilities: A Multidisciplinary Journal, 17*(3), 113–122.

Moody, S.W., Vaughn, S., Hughes, M.T., & Fischer, M. (2000). Reading instruction in the resource room: Set up for failure. *Exceptional Children, 66,* 305–316.

No Child Left Behind Act of 2001, PL 107–110, 20 U.S.C. §§ 6301 *et seq.*

Pennsylvania Department of Education, Bureau of Special Education. (2006). *Fact sheet: Supplementary aids and services.* Retrieved from http://www.pealcenter.org/images/2nd_FINAL_SAS_fact_sheet_12-18-06.pdf

Smith, T.E.C., Price, B.J., & Marsh, G.E. (1986). *Mildly handicapped children and adults.* St. Paul, MN: West Publishing.

U.S. Department of Education, National Center for Education Statistics. (2011). *The condition of education: Children and youth with disabilities.* Retrieved from http://nces.ed.gov/programs/coe/indicator_cwd.asp

Villa, R.A., Thousand, J.S., & Nevin, A.I. (2004). *A guide to co-teaching: Practical tips for facilitating student learning.* Thousand Oaks, CA: Sage Publications.

CHAPTER **7**

Co-Instruction

As a reading support teacher, I spend Monday and Friday each week pushing into general education classrooms for differentiated instruction. What I do during this time is a form of co-teaching. The general education teachers and I usually use either the one teach/one assist, station teaching, or alternative teaching models. The general education teachers and I share responsibilities in planning, presentation, evaluation, classroom management, and preparation for activities.

For the most part, co-teaching has been a wonderful experience. I love having another professional to share ideas with. I have learned an abundant amount of information from the veteran teachers with whom I have co-taught. The only problem I can report is that one particular teacher had a hard time sharing responsibilities. Sometimes the teacher would put all of the responsibility on me. At other times, I felt useless. Some teachers may have a hard time finding the happy medium that must be reached. I think a major key in successful co-teaching is the willingness and open-mindedness that both teacher participants must possess.

By Jill Torchia, special education graduate student at Slippery Rock University

The Co-Design Model takes collaboration beyond co-teaching by considering the element of co-instruction. The element of co-instruction stresses the importance of collaboration in an inclusive setting through instruction as well as professionalism. This element examines the instructional aspects of executing lessons via five specific models of co-teaching. Also encompassed in this element is professionalism on the part of both co-teachers. The element of co-instruction drives home the fact that there is a continual need for professional conduct while the teacher implements lessons within the room. When co-instruction occurs in a positive, professional environment and on a consistent basis, trust and respect by professionals for each other are likely to develop (Barger-Anderson, Isherwood, & Merhaut, 2010). Developing common principles in the classroom is suggested as a means for teachers to improve their collaborative teaching relationship, particularly in this element.

As Jill Torchia stated, teaching arrangements for the element of co-instruction are presented through models of co-teaching. The models of co-teaching that are promoted in this design are five models taken from Marilyn Friend's research and abundant contributions to the field of education. These models are one teach/one assist, stations, parallel, alternative, and team. These models of co-teaching are explained in detail in Chapter 13.

The area of professionalism is discussed throughout many elements of the Co-Design Model, but it is a particular focus within the element of co-instruction. Specifically, respect and trust through parity are examined. Parity is realized when each teacher recognizes the other's skill set. The skill sets of co-teachers do not need to be equal. In fact, teachers in this kind of collaborative relationship benefit from learning from each other's talents. Finally, the teachers need to agree on common principles for managing and executing a collaborative classroom. A suggested activity for identification and discussion on common principles is included. This activity promotes finding and developing agreements about common principles in areas such as student groupings and homework policies. Figure 7.1 shows the issues involved in the co-instruction element.

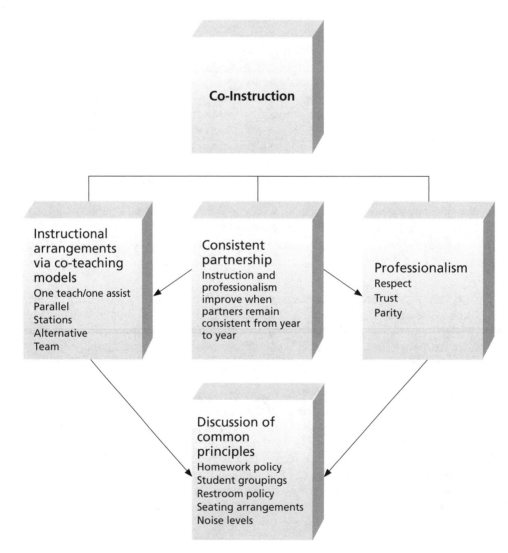

Figure 7.1.   Co-instruction.

CO-INSTRUCTION: AN EXPLANATION

Friend and Bursuck (2006) report that collaboration is a vital component of a successful inclusion program. Collaboration, via co-teaching, is a proven recommended practice for the education of all students when implemented effectively (Friend, 2011; Isherwood, Barger-Anderson, Merhaut, Badgett, & Katsafanas, 2011). Rice and Zigmond (2000) have concluded that well-implemented co-teaching can be beneficial to students with and without disabilities. For purposes of the Co-Design Model, co-instruction is defined as professionals engaged in consistent and routine collaborative efforts for the implementation of instructional practices within an educational setting (Barger-Anderson et al., 2010). The two components of co-instruction are 1) instructional arrangements through co-teaching models and 2) professionalism.

Instructional Arrangements: Models of Co-Teaching

Co-teaching is the foundation of the element of co-instruction. To clarify, co-teaching is not an element of the design but a strategy. This teaching strategy has been proven as a recommended practice and promotes collaboration. For the element of co-instruction, the purpose of recommending the consistent use of the five models of co-teaching is to reinforce that both teachers are to be involved in all of the instruction in some way, shape, or form.

Some days, one teacher may take the lead because he or she has content expertise. This is an example of one teach/one assist. Other days, both teachers may "share the stage" with equal responsibilities. This is the model of team teaching. As long as both teachers are contributing to the lesson, co-teaching is occurring. Teachers are strongly discouraged from overusing any one of these models. Typically, the one teach/one assist model is the default model. Many co-teaching pairs rely too heavily on this model and do not try any of the other models. Many times, the same teacher will serve as the "teacher" and the other as the "assistant," and too often it is the special education teacher serving as the assistant. Co-teaching is discussed in Chapter 13.

Professionalism

The second part of the co-instruction element is the professional relationship that develops between the partners via consistency and steady sharing of classroom management and instructional responsibilities. The relationship between partners depends on communication of and respect for each other's principles, beliefs, and skill sets. Smith and Tyler (2010) report that collaboration is one of the key components to finding success in education.

In an inclusive setting, it is particularly important to promote collaboration between professionals. Educators should feel reciprocity in sharing expertise with instructional tactics as well as with content and skill sets. Partners should be comfortable approaching their colleagues for support when planning for a student with unique needs or designing a lesson plan for a specific content area without fear of losing the respect of those colleagues. In both of these situations, co-teachers should not be judged by their partners if their skills are not the same. As discussed in Chapter 6, this attitude is referred to as parity. Recognizing the strengths of other educators is an important step in promoting respect for each other's philosophies and beliefs (Cook & Friend, 1996; Friend, 2007).

Another contributor to the success of co-instruction is for collaborative teams to remain together for more than a year at a time. Parrott (2004) reports that confidence and trust are gained when co-teaching pairs are maintained from year to year. In such a situation, a trusting relationship can grow, the teachers are able to build on past experience with lesson implementation, and recognition of skill sets is established. The co-instruction components of instructional arrangements and professionalism are both enhanced when co-teaching partners remain consistent over time.

COMMON PRINCIPLES FOR CO-INSTRUCTORS

It is central for partners taking a role in co-instructional practices to discuss common principles within the shared venue. Figure 7.2 shows a sample discussion starter form that can help partners confer about common beliefs. (A reproducible version of this form is provided in the appendix.) One of the issues on the example form is sharpening of pencils. Discussion on when to sharpen pencils may seem trivial to some teachers, but when partners are sharing a classroom, it is sometimes these smaller issues that snowball into bigger problems. Other ideas that co-teaching partners may need to discuss include grouping of students for instruction, seating charts, noise levels during group work, and a routine for distributing materials. The discussion and decisions prompted by using the form in Figure 7.2 may help the co-teachers identify which co-teaching model(s) will work best for certain topics and lessons.

Differing teaching philosophies were the second highest category of concern for co-teaching identified by Ashton (2003). Concerns with earning trust and issues of control were two other areas identified by Ashton. This is not to say that the professionals must agree in all areas. Yet teachers should discuss issues that are important

Developing Common Principles with Your Co-Teaching Partner

List of principles	My principles	Your principles	Possible solutions
Homework policy	Graded for completion, not accuracy. Must be on time.	Graded for accuracy. Must be on time.	Grade some homework assignments for completion only and some for accuracy. Make joint decisions one assignment at a time.
Restroom policy	The pass is available near the front of the room. The sign-out sheet is next to the pass. The students may use this pass at any time during the lesson. There is only one restroom pass available.	The pass is available near the front of the room. Each student may use it one time per period. The sign-out sheet is next to the pass. The students may use this pass only during the first 5 minutes of class or the last 5 minutes of class.	Discuss the possible disruption caused by students exiting and entering the classroom throughout the lesson. Decision: restroom passes are only good during the first and last 5 minutes of class and emergencies.
Sharpening pencils	Students may sharpen pencils any time during the period.	Students must arrive with a sharpened pencil and ready for the lesson.	Allow students to sharpen pencils only during the first 5 minutes of the class. If the student breaks a pencil point during the lesson, a new pencil will be provided to the student.

Figure 7.2. Example of completed Developing Common Principles with Your Co-Teaching Partner form. (Copyright © 2013 by Keystone Educational Consulting Group. http://www.keystone-educational.com. Reprinted by permission.)

for the shared governance of the room. This brief activity to help communicate and find common ground for principles can help promote discussion between the co-teachers that is necessary for the collaborative classroom.

Students will recognize and appreciate the unified environment created by the collaborative partners (Barger-Anderson et al., 2010). The following comments are from a practitioner involved in a successful collaborative relationship. They emphasize the potential for success promoted via collaboration.

The reason that I love co-teaching so much is because, as an inclusion learning support teacher, I rarely have the opportunity to instruct an entire class of learners. In addition, I truly enjoy co-teaching in my school as a result of the wonderful seventh-grade teachers that I have surrounding me. We are all friends who do things together outside of school and honestly enjoy working together. This relationship makes planning and instructing so much easier and fun to do. Since we have such a fantastic rapport with one another and constantly share our instructional ideas, as well as fears, we have also developed great communication with one another, which can be witnessed in and out of the classroom. During any of their classes, they never object to me interjecting a piece of information to help the learners better understand the material. In fact, as a result of my fantastic relationship with my team members, our district curriculum coordinator refers to me and my reading teacher as The Regis and Kelly of co-teaching.

S. Katkich (personal communication to Richael Barger-Anderson, July 13, 2010)

CONCLUSION

Co-instruction emphasizes the need for professionalism and parity between partners. Teachers need time to develop trust and respect for each other within the co-teaching relationship. Friend and Hurley-Chamberlain (n.d.) state the length of the partnership for co-teachers is an influencing factor to consider when measuring the outcome. When the partners realize that collaborative efforts are important and are a priority, the dynamics shift. A trust begins to develop, as well as a dependency on each other.

Finally, it is important for teaching partners to communicate regarding each other's principles for teaching and managing a classroom. Zigmond and Magiera (2001) conclude that successful co-teaching results from careful planning, ongoing co-planning, and enthusiastic pairs of teachers compatible in philosophy. Collaboration is vital for the success of students with and without disabilities (Dettmer, Thurston, & Dyck, 2005; Kochhar-Bryant, 2008; Shapiro & Sayers, 2003, as cited in Heward, 2009). Co-taught inclusive classrooms are a means to ensure success for all students as well as to permit students with disabilities to receive necessary modifications and instruction from a content expert (Murawski & Dieker, 2004).

REFERENCES

Ashton, T.M. (2003). What are teachers' greatest co-teaching concerns? *Academic Exchange Quarterly, 7*(3), 100–104.

Barger-Anderson, R., Isherwood, R., & Merhaut, J. (2010, February). *The Co-Design Model: A collaborative approach to inclusive education.* Paper presented at the 47th Annual International Conference of the Learning Disabilities Association of America, Baltimore, MD.

Cook, L., & Friend, M. (1996). Co-teaching: Guidelines for creating effective practices. *Focus on Exceptional Children, 28,* 1–16.

Dettmer, P., Thurston, L.P., & Dyck, N.J. (2005). *Collaboration, consultation and teamwork for students with special needs* (5th ed.). Boston, MA: Pearson Education.

Friend, M. (2007). *Co-teaching defined.* Retrieved from http://www.marilynfriend.com/basics.htm

Friend, M. (2011). *Special education: Contemporary perspectives for school professionals* (3rd ed.). Boston, MA: Pearson.

Friend, M., & Bursuck, W.D. (2006). *Including students with special needs: A practical guide for classroom teachers* (4th ed.). Boston, MA: Allyn & Bacon.

Friend, M., & Hurley-Chamberlain, D. (n.d.). *Is co-teaching effective?* Retrieved from http://www.cec.sped.org/AM/Template.cfm?Section=Home&CONTENTID=7504&TEMPLATE=/CM/ContentDisplay.cfm

Heward, W.L. (2009). *Exceptional children: An introduction to special education* (9th ed.). Upper Saddle River, NJ: Pearson Merrill Prentice Hall.

Isherwood, R., Barger-Anderson, R., Merhaut, J., Badgett, R., & Katsafanas, J. (2011). First year co-teaching: Disclosed through focus group and individual interviews. *Learning Disabilities: A Multidisciplinary Journal, 17*(3), 117–122.

Kochhar-Bryant, C.A. (2008). *Collaboration and system coordination for students with special needs: From early childhood to the postsecondary years.* Upper Saddle River, NJ: Merrill.

Murawski, W.W., & Dieker, L.A. (2004). Tips and strategies for co-teaching at the secondary level. *Teaching Exceptional Children, 36,* 52–58.

Parrott, P. (2004). *Collaborative working relationships.* Retrieved from http://www.vcld.org/pages/newsletters/03_04_fall/collaboration.htm

Rice, D., & Zigmond, N. (2000). Co-teaching in secondary schools: Teacher reports of developments in Australian and American classrooms. *Learning Disabilities Research and Practice, 15*(4), 190–197.

Shapiro, D.R., & Sayers, L.K. (2003). Who does what on the interdisciplinary team regarding physical education for students with disabilities? *Teaching Exceptional Children, 35*(6), 32–38.

Smith, D.D., & Tyler, N.C. (2010). *Introduction to special education: Making a difference* (7th ed.). Upper Saddle River, NJ: Merrill.

Zigmond, N., & Magiera, K. (2001). *A focus on co-teaching (use caution)* (Current Practice Alert No. 6). Retrieved from web site of the Division for Learning Disabilities of the Council for Exceptional Children, http://www.dldcec.org/alerts/

CHAPTER 8

Classroom Management

Classroom management in a co-teaching environment is a successful venture if the participants can work together as a team. Comparing the characteristics and roles of the co-teachers to those of two dancers provides a metaphor by which the relationships can be best understood. In both cases, the team members need to be informative, consistent, and supportive.

Just as two dancers need to be aware and informed of the particular steps and rules of the dance, so too do the co-teachers need to be aware of the rules. In particular, the co-teachers need the students' input when creating the rules. Afterward, both teachers need to teach the rules explicitly so the students understand what is expected of them. When both the students and the co-teachers understand the rules and expectations, the environment will be much more predictable. Last, teachers are the biggest role models in the classroom, so both teachers need to model the rules themselves.

Just as consistency in practice and performance enables two dancers to perform their best routine, consistency between co-teachers enables them to manage their classrooms in the most successful manner. Both teachers need to demonstrate consistency in discipline as well as praise. Furthermore, both teachers need to develop an understanding of each other's roles in the classroom. Students thrive in environments in which clear expectations exist. Consistency in both discipline as well as roles will enable co-teachers to create this environment for their students.

When two individuals, such as dancers or co-teachers, are put into a situation in which each individual's performance affects the team's performance, both individuals need to be supportive of each other. General educators and special educators are now partners in the same classroom, and it is going to take time for teachers from both backgrounds to get comfortable with new models of co-teaching and classroom management. There will be triumphs and frustrations, but each teacher needs to support the other throughout the process of becoming successful and efficient in managing and disciplining students who are not thought of as "mine" or "yours" but "ours."

Effective co-management of a classroom can appear to be as smooth as a waltz or as synchronized as a cha-cha. By being informative, consistent, and supportive, co-teachers will have the greatest chance of success in not only managing the environment but also effectively teaching their students.

By Jason Kight, Ed.D., Assistant Professor of Special Education at California University of Pennsylvania (2010), and Robert Bost, Ed.D., Associate Professor of Special Education at Slippery Rock University

Achieving success with classroom management involves many facets found in the Co-Design Model. These facets include personality compatibility, sharing of common beliefs, administrative support, and action planning to develop behavior plans to meet both individual behavior and classwide behavior needs. As discussed by Gately and Gately (2001) and in "Classroom Management Theorists and Theories" (n.d.), personality types affect many aspects of co-teaching, including establishing classroom management strategies (see Chapter 11). As evidenced by multiple observations of successful co-taught classrooms, classroom management issues are practically nonexistent when the co-teachers have a common belief system. However, in order for classroom management to be successful in the co-taught classroom, both teachers must first review and discuss their belief systems or common principles so that potential conflicts can be identified and addressed (see Chapter 7 for a worksheet that supports discussion of principles). Establishing strategies such as working through an action planning process and having daily discussions about student and classwide behavior and management processes leads to successful implementation of the Co-Design Model (Barger-Anderson, Isherwood, & Merhaut, 2010). Figure 8.1 shows a behavior management guide to start discussions about ways of meeting students' individual needs. (A reproducible version of this form is provided in the appendix.)

According to Webber and Plotts (2008), the number of students with emotional and behavioral disorders is on the rise. Because it is likely for co-teachers to have a mixture of ability and behavioral disabilities in one classroom, they need to discuss potential strategies for dealing with such a diverse group.

RIGHT FROM THE START

Effective classroom management involves two major components: relationship building and the structure of the classroom environment (Burden, 2003). In most cases, both of these components take substantial time to develop. Gately and Gately (2001) explain that rules and routines structure the learning environment. Once the collaborating teachers decide together on the "how" of behavior management, students begin to feel a sense of community. According to Garnett (2010), because the classroom is a busy place, it is important for co-teachers to work on developing an atmosphere of community.

As mentioned previously, structure and relationship building between the co-teachers is essential for effective classroom management. The teachers need to have clear and consistent expectations for student behavior (Cook & Friend, 1995). In the absence of clear expectations, students tend to create and exploit a "good cop, bad cop" dynamic between the two teachers. Enforcement of rules needs to be consistent as well. That said, both teachers must communicate the key points to each other in the early stage of building their relationship. It is vital that both teachers understand their roles within the classroom and the rules of the room. If the teachers' roles are established early on, then rules and their enforcement become second nature. Typically, in the early stages of the co-teaching relationship, the special education teacher takes on the role of behavior manager. This is not a bad thing, but for the structure of the room to be consistent, both teachers need to share this role equally.

Co-teachers will eventually get to a collaborative relationship in which rules and routines are consistent and shared. For students who need an individual behavior plan, the plans are co-developed by the two teachers, and application of contracts, tangible reinforcers, and other types of social-skill development is shared between the two teachers. The co-teachers may collectively agree that a classwide behavior

Behavior Management Discussion Starter

Does anyone have an individualized education program (IEP)?
    Names
    Roles for execution
	Discussion tips: During the planning process, both teachers should discuss this question to determine which students in the classroom have IEPs and what specially designed instruction is required for them.
	
	Jake Q.: IEP with behavior plan included.
	
	Ian K.: IEP with behavior plan included.
	
	Both teachers: Take part in execution of the plan. Mrs. Tall (special education teacher) will ensure the plan is being met in other inclusion classes.

Class rules
    Expectations
    Who will develop rules?
    How many rules?
    Posting of rules
	Discussion tips: When setting up the behavior management plan, the teachers need to discuss and reach agreement on student expectations. Who will develop the rules for the classroom, or will this be decided together?
	
	How many rules will there be, and how will they be displayed in the classroom?
	
	Both teachers: Decide expectations and develop rules. The number of rules will not exceed a total of 5. Mrs. Clever (general education teacher) will post the rules in the classroom. All rules will be written as positive statements.

Consequences
    Positive
    Negative
	Discussion tips: Both positive and negative consequences should be used for behavior management. Both teachers need to discuss exactly how the consequences will be handed down. A positive consequence can be as simple as assigning a percentage of the student's grade for appropriate behavior.
	
	A negative consequence could be as simple as having a behavior grade that starts at 100% and slowly taking points away for inappropriate behavior.
	
	Both teachers: Follow the behavior plans as written in the IEPs for both Jake Q. and Ian K.

Need for classwide behavior plans
    Types of reinforcers:
        Intrinsic
        Extrinsic
	Discussion tips: Most teachers would agree that intrinsic reinforcement is best. Students need to feel good about doing something good or doing well on an assignment. Praising the student helps to intrinsically reinforce positive actions. Extrinsic reinforcement focuses more on giving the student some type of reward for doing well. In the planning process, the co-teachers need to decide what works best for which students.
	Both teachers: Watch for a need for a classwide behavior plan. Currently, there is not a need for one to be developed.

Figure 8.1. Example of completed Behavior Management Discussion Starter form. (Copyright © 2013 by Keystone Educational Consulting Group. http://www.keystone-educational.com. Reprinted by permission.)

plan is in order. Again, the two teachers should develop this plan together and co-present it to the class.

Gately and Gately (2001) explain that the relationship between co-teachers develops in three stages. In the beginning stage, the teachers begin to get comfortable with each other. In the compromising stage, the relationship starts to become a give and take. In the final stage, the collaborative stage, they arrive at the most effective relationship. Upon entering the classroom of co-teachers who are in the collaborative stage, one is not able to tell who is the content teacher and who is the special education teacher, speech therapist, or other type of collaborative professional. The back-and-forth interactions between the co-teachers become seamless and effortless. To arrive at this level of classroom management, administrative support is necessary to help make time for the communication and planning that are necessary to build and strengthen the collaborative relationship.

POSITIVE BEHAVIORAL SUPPORTS

Often teachers and administrators punish students for inappropriate behavior without really looking at the behavior and cause of it (Fixen, Naoom, Blasé, Friedman, & Wallace, 2005). With positive behavioral supports in place and embedded in the classroom management plan, punishment of students is likely to be less necessary. These positive behavioral supports could involve changing the environment or looking for antecedents (i.e., a stimulus that occurs right before the behavior) that can cause the student to act out. The goal in all of this is to reduce future behavioral outbursts.

Webber and Plotts (2008) identified seven important characteristics of positive behavioral support:

1. Person-centered planning

2. Collaborative planning

3. Functional behavioral assessment

4. Hypothesis development

5. Multicomponent planning

6. Evaluation

7. System change

For the purpose of this chapter, the focus on collaborative planning is highlighted, given the context of co-teaching. Because positive behavioral support is considered a scientifically based recommended practice, training to implement all of the components would be necessary. In our discussions with hundreds of teachers, a recurring theme is that, in most cases, the opportunity for collaborative planning of positive behavior supports does not exist during the school day. Again, teachers need to make time to plan whether the planning time is available in their daily schedules or not (Barger-Anderson et al., 2010). This may be difficult to achieve. For more information on the importance of finding time for planning, see Chapter 12.

COMMON PRINCIPLES OF CLASSROOM MANAGEMENT

As previously mentioned, the most important part of co-instruction, when it comes to classroom management, is that the two co-teachers discuss their own principles and belief systems (Stainback & Stainback, 1996). Lane, Kalberg, and Menzies (2009) agree that even though developing common beliefs may be a challenge, in order for positive change to occur, teachers have to work together. In the course of multiple discussions with hundreds of co-teachers, we were amazed at how many of co-teaching teams struggled in the beginning of their partnership with the stage of establishing a common belief system regarding classroom management. For this reason, it is essential that newly established co-teaching teams work through the action planning process to help discover and resolve some of the issues surrounding classroom management before the issues evolve into deeper problems. The Developing Common Principles with Your Co-Teaching Partner form (appendix and Figure 7.2) promotes sharing of common beliefs and finding common ground. The Behavior Management Discussion Starter form (appendix and Figure 8.1) prompts the co-teachers to identify and discuss particular students and their individual needs in the area of classroom management, as well as the possible need for classwide systems.

Baker, Wang, and Walberg (1994) discuss the negative impact that the behavior of students can have on other students within the classroom. One of the major reasons for establishing common principles or beliefs is to help minimize or even eliminate the negative impact of challenging behavior on student learning. However, as stated by Staub and Peck (1994), Peck, Staub, Gallucci, and Schwartz (2004), and Jordan, Glenn, and McGhie-Richmond (2010), although the research is limited, the available studies consistently indicate that inclusion classrooms do hold back the progress of students without disabilities. Some critics of inclusion believe that the general education students may stagnate or even move backwards. Other researchers hold that general education students become resilient to some of the distractions that may occur in the co-taught or inclusive classroom. From some observations we have seen, it may be the teachers who are more distracted by classroom disruptions than the students are.

So, what tends to cause the biggest issues? Ashton (2003) reports that differing teaching philosophies is the second highest concern of teachers within this context (first being co-planning time). However, having teachers with differing teaching philosophies can sometimes be an advantage to the students in a co-taught environment: Some students may connect better with one teacher than the other. Also, a difference in classroom management styles means that a broader range of behavior management skills and strategies are available. New co-teaching teams are encouraged to not get frustrated early on: Over time, balancing teaching styles and behavior management styles becomes more fluid as the relationship grows stronger.

ACTION PLANNING

Once the co-teaching teams are established and receiving training, supported by school leaders, to help facilitate the process, they should go through the action planning process (Barger-Anderson et al., 2010). This process includes in-depth conversation between the two teachers in which they discuss concepts such as the identification of student needs, classroom management styles, teacher roles, common belief systems for handling behavior concerns, and so forth. In terms of classroom management, an action plan may start with consulting previous teachers, guidance counselors, other professionals, or parents to gather all pertinent information that will help the teachers meet not only the academic but also the behavioral needs of individual students. Discussions should also involve identifying which students are gifted students and which students may be at risk for learning and behavioral difficulties. This step is essential because with this information, co-teachers can make better differentiated lesson plans and better groupings because they will know which students can work together well. At times, the gifted student or a nonidentified student could be a behavior problem, so planning and discussion regarding these students are necessary.

With most classrooms being grouped heterogeneously, teachers must discuss how they will differentiate instruction and behavior management to meet the needs of students with varying abilities and behaviors. At times, purposeful grouping of the students is important. Purposeful grouping, as opposed to random grouping, occurs when the co-teachers decide which learning groups include which students. Data from past performance are used in establishing groups. Purposeful grouping can be implemented any time cooperative learning groups are used in the room. Instead of random grouping or the students selecting their own groups, teachers may elect to do purposeful grouping for several reasons and in several different ways. Purposeful grouping may include all groups being comprised of students who are similar in terms of academic ability or may have students of high, medium, and low dispersed equally among the group. In terms of classroom management, teachers who use purposeful grouping need to rely on information about past behavior. This information helps them judge which students can work together and which students are best kept separated. Learning groups may be used if the co-teachers decide to instruct with a stations teaching model, in which the students are assigned to specific groups. Another example is purposeful grouping as used in the parallel model of co-teaching. Co-teaching models and instructional groupings are discussed in Chapter 13.

Along with planning for individual behaviors, co-teachers can use another simple strategy: Refrain from engaging in power struggles with students or getting overly emotional about their behavior. Often teachers take a student's behavior personally when clearly it is simply an extension of the student's disability. The classroom teacher is there to teach the children how to make appropriate choices and decisions. The best way to do this is to lead by example, by modeling positive behavior. *Children learn from our actions.* Co-teachers should model appropriate behavior in all situations.

Finally, here are some basic reminders that can be worked into plans for positive behavior approaches:

- Ask the child (in a nonhumiliating way) to state what he or she did. Ask whether that behavior is allowed at school, at home, and so forth.

- Probe the child to tell what classroom rule was not followed and how the situation could have been handled better (e.g., "What was a better choice?").

- Discuss what the child might do differently if this situation were to happen again. What are other appropriate options?

- Be consistent with rules and consequences.

- Privately discuss inappropriate choices with a child.

These suggestions and strategies may be helpful when teachers design the classroom management plan. Co-teaching partners should decide together which strategies and suggestions work best for them.

CONCLUSION

In the current educational system, general education classes are likely to be more diverse and inclusive of students with disabilities than ever before. The points raised in this chapter offer a starting point for positive classroom management and collaborative practice for co-teachers working with students with a wide range of abilities. The co-teachers should identify and access the supports they need to create an inclusive classroom community that ensures membership and opportunities for friendships, collaboration, and parent involvement (Soodak & Erwin, 2000). In inclusive settings, teachers also need to consider the benefits of using positive approaches to behavior management rather than punitive and exclusionary methods. Classroom management plans should include a shared belief system, clear and consistent establishment of rules and routines, and development of both classwide and individual behavior management plans when needed. Clearly, administrative support is necessary to allow for professional development opportunities and time for co-teachers to discuss and plan classroom management issues.

REFERENCES

Ashton, T.M. (2003). What are teachers' greatest co-teaching concerns? *Academic Exchange Quarterly, 7*(3), 100–104.

Baker, E., Wang, M., & Walberg, H. (1994). The effects of inclusion on learning. *Educational Leadership, 52,* 33–35.

Barger-Anderson, R., Isherwood, R., & Merhaut, J. (2010, February). *The Co-Design Model: A collaborative approach to inclusive education.* Paper presented at the 47th Annual International Conference of the Learning Disabilities Association of America, Baltimore, MD.

Burden, P.R. (2003). *Classroom management: Creating a successful learning community* (2nd ed.) Hoboken, NJ: Wiley.

Cook, L., & Friend, M. (1995). Co-teaching: Guidelines for creating effective practices. *Focus on Exceptional Children, 28,* 1–16.

Fixen, D.L., Naoom, S.F., Blasé, K.A., Friedman, R.M., & Wallace, F. (2005). *Implementation research: A synthesis of the literature* (Louis de la Parte Florida Mental Health Institute Publication No. 231). Tampa, FL: University of South Florida, Louis de la Parte Florida Mental Health Institute, National Implementation Research Network.

Garnett, K. (2010). *Thinking about inclusion and learning disabilities: A teacher's guide* (pp. 7–12). Arlington, VA: Division of Learning Disabilities, Council for Exceptional Children.

Gately, S.E., & Gately, F.J. (2001). Understanding co-teaching components. *Teaching Exceptional Children, 33*(4), 40–47.

Glasser, W. *Classroom management theorists and theories.* Retrieved from http://en.wikibooks.org/wiki/Classroom_Management_Theorists_and_Theories/William_Glasser

Jordan, A., Glenn, C., & McGhie-Richmond, D. (2010). The Supporting Effective Teaching (SET) project: The relationship of inclusive teaching practices to teachers' beliefs about disability and ability, and about their roles as teachers. *Teaching and Teacher Education, 26*(2), 259–266.

Lane, K.L., Kalberg, J.R., & Menzies, H.M. (2009). *Developing schoolwide programs to prevent and manage problem behaviors: A step-by-step approach.* New York, NY: Guilford.

Peck, C., Staub, D., Gallucci, C., & Schwartz, I. (2004). Parent perception of the impacts of inclusion on their nondisabled child. *Research and Practice for Persons with Severe Disabilities, 29*(2), 135–143.

Soodak, L.C., & Erwin, E.J. (2000). Valued member or tolerated participant: Parents' experiences in inclusive early childhood settings. *Journal of the Association for Persons with Severe Handicaps, 25,* 29–44.

Stainback, W., & Stainback, S. (1996). Structuring the classroom to prevent disruptive behaviors. In S. Stainback & W. Stainback (Eds.), *Inclusion: A guide for educators* (pp. 343–348). Baltimore, MD: Paul H. Brookes Publishing Co.

Staub, D., & Peck, C.A. (1994). What are the outcomes for nondisabled students? *Educational Leadership, 52,* 36–40.

Webber, J., & Plotts, C. (2008). *Emotional and behavioral disorders: Theory and practice.* Boston, MA: Allyn & Bacon.

CHAPTER 9

Adaptations, Accommodations, and Modifications

Often a parent's first IEP meeting is overwhelming, fast paced, and full of incomprehensible legal terms. That's how it was for my daughter Laura and me when we walked into my grandson's IEP meeting at the end of his kindergarten year. Ryan had been diagnosed with autism when he was 2½ and had participated in 3 years of early intervention before entering public school. My daughter and I are both educators, and we believed strongly in inclusion. We had seen firsthand the benefits of an inclusionary setting in Ryan's placement at the age of 5 in Learning Experiences: An Alternative Program for preschoolers and parents (LEAP), a preschool program modeled on the TEACCH principles (University of North Carolina, 2012). When he entered a half-day kindergarten in public school, we agreed that he could participate in the "autistic support classroom" in the morning, where we felt he would benefit from one-to-one support, but also we requested that he participate in a "typical" afternoon kindergarten, where we felt he could develop social skills alongside his neurotypical peers. We were quite disappointed in the year's experience, because Ryan, who was verbal with no behavior problems, was treated as a "visitor" in the afternoon kindergarten classroom. When we visited for parents' day, his name was not on the job chart, and there was no evidence of his participation in the kindergarten activities—no art on the bulletin board, no birthday cake with his name on the birthday calendar. He was obviously not looked upon as a member of the kindergarten community.

In May, my daughter and I both attended his IEP meeting, in which first-grade placement was to be discussed. When Laura and I walked into the room, there were no fewer than 10 people already sitting around the table. I couldn't help but think how intimidating such a setting would be for a parent who was nervous about how to communicate a son or daughter's need and hoping to trust that the experts around the table would know best. The meeting began with a "report" from the autistic support teacher and the kindergarten teacher. For at least 15 minutes Laura and I sat there listening to both educators discuss everything Ryan could *not* do—he wasn't able to answer "why" questions; he had poor social skills; his reading and listening comprehension scores were low; he often seemed to be on the periphery of the group; he still walked in circles on the playground and sometimes flapped his hands when excited. They kept emphasizing how he would be best served in an autistic support classroom.

It was obvious to Laura and to me that the assessment of Ryan's learning was certainly based on an impairment model. We weren't going to hear about all the growth we had seen in Ryan that year. What about the fact that he was now reading and following schedules? What about the fact that he transitioned throughout the day with no difficulty? What about the fact that his math skills were excellent? What about the fact that he loved maps and obviously had an amazing memory?

Although we were disheartened, I waited for the teacher to take a breath.

"Excuse me," I interrupted. "We realize Ryan still has autism, but his mother feels that the least restrictive environment for Ryan is a 'typical' first-grade classroom. Ryan is no danger to himself or others and is progressing quite well. I think it's best that we now begin to discuss how we will all support Ryan in first grade."

There were a few moments of silence and surprised looks around the table. It wasn't long before the special education coordinator acknowledged that I was correct and agreed that we should begin to talk about what, if any, adaptations or modifications would be necessary for Ryan's success.

That was 9 years ago. Of course Ryan is still on the autism spectrum, but he is now a ninth-grader in middle school. He is included in most academic subjects; he is on the honor roll, participates on the cross-country team, and wrote his first computer program last summer. I often wonder about the path Ryan's academic life would have taken had I not spoken up and advocated for my grandson at that first IEP meeting in kindergarten.

By Kathleen Strickland, Ph.D., Dean of the College of Education
at Slippery Rock University

Many people may use the terms *accommodation, modification,* and *adaptation* interchangeably. This is understandable. They are comparable terms but may have either conflicting or similar definitions, depending on your source. This chapter presents the definitions used in the Co-Design Model. However, the primary purpose of this chapter is to move beyond definitions to examine appropriate adaptations to help students achieve success. Along with looking at appropriate adaptations, this chapter also discusses responsibility for making adaptations, issues of fidelity of implementation, and the role of supplemental aids and services for meeting individual needs of students.

Supplementary aids and services may be delivered via adaptations, accommodations, modifications, or some combination thereof. Supplementary aids and services are addressed in current special education law: specifically, aids, services, or supports, or a combination thereof, must be provided in the general education or other related educational settings to assist students when appropriate (Friend, 2011; IDEA 2004).

DEFINITIONS: ADAPTATION, ACCOMMODATION, MODIFICATION

This section defines the terms *adaptation, accommodation,* and *modification.* Although many definitions exist for each term, a single definition per term was selected for the Co-Design Model, for clarity. Table 9.1 summarizes these definitions. Adaptation is an umbrella term that includes the other two. An *adaptation* is any type of change in the typical way a teacher would implement instruction or assessment. The *means* to attain the change is a modification or an accommodation (Algozzine, Ysseldyke, & Elliott, 1997; Smith, Polloway, Patton, & Dowdy, 2011; Thurlow, 2002). Thus, modifications and accommodations are two kinds of adaptation. The changes to meet the needs of students may involve aspects of the environment, curriculum, instruction, or assignments. If a teacher says he or she is making an adaptation, a good question to ask is, "Will the adaptation be a modification or an accommodation?" Once again, making an adaptation simply means making a change.

Table 9.1. Definitions of adaptation, accommodation, and modification

Term	Definition
Adaptation[a]	Any type of change in the typical way a teacher would implement instruction or assessment. The means to attain the change is achieved via modifications or accommodations (Thurlow, 2002).
Accommodation	Changes that help students with disabilities demonstrate their abilities by working around or overcoming the obstacles presented by their disability (National Dissemination Center for Children with Disabilities, 2010).
Modification	Change in the expectations for learning from the approved curriculum and standards. Making a modification may include changing content or altering goals for meeting various needs of students (National Dissemination Center for Children with Disabilities, 2010; Pennsylvania Training and Technical Assistance Network, 2010; Smith, Polloway, Patton, & Dowdy, 2006).

[a]Adaptations include both accommodations and modifications.

Accommodations are one type of adaptation that teachers may use in the classroom. Accommodations are changes in the materials and procedures that give students with disabilities the same access to the curriculum and assessments as their peers without disabilities (Thurlow, 2002). Accommodations are implemented to allow students with disabilities to demonstrate their learning, knowledge, and ability to succeed by working around or overcoming the obstacles presented by their disability (National Dissemination Center for Children with Disabilities, 2010). When an accommodation is made, the student is expected to complete the same assignment as his or her peers without a disability. However, with the accommodation, a different route to accomplish the same task is provided. Examples of accommodations include having a test read aloud or the use of math manipulatives during a math assessment. In either scenario, the student is completing the same assignment as other students but is afforded assistance to help overcome her or his disability. Accommodations can be particularly helpful in assessments (Salvia, Ysseldyke, & Bolt, 2009), because the changes do not alter the content or level of complexity within the curriculum (Hallahan, Kauffman, & Pullen, 2009). Examples are giving a test orally, providing for additional time, or allowing a keyboard for extended writing assignments. Other accommodations can also be made in the classroom to promote the way the student learns best, such as arranging peer support or using a computer for notetaking, using graph paper to help organize and line up math problems, or tape-recording lectures. Accommodations in the physical environment may include provision of a ramp or elevator.

Modifications are defined as adaptations made to the curriculum, instruction, assessment, or environment, or to some combination of these, that change the expectations of learning from the general curriculum and standards. Modifications provided in the classroom allow for changes to the level, the content, and learning objectives (Castagnera, Fisher, Rodifer, & Sax, 1998). Making a modification may include changing content or altering goals for meeting various needs of students (Pennsylvania Training and Technical Assistance Network [PaTTAN], 2010; National Dissemination Center for Children with Disabilities, 2010; Smith et al., 2011. Modifications to instruction include alternate materials and assignments. For example, if students are reading below grade level, they might be provided the same novel as their peers without disabilities but in a version edited to the appropriate reading level. A modified or alternate assessment might ask yes-or-no questions rather than multiple-choice questions.

WHO IS RESPONSIBLE FOR MAKING THE CHANGES?

When we hold professional development sessions with teachers, we are often asked who is responsible for making the adaptations. As with many other important questions in education, there is no one simple answer. Unless there is a directive from the school administration specifying where the responsibility lies, two areas should be considered: 1) curriculum updating and cyclical textbook adoption and 2) division of responsibility between co-teachers (Barger-Anderson, Isherwood, & Merhaut, 2010).

Curriculum Updating and Cyclical Textbook Adoption

If curriculum is being rewritten or textbook adoption is a district initiative, the availability of adaptations should be a criterion for selection. Having a textbook or curriculum that explicitly addresses adaptations may assist with determining responsibility within co-teaching pairs. The following are some questions to consider during the selection process. Does the teacher's edition of the text provide ideas for differentiating instruction? Are appropriate ancillary materials included? Is a parallel curriculum available? Is technology augmentation available? Finally, do the text and other materials facilitate the use of alternative types of assessment to meet the needs of diverse learners? Consideration of curriculum development is an excellent starting point for not only the creation of appropriate adaptations but also identification of responsibility for the follow-through. The follow-through includes planning and delivering instruction as well as monitoring student progress.

Division of Responsibility Between Co-Teachers

Whether or not a school is in the process of updating curriculum or adopting a new textbook, it is necessary to divide responsibility between the co-teachers. The best approach to finding an answer is to go straight to the source: the co-teachers. They are the ones who need to ensure that specially designed instruction, as stated in the IEP, occurs. As long as the IEP goals are addressed, there is no right or wrong answer for who does what and how much. Both teachers in the co-teaching relationship are responsible for educating all students. As addressed in the discussion of co-instruction element, both teachers share in the responsibilities for making and implementing the adaptations, and they should play off each other's strengths. However, the way to do this may differ from pair to pair.

Various approaches can be taken by the collaborative pair to decide on the appropriateness of changes and who will be responsible for them. It is always best for collaborative partners to communicate clearly when designing and delivering adaptations. Whether the adaptations are for assessments, instruction, environment, or assignments, fidelity of implementation is an important concern. It may be that the special education teacher will take the lead and create some of the adaptations, with the general education teacher providing input and implementation. Other times, the reverse may be true, or it may be a sort of hybrid collaboration. Any of these options are okay as long as the co-teachers accept the shared work load, the needs of the students are being met, and fidelity of implementation is realized. As mentioned earlier in this chapter, supplementary aids and services must be provided when necessary. Adaptations are not an option; they are mandated. In special education law, aids, services, or supports (or some combination of these), when deemed appropriate, must be provided in the general education or other related educational settings to assist students (Friend, 2011; IDEA 2004). Supplementary aids and services include implementation of research-based practices such as collaboration via co-teaching. More information on other supplemental aids and services is provided on the Special Education page in the Student Service/Special Populations section of the Pennsylvania Chapter 12 Student Services Toolkit web site (http://www.pachapter12toolkit.info/index.cfm?pageid=3605). This web site provides a full range of supplemental aids and services that must be considered for identified students.

As always, it is important that collaborative partners agree on the appropriateness of the adaptations. Figure 9.1 is an example of a matrix of student needs. This matrix may be used as a discussion starter for examining individual needs of specific students. Although assessments are discussed in Chapter 10, it is worth calling attention here to Figure 10.1, which is a guide sheet to help promote dialogue about responsibilities for ensuring that appropriate adaptations are being made in the area of assessments. (A reproducible version of both these forms is provided in the appendix.) Similar guides may be created for the areas of planning, delivering, and implementing instruction. Table 9.2 gives examples of possible adaptations for instruction, assignments, environment, and testing situations.

CAN A STUDENT WITHOUT AN INDIVIDUALIZED EDUCATION PROGRAM BENEFIT FROM ADAPTATIONS?

Can a student without an IEP have the benefit of instruction, environments, assignments, or assessments that have been adapted? The answer is yes, which seems to surprise some people. Some educators assume that only students with identified needs can be the recipients of adaptations in the classroom. One example is through the RTI initiative (or the RtII approach specific to Pennsylvania and other states).

First, consider initiatives at the national level. The RTI model is a direct result of some of the provisions stated in the reauthorization of IDEA in 2004. The reauthorization allows for provisions that could lead to changes in the identification process for students with SLDs. One of these allowances is that, when identifying such students, the local educational agency may consider the students' RTI with scientifically based instruction. In other words, the diagnosis of an SLD does not require a severe discrepancy in achievement versus ability. This new model differs from the discrepancy model in that a child does not have to fail in order to be identified. In this model, an RTI

Matrix of Student Needs

Student name	Area identified	Sources for identification	Other
Sue Snowflake	At risk for oral reading performance	Previous teacher, parents, grades	Preferential seating in the general education classroom
Sam Summer	Specific learning in the area of mathematics	Individualized education program	

Figure 9.1   Example of completed Matrix of Student Needs form. (Copyright © 2013 by Keystone Educational Consulting Group. http://www.keystone-educational.com. Reprinted by permission.)

Table 9.2.   Examples of adaptations

Instruction/assignment/environment	Assessment
Peer support for notetaking	Tests read aloud
Graph paper to help with organization	Additional time
Math manipulatives	Oral response
Additional time	Assistive technology
Computers used for extended writing projects	Graphic organizers
Tape recording of lectures	Examples for practice
Computers used for notetaking	Underlining of key words in directions or
More than one learning modality used	questions
Peer tutoring	Lists for fill-in-the-blank answers
Breaks	Reduced choices in multiple-choice answers
Extra lighting	Test administered in an alternative setting
Preferential seating	

From Barger-Anderson, R., Isherwood, R., & Merhaut, J. (2010, February). *The Co-Design Model: A collaborative approach to inclusive education.* Paper presented at the 47th Annual International Conference of the Learning Disabilities Association of America, Baltimore, MD; adapted by permission.

analysis considers a child's ability to respond to research-based practices (Heward, 2009). RTI features a tiered intervention plan to meet the academic and behavioral needs of all students, along with progress monitoring to track academic achievement (see Chapter 1).

A major reason for this change was that educators could not confidently say whether a diagnosis of an SLD resulted from the child's ability or from lack of appropriate instruction provided in the general education classroom. The National Research Center on Learning Disabilities states that RTI is one element for consideration when identifying SLDs (Johnson, Mellard, Fuchs, & McKnight, 2006). Some states are going beyond the federal mandates of the RTI initiative. Pennsylvania and California are two states that have opted to do this. For example, in Pennsylvania, instead of implementing the RTI initiative, the state is using the Response to Instruction and Intervention (RtII) model. As introduced in Chapter 1, PaTTAN defines the RtII model as "a comprehensive, multi-tiered standards aligned [*sic*] strategy to enable early identification and intervention for students at academic or behavioral risk" (2010, n.p.). The purpose of RtII is to give teachers a standard that helps with identifying needs and providing assistance with both academic and behavioral difficulties before the student fails. Data for decision making to determine possible eligibility for special education services is provided with the use of the RtII model (PaTTAN, 2010). The discrepancy model of the method for identifying SLDs before the reauthorization of IDEA in 2004 still remains a method for identification of SLDs.

A FINAL QUESTION: DOES FAIR MEAN EQUAL?

Parents, students, colleagues, and community members may wonder whether it is fair for some students to receive changes in their curriculum yet still receive the same grades as students without changes. The plain truth is that fair is not always equal. For example, some people need glasses to see distances far away. Is it fair that some people get to wear glasses and others do not? The answer, most would agree, is "yes." Is it equal? No, because not everyone is wearing a pair of glasses. Why would someone who can see at a distance without glasses wear them? In this example, the glasses are an appropriate adaptation, or supplemental aid, to ensure access. If a student can be assisted by wearing glasses, why not give him or her the glasses? If a student does not need an adaptation, why provide it? Supplemental aids and services are addressed in special education law and must be applied when appropriate. Aids, services, and supports must be provided in the general education or other related educational settings to assist students when appropriate (Friend, 2011; IDEA 2004). Adaptations are required to ensure that everyone is afforded the same opportunities for learning and success and should be used only when appropriate.

CONCLUSION

The Co-Design Model promotes the appropriate use of adaptations in the collaborative classroom for all students. Through the use of adaptations, the playing field is leveled and all students have access to learning and an opportunity to succeed. Communication and collaboration are promoted between co-teachers to ensure that both partners agree upon the adaptations being provided and the implementation of adaptations is done with fidelity.

Adaptations are an important part of today's diverse and ever-changing classroom dynamics. When two teachers are present to assess the learning needs of all students and determine appropriate adaptations, the workload is shared and opportunities to teach and interact with all students are increased: Every student can have access to an appropriate learning and social environment.

REFERENCES

Algozzine, B., Ysseldyke, J., & Elliott, J. (1997). *Strategies and tactics for effective instruction*. Longmont, CO: Sopris West.

Barger-Anderson, R., Isherwood, R., & Merhaut, J. (2010, February). *The Co-Design Model: A collaborative approach to inclusive education.* Paper presented at the 47th Annual International Conference of the Learning Disabilities Association of America, Baltimore, MD.

Castagnera, E., Fisher, D., Rodifer, K., & Sax, C. (1998). *Deciding what to teach and how to teach it: Connecting students through curriculum and instruction.* Colorado Springs, CO: PEAK Parent Center.

Friend, M. (2011). *Special education: Contemporary perspectives for school professionals* (3rd ed.). Boston, MA: Pearson.

Hallahan, D.P., Kauffman, J.M., & Pullen, P.C. (2009). *Exceptional learners: An introduction to special education* (11th ed.). Boston, MA: Pearson.

Heward, W.L. (2009). *Exceptional children: An introduction to special education* (9th ed.). Upper Saddle River, NJ: Pearson Merrill Prentice Hall.

Individuals with Disabilities Education Improvement Act (IDEA) of 2004, PL 108-446, 20 U.S.C. §§ 1400 *et seq.*

Johnson, E., Mellard, D.F., Fuchs, D., & McKnight, M.A. (2006). *Responsiveness to Intervention (RTI): How to do it.* Lawrence, KS: National Research Center on Learning Disabilities.

National Dissemination Center for Children with Disabilities (2010, September). *Supports, modifications, and accommodations for students.* Retrieved from http://www.nichcy.org/EducateChildren/Supports/Pages/default.aspx

Pennsylvania Training and Technical Assistance Network. (2010). *What is the difference between adaptations and modifications?* Retrieved from http://www.pattan.net/FAQs.aspx?PageNumber= 0&Contains =adaptations [source no longer online]

Salvia, J., Ysseldyke, J., & Bolt, S. (2009). *Assessment in special education and inclusive education* (11th ed.). Belmont, CA: Wadsworth.

Smith, T.E.C., Polloway, E.A., Patton, J.R., & Dowdy, C.A. (2011). *Teaching students with special needs in inclusive settings* (6th ed.). Boston, MA: Pearson.

Thurlow, M. (2002). *Accommodations for students with disabilities in high school* (Issue Brief, Vol. 1, No. 1). Retrieved from National Center on Secondary Education and Transition web site: http://www.ncset.org/publications/viewdesc.asp?id=247.

University of North Carolina at Chapel Hill School of Medicine. (2012). *TEACCH Autism Program.* Retrieved from http://teacch.com

CHAPTER 10

Assessment

Multifaceted assessment is elemental to the diagnosis and prediction of all behavior. Thus, to understand where kids are and why, or where they are going or could go, educators turn to appropriate assessment for answers. Moreover, it is important to understand that assessment applies to every student in both the general and the inclusionary classroom, at every cognitive level, and in every academic area.

Because the quality of instruction can be determined only through the quality of the assessment used, it is important that the general and the special education teacher collaborate in their instruction and assessment if they are to maximize the academic enhancement of all their students. At the very outset of this collaboration, it is essential that both teachers understand that a fusion of their respective areas of content and methodological expertise will be conducive to higher levels of instruction and assessment. The effectiveness of the collaboration will increase further if both teachers also understand that students with special needs can ascend through any cognitive hierarchy in an academically honest fashion.

Appropriate assessment, when collaboratively designed to measure learning at different cognitive levels, enables co-teachers to decide what is working and what needs to be redirected. Conversely, using indiscriminate, one-size-fits-all assessment in the inclusionary classroom is equivalent to using a sundial at a track meet. Hence, teachers must determine what, whom, and which levels they want to assess. Then, they can collaboratively determine the directions in which to proceed.

By John Badgett, Ph.D., Professor of Secondary Education at
Slippery Rock University

Assessment is identified as one of the nine elements in the Co-Design Model. Adequately addressing assessment, which encompasses students' needs for appropriate evaluation techniques, is necessary for the success of the inclusive classroom (Barger-Anderson, Isherwood, & Merhaut, 2010). Gately and Gately (2001) concur that assessment is an area that educators who share a common class assignment must address together. Educators may ask themselves, "How will I assess this content? Will I assess all students the same way? What will I do when not all of my students meet the objectives?" This chapter looks at assessment and some of the challenges it may present.

A principal reason for conducting assessments is to gather information that will assist with effective decision making (Badgett & Christman, 2009; Salvia & Ysseldyke, 2004; Salvia, Ysseldyke, & Bolt, 2007). Salvia and Ysseldyke state that

> In the educational system, assessments help teachers, administrators, psychologists, and parents make at least five kinds of decisions: 1) screening, 2) identifying strengths and weaknesses, 3) determining eligibility and making diagnoses, 4) doing instructional and program planning, and 5) determining program planning effectiveness. (p. 4)

Assessment, in the educational arena, is especially diverse, given the many types, purposes, and definitions of the term (Newton, 2007). In this chapter, only two forms of assessment are considered. This chapter does not address state assessments. Nor does the chapter discuss schoolwide assessments or norm-referenced, formal assessments to assist in determining eligibility requirements for special education services and establishment of IQ. Rather, the two assessments examined in this chapter are the formative and summative types. These two forms of assessment are to be conducted and the results used within the daily routines of the classroom. The results from these assessments should drive daily data-managed decisions (Mercer & Mercer, 2005). As Tomlinson states, "Informative assessment isn't an end in itself, but the beginning of better instruction" (2007/2008, p. 11).

ASSESSMENT TYPES

This chapter focuses on summative and formative assessments. Summative assessment is defined as assessment proctored at the end of a unit or time frame to determine how much learning has occurred (Dodge, 2009). Fisher and Frey (2007) define formative assessment as continuous evaluation, summaries, observations, and reviews used daily to provide teacher information and student feedback.

Stiggins (2007) explains that the focus of formative assessment is assessment for learning. Formative assessments do not necessarily require grading. They serve as practice for the summative assessment. Formative assessments check for understanding along the way and provide feedback. They also help teachers differentiate (see Chapter 14). Some take longer to administer (such as writing assessments); however, many are quick and easy. Formative assessments allow opportunities for both individual and group work (Dodge, 2009).

It is important for teachers to identify appropriate daily instructional goals. Clear instructional objectives can serve as "baselines for the formative assessments" (Badgett & Christman, 2009, p. 39). Badgett and Christman suggest three categories for assessment: "paper-and-pencil tests," "performance-based activities," and "the portfolio process" (p. 39).

Paper-and-pencil assessments include multiple-choice, true/false, matching, completion items, and short-answer/essay types. Performance-based assessments measure product or process by rubrics, checklists, or rating scales. Table 10.1 lists possible structured and unstructured assessments that fall into the pencil-and-paper and product categories. These may serve as either summative assessments, formative assessments, or both.

Portfolios include work samples produced by students. Student growth is considered in this model of assessment (Badgett & Christman, 2009). Many definitions of portfolio assessment exist, but the following components listed by Salvia et al. seem to be the most common:

Table 10.1. Ideas for formative and summative assessment

Assessment Type	Suggestions
Checklists	These may be simple class lists with "yes/no" or "satisfactory/unsatisfactory" marked next to the students' names. The teacher may use a clipboard for organization of the checklists.
Rating scales	Rating scales are a type of continuum. Typically, teachers rate students on preestablished criteria on a scale from 1 to 3 or 1 to 5.
Rubrics	When using rubrics, the teacher should clearly define the objectives for the students. The more specific the rubric, the less chance of scoring biases to occur. A free site that can help in generating rubrics is http://rubistar.4teachers.org.
Charts and other graphic organizers	Graphic organizers are useful for having students demonstrate knowledge in a variety of forms. Charts or organizers may take the form of a Venn diagram, T chart, wagon wheel, or many others. Teachers may offer the students the option to select their favorite chart or graphic organizer. This choice may increase student motivation. A source for finding graphic organizer templates is http://www.freeology.com.
Cloze tests	This form of assessment may be administered as oral or written. Brief chunks of text are provided with blanks. The student must fill in the blanks.
Writing	Writings may be short answers, essays, summaries, or reflections. They may also be in the form of logs or journals. Writings may be the most time-intensive assessment but are meaningful.
Debates	Debates are helpful in determining oral skills in addition to content knowledge of a topic. Debates promote higher-level thinking skills, such as critical thinking, analysis of information, evaluation of content, as well as public speaking skills.
Experiments	This form of assessment is especially useful for assessing application of knowledge learned from prior lessons. Experiments are helpful because they provide immediate feedback on whether skills have been mastered or reteaching is needed.
Story retelling	This type of assessment may be completed in a variety of forms. It may be performed orally. It may be completed in a written form consisting of words or visuals. It may take the form of a comic strip. It may be a video created by students—for example, on a site such as http://www.xtranormal.com. Some of these ideas may also provide ways to differentiate instruction to the appropriate levels.
Running records/miscue analysis	Running records and miscue analyses are assessments for measuring a student's oral reading performance. A running record measures the student performance against established benchmarks. A miscue analysis measures errors in a student's oral reading performance. Up to six different types of errors may be documented: omissions, corrections, repetitions, substitutions, insertions, and reversals.
Entrance/exit slips	Entrance/exit slips are a quick and easy way to gather assessment information on a topic. Entrance slips may be used as a springboard into the day's lesson. Exit slips may check for comprehension. See http://www.educationworld.com/a_curr?profdev/profdev091.shtml for a brief yet informative article on using these assessments.

Sources: Badgett and Christman (2009); Dodge (2009); Jenkins (2009); Newton, 2007; and Navarrete, Wilde, Nelson, Martinez, and Hargett (1990).

Targets valued outcomes for assessment (analysis, synthesis, and evaluation), uses tasks that mirror work in the real world, encourages cooperation among learners and between teacher and student, uses multiple dimensions to evaluate student work, encourages student reflection, and integrates assessment and instruction. (2007, p. 253)

There are several different styles and possibilities of content that make up a portfolio. It depends on the intent of the portfolio. The wide variation in the content of a portfolio leads many to raise concerns about criteria selection, student involvement in selection of content, "sufficient content generated by a student to reach valid decisions," reliability concerns, "biased scoring, instructional utility, and efficiency" (Salvia et al., 2007, p. 267).

Gunning (2010) provides advice for addressing concerns associated with use of portfolios. First, inclusion of material in the portfolio needs to be based on a discussion with an individual student about his or her goals for the year. These goals may change throughout the year depending on progress and acquisition of new skills. It is important to revisit goals occasionally and alter them if needed. Next, in addition to setting the goals, teachers must select a way to determine whether the goals are being met at an acceptable standard. In other words, not only should the portfolio include a checklist of what is included but there should also be regular quality-assurance checks. And finally, the portfolio should be managed and evaluated by both the teachers and the student. Management includes making decisions about which artifacts are included and excluded throughout the year. Evaluation encompasses holding conferences with the student to discuss the contents and completion of various types of assessment, which may take the form of a rating scale or rubric.

As one example of how portfolios can be used, a teacher from Karns City, Pennsylvania, comments,

I have used portfolios but more as a culminating activity to show long-term growth from the beginning of the year until the end. My students really enjoyed the project! It was time-intensive and expensive to buy the folders each year. Another negative to portfolios was the space in my room it took to house all of the work they collected for the portfolio. Even with these drawbacks, I found it meaningful. The students reflected on their work and they were proud of their accomplishments. It showcased their best work as well as their improvements.

(M. Twentier, personal communication to Richael
Barger-Anderson, February 13, 2011)

APPLICATION TO THE CLASSROOM

Preassessment and postassessment techniques should be conducted frequently and on a cyclical basis to drive instruction. In other words, preassessment information provides a baseline for student understanding and should help identify learning objectives and drive the direction of instruction. Postassessment data should be collected and used to guide new daily objectives. Frequent progress monitoring, via formative assessments, should be conducted to determine the individual needs of the students and ensure that progress is indeed being made (Mercer & Mercer, 2005).

Informal types of assessment must be planned carefully (Naverrete, Wilde, Nelson, Martinez, & Hargett, 2011). Salvia et al. note, "Because teacher-made tests are seldom subject to public scrutiny, many tests theorists have doubts about their technical adequacy" (2007, p. 247). Newton (2007) found that many teachers use an assortment of testing techniques to measure student knowledge and cautions teachers to ensure the measurements employed are suitable. It is possible for formative and summative measures to be reliable and valid (Navarrete, Wilde, Nelson, Martinez, &

Hargett, 1990), but teachers need to realize that it is important for any assessment to align with the content being delivered and the standards that are set.

Dodge (2009) asserts that once the assessments are given, data must be collected and tracked. The task of tracking data should not be time-intensive and burdensome. Tracking may be completed via use of a clipboard and sticky notes. Anecdotal notes may also be kept on a class list. Beside the student names, specific skills may be itemized. A simple "yes" or "no" may be enough to track the progress of each student. A system of plus/minus or the numbers 1–4 can be assigned to the tasks to document levels of proficiency. Figure 10.1 shows a completed example of a "yes/no" progress sheet for tracking syllabication skills of sample consonants + -le words for a student named Colben. Each student working on this skill would have a progress sheet on which data would be recorded. The skill sheets may be kept together on a clipboard to help with organization.

Guskey (2007/2008) reminds teachers that it is important for assessments to be included as part of the development of instruction. He cautions teachers not stop short, though. Yes, formative assessments must be completed, but the most important step in this process is using the collected data to determine the next step in the educational process.

Badgett and Christman (2009) state that assessment results should be instrumental in the decision-making process for determining instructional goals. If assessment results are revealing that students are not making progress, instruction should be altered to allow for another chance and promote success for all students (Guskey, 2007/2008; Mercer & Mercer, 2005). As has been highlighted through several elements of the Co-Design Model, determining how the data are collected and used should be discussed and agreed upon by both teachers collaboratively (Barger-Anderson et al., 2010).

SKILL: Syllabication of Sample Consonant + -*le* Words

Student name: _____Colben_____

Word	Yes	No	Comments
Bubble	X		
Angle		X	
Apple	X		
Double		X	
Sample	X		
Needle	X		
Battle	X		
Wiggle	X		
Puzzle	X		
Jungle	X		
Saddle	X		
Simple	X		
Sparkle		X	
Noble	X		
Little	X		

Figure 10.1.   Sample yes/no progress sheet.

WHAT ASSESSMENT MIGHT LOOK LIKE IN A SHARED ENVIRONMENT

Assessment is identified in the Co-Design Model as a critical component of the design and therefore must be addressed in terms of collaboration in the inclusive classroom (Barger-Anderson et al., 2010). Figure 10.2 is a shared assessment form that can promote dialogue between collaborative partners for making joint assessment decisions. (A reproducible version of this form is provided in the appendix.) In the completed example form in Figure 10.2, the two types of examples showcased are story retelling and debates. From these examples, you can see the importance of collaboration to identify the type of assessment as well as decide who will take responsibility for creating the assessment, evaluating the assessment, and making any necessary adaptations.

Within the area of assessment, partners must collaborate to reach agreement on making adaptations to assessments. Careful consideration for adaptations (either accommodations or modifications) of assessments for students with disabilities or individual needs must be applied. As Salvia et al. recommend,

> The most important principle to keep in mind is that assessment accommodation decisions should be made carefully, taking into consideration the student's individual needs, the test purpose, the accommodations that student receives during instruction, and the skills the test is intended to measure. Students should not, on the day of testing, suddenly be given accommodations they have never previously experienced. (2007, p. 169)

See Chapter 9 for more information on adaptations.

When addressing the element of assessment, collaborating with a partner should allow for more responsiveness to student learning and achievement. With two

Shared Assessment

Type of assessment	Adaptations	Responsibility
Story retelling	Highest level—written version of story with a minimum of 3 paragraphs. Must include a beginning, middle, and end. Lower level—may include visuals. Must include a beginning, middle, and end.	Mrs. McMillan and Mrs. Miller will share responsibility for grading both versions of the story retelling. Mrs. Miller will be responsible for the creation of the rubric to score the higher level. Mrs. McMillan will be responsible for creating the rubric for the lower-level version of the assignment.
Debate	The debate teams will be heterogeneously grouped according to ability. Questions will be teacher selected depending on the student who is responsible for addressing the question. Questions will be created at each level in alignment with Bloom's Taxonomy.	Mrs. McMillan and Mrs. Miller will create the groupings of students and the scoring chart for the debate together. Mrs. McMillan will create questions at the lower level of Bloom's Taxonomy. This includes questions that require recall, matching, listing, summarizing, and defending. Mrs. Miller will create questions at the higher level of Bloom's Taxonomy. This includes questions that require demonstration, compare/contrast, distinction, problem solving, creation, justification, and appraisals.

Figure 10.2. Example of completed Shared Assessment form. (Copyright © 2013 by Keystone Educational Consulting Group. http://www.keystone-educational.com. Reprinted by permission.)

professionals sharing tasks and accountability for student advancement, it should be possible to take action for all students to help ensure daily progress monitoring is happening (Barger-Anderson et al., 2010).

CAUTIONS ABOUT TESTING

Assessment is not synonymous with testing. Assessment is a larger concept. Testing is only one possible component of assessment (Overton, 2003; Salvia et al., 2007). Educational testing is an important contribution by behavioral science. Tests continue to be improved, and educators are making better use of the results. However, the inappropriate use of test results can be damaging to both students and others who are affected by decisions based on test results, both during school age and beyond (Salvia et al., 2007). As educators, we may often contemplate the importance of testing for school-age students. Testing can profoundly affect many people far beyond the K–12 system: Consider college entrance exams, state examinations for teachers, the bar exams for attorneys, medical boards, and so forth. Do these examinations really assess knowledge in these areas? Are these testing procedures fair? And, finally, are they culturally biased considering the heterogeneous makeup of today's society?

CONCLUSION

Gunning (2010) states that assessment and instruction are blended components of education that cannot be separated. Many experts in the field agree that an important reason for conducting assessments is to help with making data-driven decisions for instruction (Badgett & Christman, 2009; Mercer & Mercer, 2005; Salvia & Ysseldyke, 2004; Salvia et al., 2007).

The element of assessment builds on the element of collaboration within the Co-Design Model. Professionals who collaborate within a shared learning environment often promote successful and appropriate assessment techniques by way of paper-and-pencil tests, performance-based assessments, and portfolio assessments. This collaboration occurs during planning, executing, and evaluating instruction and assessment in their daily routines. Open dialogue between the collaborative partners is a must. No matter which type of assessments are given or how co-teachers divide the labor, assessments should be given frequently, including both pre- and post-assessments to develop objectives, drive instruction, and monitor progress.

Assessment and instruction are two areas that work in tandem (Badgett & Christman, 2009; Salvia & Ysseldyke, 2004; Salvia et al., 2007). It is important to keep in mind the differences between testing and assessment (Overton, 2003; Salvia et al., 2007). Thoughtful development and use of formative and summative assessments to make informed decisions, along with having a collaborative partner, should help teachers gather useful information to measure and promote learning of all students (Barger-Anderson et al., 2010).

REFERENCES

Badgett, J.L., & Christman, E.P. (2009). *Designing elementary instruction and assessment using the cognitive domain.* Thousand Oaks, CA: Corwin.

Barger-Anderson, R., Isherwood, R., & Merhaut, J. (2010, February). *The Co-Design Model: A collaborative approach to inclusive education.* Paper presented at the 47th Annual International Conference of the Learning Disabilities Association of America, Baltimore, MD.

Dodge, J. (2009). *25 quick formative assessments for a differentiated classroom.* New York, NY: Scholastic.

Fisher, D., & Frey, N. (2007). *Checking for understanding: Formative assessment techniques for your classroom.* Alexandria, VA: Association for Supervision and Curriculum Development.

Gately, S.E., & Gately, F.J. (2001). Understanding co-teaching components. *Teaching Exceptional Children, 33,* 40–47.

Gunning, T.G. (2010). *Assessing and correcting reading and writing difficulties* (4th ed.). Boston, MA: Allyn & Bacon.

Guskey, T.R. (2007/2008). The rest of the story. *Educational Leadership, 65*(4), 28–35.

Jenkins, S. (2009, September 17). *Formal and informal assessments: Testing methods.* Retrieved from www.associatedcontent.com<http://www.associatedcontent.com/>

Mercer, C.D., & Mercer, A.R. (2005). *Teaching students with learning problems* (7th ed). Upper Saddle River, NJ: Prentice Hall.

Navarrete, C., Wilde, J., Nelson, C., Martinez, R., & Hargett, G. (1990). *Informal assessment in educational evaluation: Implications for bilingual education programs.* Washington, DC: National Clearinghouse for Bilingual Education.

Newton, P.E. (2007). Clarifying the purposes of educational assessment. *Assessment in Education: Principles, Policy, and Practice, 14*(2), 149–170.

Overton, T. (2003). Promoting academic success through assessment of the academic environment. *Intervention in School and Clinic, 39*(3), 147–153.

Salvia, J., & Ysseldyke, J.E. (2004). *Assessment* (9th ed.). Boston, MA: Houghton Mifflin.

Salvia, J., Ysseldyke, J.E., & Bolt, S. (2007). *Assessment in special and inclusive education* (10th ed.). Boston, MA: Houghton Mifflin Company.

Stiggins, R. (2007). Assessment through student eyes. *Educational Leadership, 64*(8), 22–26.

Tomlinson, C. (2007/2008). Learning to love assessment. *Educational Leadership, 65*(4), 8–13.

CHAPTER 11

Personality Types

During 3 years of teaching in my district, I have witnessed many, many benefits of co-teaching. I have been involved in a co-teaching relationship in reading for all 3 years. During that time, the reading teacher and I have reached the point where we can finish each other's sentences. In fact, our director has often referred to our working relationship as a marriage. (Because her name is Lora, we've received many "Luke and Lora" jokes—though I truly don't know what show that comes from.) We both know that we can rely on each other. Also, there have been numerous times when we have needed to be flexible and knew that "our" kids would be all right with the other person. She knew that I knew the curriculum well enough to take over (something many teachers struggle with), and I knew that if I was somewhere else, the students on my roster would be okay with her (no small feat considering the size of my roster this year!).

Most of my other co-teaching relationships have been one teach/one assist. This situation can become frustrating for a support teacher who feels they could be doing more. However, as long as my students are learning, I can accept this role. This year I entered another co-teaching partnership. This partnership was harder to mesh because, though we got along well outside the classroom, we had polar opposite teaching styles. As the year went along, we moved more into a one teach/one assist model with me as the lead teacher. I believe we needed more time to truly plan for each class because we did not have the benefit of the relationship I share with the reading teacher. It is my belief that for co-teaching to work, the general education teacher must be open and inviting to the co-teaching initiative.

By Luke Travelpiece, special education teacher at
Riverside Area School District, Ellwood City, Pennsylvania

What is personality? How many types of personality are there? Personality is another important element of the Co-Design Model (Barger-Anderson, Isherwood, and Merhaut, 2010), and this chapter looks at how personality plays a role in the collaborative classroom. Professionals in a co-teaching relationship should take ownership of the responsibility for all students and must be respectful of each other's skill sets and training (Cook & Friend, 1996; Friend, 2007). Gately and Gately (2001) state that personality type is a factor to be considered in order to promote successful collaborative efforts within a shared setting.

Because of the intimacy of sharing classroom space and responsibilities, collaboration between professionals in a common educational environment has been likened to a marriage (Villa, 2008). As comedian Billy Connolly has been quoted as saying, "Marriage is a wonderful invention; then again, so is a bicycle repair kit." In other words, marriage is wonderful, but if some areas are not working properly, those may cause the entire experience to deteriorate. However, there are tools available to assist with "repairs" to a marriage, to a bicycle, and yes…to a co-teaching relationship. This chapter examines the intricate relationship between collaborative partners in education in terms of personality types and provides some tools for a "repair kit."

UNDERSTANDING PERSONALITY TYPES

Some pairs of co-teachers just "hit it off." It may be their first year together, but it seems like they have been co-teaching for years. Other co-teaching pairs may take as long as 3 years to reach this level of collaboration. Some co-teaching pairs never make it to the collaborative stage, and personality has a lot to do with it.

To understand personality traits and styles, we often use the Four Temperament Model proposed by Robert Rohm (2008). This model offers four profile types to define a person's temperament, or personality. This particular model is easy to connect with and understand. During professional development workshops that promote the Co-Design Model, teachers and administrators are interested in acquiring information to help establish partnerships that will thrive. Understanding certain personality traits via the Four Temperament Model may help with this task. Rohm's work consists of four characterizing traits that are presented in pairs: people-oriented versus task-oriented and outgoing versus reserved. These four characterizing traits are used in combinations to identify the four temperaments or personalities found within this model.

The Four Temperament Model we use was published in 1928 by W.M. Marston and draws on traditional concepts of temperaments. Rohm has since contributed to and expanded topics in this area of research. This model uses a four-quadrant display to describe personality types. The personality traits are (Rohm, 2008)

- *D* type: dominant or "outgoing" and "task-oriented"
- *I* type: inspiring or "outgoing" and "people-oriented"
- *S* type: supportive or "reserved" and "people-oriented"
- *C* type: cautious or "reserved" and "task-oriented"

This formulation is often known as the DISC Model, for "dominant, inspiring, supportive, cautious."

The exact mix of these four traits is called a person's "style blend." For a teacher to achieve the highest potential of effectiveness within the classroom, he or she must be comfortable within the environment. Knowing and understanding one's own "style blend" and the personality type and "style blend" of one's collaborative partner will promote better communication within the learning environment and allow greater comfort for working effectively as a team (Rohm, 2004, 2008).

Often teachers or administrators think people with similar personality types will make the best co-teaching teams, but this is not always true. Sometimes the most successful teams have opposite personality types. Identifying personality types and pairing teachers according to the results does not guarantee success in a collaborative environment. However, it is one way to make a more informed decision.

ADDITIONAL TOOLS IN THE REPAIR KIT

Through better understanding of personality traits, additional tools become available for struggling co-teaching pairs. Co-teaching pairs who are doing well but still want to improve may benefit from a few of these tools as well (see Table 11.1). Understanding one's own personality style blend and that of others is a helpful tool to keep handy in the repair kit. Other tools include

1. Consideration of personality traits by administrators before creation of the master schedule

2. Intervention by an administrator or outside consultant via the use of problem-solving models to improve communication

3. Recognizing individual strengths and contributions by the co-teachers

4. Termination of unsuccessful pairings

Administrators should take faculty members' personality traits into consideration before assigning collaborative teams in the master schedule. Administrators especially need to consider personality styles in situations where co-teachers have multiple collaborative partners. For example, a special educator in an elementary school may be required to co-teach with two different fourth-grade teachers. She may also work with the art and physical education teachers. This complex schedule adds another layer of concerns: The more partners a teacher is working with, the more flexibility and understanding is required by each of the partners. Also, more time will need to be devoted to getting to know each other and learning each other's personality traits, in addition to time for planning and instructional concerns. Administrators should look for ways to decrease the number of co-teaching pairs within a daily schedule. Also, when administrators see a successful co-teaching partnership, efforts should be made to keep them together. Scheduling concerns are addressed in the discussion of leadership in Chapter 4.

Previous chapters have already addressed the importance of communication in the co-taught classroom. Communication, both verbal and nonverbal, is one of the factors required to make collaboration in the classroom effective (Barger-Anderson et al., 2010; Friend, 2011; Gately & Gately, 2001). Communication skills include a person's ability to convey thoughts and meaning through body language as well as spoken words (DeVito, 2009). Understanding your educational partner's personality may help to improve communication skills (Rohm, 2004; 2008).

It is vital for teachers to convey concerns, via effective communication techniques, to co-teaching partners as they arise, rather than waiting to see if it "works out" or thinking, "Well, I'll let it go this time." It is amazing how small issues and disagreements snowball into bigger issues and discord. If the conflicts and feelings

Table 11.1. Tools in the co-teaching repair kit

Tools for co-teachers
Understanding personality traits of self and others
Administration consideration of personality traits before creation of the master schedule
Intervention via problem-solving models to improve communication
Recognition of individual strengths and contributions by the co-teachers
Termination of unsuccessful pairings

of resentment grow to an extent that is beyond reconciliation, it is recommended that intervention be sought via an administrator or consultant (Barger-Anderson et al., 2010).

The administrator or consultant may share a problem-solving model with these individuals (Friend, 2011). These problem-solving models often offer ways to improve upon existing skills. Friend (2011) names four skills that are important to effective communication. These skills are often included in the models shared for problem solving. The four skills are 1) listening skills (Johnson, 2009), 2) nonverbal signs that one wants the conversation to continue (Egan, 2001; Johnson, 2009), 3) trying to phrase concerns in a light that is nonjudgmental, and 4) questioning techniques that promote the conversation to continue. Understanding personalities and temperaments will increase the likelihood of effective communication with all personality types (Rohm, 2008).

Kloo and Zigmond (2008) state that collaborative partners must recognize the individual strengths of each professional in order to be successful when sharing classroom responsibilities. The special education teacher may feel a loss of "turf" when required to push into the general education rooms, especially if resource rooms are lost. The general education teacher may feel the presence of the special education teacher as an intrusion. This may also cause a feeling of a loss of territory. Through effective and positive communication to acknowledge a partner's worth in a collaborative classroom, a sense of ownership and sharing of responsibilities may be achieved more rapidly.

There will occasionally be times when counseling or the use of a problem-solving model to improve communications is futile; in such cases it is in everyone's best interest—recalling the comparison of collaborative relationships to marriage—to call for a "divorce." Saying that it is necessary to terminate the relationship does not mean the two teachers are ineffective at their trade. It simply means that they are best suited to *not* share a classroom. As always, teachers and administrators must make decisions based on the best interests of the students.

CONCLUSION

According to the DISC Model of personalities, each of us has some features of each of the four types of personalities. A teacher who is aware of his or her dominant personality traits is better able to understand a collaborative partner and work with that partner as a team. Administrators can help set the stage for successful co-teaching by taking personality traits into consideration when assigning and scheduling pairs. When difficulties arise, intervention and training in communication skills may help, but in some cases the best solution may be to end the assignment and look for a better pairing.

A collaborative relationship between co-teachers will benefit students' academic achievement and increase positive behaviors in the shared classroom. In many cases, however, teachers and administrators do not have the luxury of selecting co-teacher partners. Many times, the schedule and minimum complement of faculty members dictate who is paired with whom. Regardless of whether they have had a choice in the pairing, co-teachers must collaborate to provide the best learning environment possible for our students. Understanding personality types is a means of helping that collaboration develop and function more smoothly.

REFERENCES

Barger-Anderson, R., Isherwood, R., & Merhaut, J. (2010, February). *The Co-Design Model: A collaborative approach to inclusive education.* Paper presented at the 47th Annual International Conference of the Learning Disabilities Association of America, Baltimore, MD.

Cook, L., & Friend, M. (1996). Co-teaching: Guidelines for creating effective practices. *Focus on Exceptional Children, 28,* 1–16.

DeVito, J.A. (2009). *The interpersonal communication book* (12th ed.). Boston, MA: Allyn & Bacon.

Egan, G. (2001). *The skilled helper: A problem management and opportunity-development approach to helping* (7th ed.). Belmont, CA: Wadsworth.

Friend, M. (2007). *Co-teaching defined.* Retrieved from http://www.marilynfriend.com/basics.htm

Friend, M. (2011). *Special education: Contemporary perspectives for school professionals* (3rd ed.). Boston, MA: Pearson.

Gately, S.E., & Gately, F.J. (2001). Understanding co-teaching components. *Teaching Exceptional Children, 33*(4), 40–47.

Johnson, D.W. (2009). *Reaching out: Interpersonal effectiveness and self-actualization* (9th ed.). Boston, MA: Allyn & Bacon.

Kloo, A., & Zigmond, N. (2008). Coteaching revisited: Redrawing the blueprint. *Preventing School Failure, 52,* 12–20.

Marston, W.M. (2011). *Emotions of normal people.* Charleston, SC: Nabu Press. (Original work published 1928).

Rohm, R. (2004). *You've got style: Your personal guide for relating to others.* Marietta, GA: Personality Insights.

Rohm, R. (2008). *Positive personality profiles.* Marietta, GA: Personality Insights.

Villa, R. (2008, February). *Restructuring for caring and effective education.* Paper presented at the Pennsylvania Department of Education Conference, Hershey, PA.

CHAPTER 12

Co-Design Time

I have had the pleasure of acting in the role of both special education teacher and co-teacher for many years at both the elementary and secondary level, working alongside some of the best general education teachers in our schools. I have learned a lot about sharing, compromising, and cooperating, the tools necessary for successful co-teaching experiences. And most important, I have come to believe wholeheartedly in the power of common planning time.

I think co-teaching is a lot like bridge building. If you would, for a moment, imagine a wide river, bordered on both sides by flourishing shores. The land on each side of the river is fertile and prosperous, growing an assortment of all kinds of delights. Then one day two brave people decide to build a bridge, to see what can be discovered, what can be shared, and what can be accomplished by building a bridge. Their independent desire to build a bridge is not enough. It takes at least two to share the vision, draw the blueprint, and share in the tasks of bridge building. After a great deal of planning and working, they meet in the middle and celebrate their success.

The art of co-teaching is like bridge building: You have to take that first step off your own turf, off that safe ground of individuality, and begin the ascent into togetherness. It takes courage, knowledge, skill, and, most of all, it takes time. Without the shared blueprint, the bridge may wobble, or it may even fall. Never underestimate the power of planning together to build bridges and to teach students.

By Jodi Katsafanas, Ph.D., Assistant Professor
of Special Education at Slippery Rock University

Common time for partners to design lessons is essential (Gately & Gately, 2001; Hawbaker, Balong, Buckwalter, & Runton 2001; Santoli, Sachs, Romey, & McClurg, 2008). This chapter addresses one of the most common complaints about implementing collaborative instruction in the classroom: lack of planning time for collaborative partners. The element of co-design time stresses the importance of common planning time and helps identify ways to "create" common planning time when it is not officially scheduled.

CONCERNS FOR FINDING CO-DESIGN TIME

Administrative procedures consider the amount of contact time between teacher and students for instructional purposes and assessment. However, little concern is directed to contact time between co-teachers for planning purposes (Ashton, 2003). Villa, Thousand, and Nevin (2004) promote open dialogue between the teachers to resolve planning issues that may arise. Open communication between partners is essential, but the question remains as to *when* common time will be allocated for the communication to occur (Barger-Anderson, Isherwood, & Merhaut, 2010). The following two quotes address concerns about lack of common time to design lessons with collaborative partners. One teacher noted,

> I had the experience of having other teachers in my school co-teach with one of the special education teachers. The general education teacher's and the special education teacher's ideas of co-teaching weren't the same. The work wasn't equally divided; the special education teacher served more as a support than a teacher. The planning wasn't divided up equally and the special education teacher pulled students out on a one–one instruction level when she didn't want to be in the room. Unfortunately, this set the precedent with the other general education teachers that this is what would happen if other special education teachers came in and co-taught with them. I signed up to be a part of the co-teaching because I think it would be a great thing if we could plan together. Sometimes the planning is hard in our district because most of the special education teachers' planning times were different than the teachers we would be co-teaching with.
>
> When I worked at Preston Academy [name changed], there were two "teachers" in every class. I put teachers in quotes because there was always a special education teacher but the other person was called a mental health specialist, but those people didn't have to have a degree of any kind and were sometimes just a body. We were supposed to work together to plan out our days of teaching and doing skills streaming activities and improve social skills. Well again, for the four years I was there I saw only two teams that were able to plan together and teach together instead of the special education teacher doing it and the other teacher doing nothing.
>
> I would hope that one day the district I am working for would allow planning time for teachers that are co-teaching so it would be more effective and more teachers would be open to it! (Anonymous teacher, personal communication to Richael Barger-Anderson, July 15, 2010)

The comment that follows echoes similar concerns about the area of common design time for implementing the Co-Design Model or any form of collaborative instruction:

> I am open to the idea of co-teaching, just have yet to experience it. The only thing that actually worries me is how much time it takes to plan. I think that if a school is going to implement co-teaching, it needs to make sure that the teachers are given enough time each week to plan. (C. Downer, personal communication to Richael Barger-Anderson, July 15, 2010)

HOW TO FIND COMMON DESIGN TIME

Finding common design time for lessons that will be implemented within a collaborative classroom is essential (Gately & Gately, 2001; Hawbaker et al., 2001; Santoli et al., 2008). Simmons and Magiera (2007) conclude that although co-teaching is different in each classroom, successful teachers appear to have a strong sense of their roles and responsibilities in each classroom because of careful planning, as well as discussion of feedback after lessons were delivered. Ashton (2003) warns that a common mistake may be to allow for common planning time at the start of the school year but not continue this practice throughout the school year. Common planning time must be ongoing.

Developing a master schedule that allows for common planning time is cited throughout the literature as a critical component of creating a successful co-teaching program (Aguilar, Morocco, Parker, & Zigmond, 2006; Halvorsen & Neary, 2001; Worrell, 2008). Yet, finding this time is a difficult challenge for most teachers engaged in co-teaching (Zigmond & Magiera, 2001). In a study conducted by Isherwood, Barger-Anderson, Merhaut, Badgett, and Katsafanas (2011), focus-group participants continually voiced frustration over the lack of common planning time in their daily schedules. Many suggested that the lessons in the co-taught classroom could be much better if teachers had time to plan. One participant put it in these words: "It's hard to use multiple co-teaching models when you are really planning on the fly. We just sort of pick and choose based on the dynamics of the moment" (Isherwood et al., 2011, p. 117).

Administrators cited that there are not enough teachers on their staff. This lack of personnel in the buildings is a major roadblock in providing common planning time, along with the "trickle-down effect" that results when major changes in the schedule are made in attempting to provide for a common planning time. One administrator described it this way:

> It's like putting a square peg in a round hole! In order for me to provide all of the co-teachers with a common planning time, I would virtually be changing every single teacher's schedule in this building. You see, the special education teachers are co-teaching with more than one general education teacher. I would have to coordinate a schedule that allowed for many of the teachers in various departments to have a common prep time with the special education teacher at the same time. This is just not possible. Who would be teaching? Who would be covering classes? These are things classroom teachers don't understand because they don't see the big picture. I don't have enough personnel to do this. (Isherwood et al., 2011, p. 117)

Almost all of the school administrators familiar with doing a master schedule expressed similar concerns. All recognized the significance of providing common planning time, but none had any substantial solutions. A high school principal provided common planning time by scheduling substitute teachers in the building once a month to provide a half day of coverage for the teachers to plan together. An elementary principal removed morning duties from the co-teachers to plan together prior to student homeroom. These two examples were practical ways administrators attempted to remedy a problem that seems to be structural in nature (Isherwood et al., 2011).

Another possible approach to the schedule dilemma that administrators face is to turn to a teaming approach by either grade level or content. One teacher is quoted as saying,

> I have found that a school with teaming helps co-teaching. In teaming each team (a teacher for each core subject and a special educator) have a 'team plan' period either daily or every few days. I have seen where part of this time can be used for co-teaching planning. The special education teacher takes time in the team meeting to discuss lesson plans with each person that they co-teach with. (M. Lewis, personal communication to Richael Barger-Anderson, July 16, 2010)

Table 12.1 lists several ways administrators can provide common design time.

However, even if administrative solutions aren't possible, co-teachers still need to work together to identify possible niches in their regular schedules. Figure 12.1 shows how a calendar can be used for this purpose. (A reproducible copy of this form is provided in the appendix.) Even if this does not work, common planning time is still needed. Teachers in this quandary have to be resourceful. One possible solution draws on technology, which may allow teachers to share planning ideas on a timeline that is convenient, without having to actually meet in person (see Table 12.1).

Table 12.1.   Ideas for finding co-design time

Administration-driven ideas
Arrange substitute coverage once or twice a month to allow for an hour or two of co-planning time with each set of co-teaching partners.
Ask co-teaching partners to keep a log of the time they have co-planned in addition to the regular school day and 1) provide compensation for their time or 2) excuse them early from a professional development day according to the number of hours logged.
Set aside professional development days for co-teaching partners to co-design.
Use a teaming approach with the master schedule to allow for common planning times by either grade level or content area.

Teacher-driven ideas
E-mail the co-taught lesson plan form back and forth for planning purposes.
Use Skype as a way to collaborate without being in the same physical location.

From Barger-Anderson, R., Isherwood, R., & Merhaut, J. (2010, February). *The Co-Design Model: A collaborative approach to inclusive education.* Paper presented at the 47th Annual International Conference of the Learning Disabilities Association of America, Baltimore, MD; adapted by permission.

Friend (2011) cautions that sometimes neither partner is committed to finding success. Such pairs may use lack of common planning time as a convenient excuse for failure. Barger-Anderson et al. (2010) agree with this observation. Uncommitted partners may use this excuse to avoid moving toward a more collaborative relationship in the inclusive classroom. The first remedy in this situation is to make sure the teachers do have co-design time on a dependable basis. If co-design time is provided

Co-Design Time Planning Calendar

Month: October

		1	2	3	4 meet in library at 8 am	5	6
	7	8	9	10	11	12	13
	14	15	16 meet in 116 at 2:45 pm	17	18	19	20
	21	22	23	24	25	26	27
	28	29	30	31 meet in conference room at 12:20 pm			

Figure 12.1.   Example of completed Co-Design Time Planning Calendar. (Copyright © 2013 by Keystone Educational Consulting Group. http://www.keystone-educational.com. Reprinted by permission.)

and the co-teaching partners are still not successful, more training in the Co-Design Model may be needed. Administrative support may also be needed. Chapter 17 discusses options for training and professional development.

CONCLUSION

Time is among the greatest concerns teachers have about implementing an inclusion program. In particular, teachers are concerned about having a suitable amount of time with other professionals to collaborate (Santoli et al., 2008). Bryant, Smith, and Bryant (2008) state that collaboration among professional partners supports inclusive educational practices. Ashton (2003) reports that adequate planning time is one of two major concerns identified by teachers for implementing successful collaborative teaching practices. Ashton also reports that teachers' fears about lack of common planning time can result in negative behavior between the teachers. The result is lack of trust and respect for each other.

Administrative support is important for the success of inclusive programming (Shade & Stewart, 2001; Villa et al., 2004), because teachers often find it difficult to arrange for common planning time on their own (Zigmond & Magiera, 2001). In particular, it is important for co-design time to be consistently available throughout the school year.

This chapter concludes the discussion of the nine elements of the Co-Design Model. The following four chapters address pathways that are promoted as means to achieve desired outcomes. These pathways include strategies and recommended practices that have been shown through research to promote a successful inclusive and collaborative environment.

REFERENCES

Aguilar, C.M., Morocco, C.C., Parker, C.E., & Zigmond, N. (2006). Middletown high school: Equal opportunity for academic achievement. *Learning Disabilities Research and Practice, 21*(3), 159–171.

Ashton, T.M. (2003). What are teachers' greatest co-teaching concerns? *Academic Exchange Quarterly, 7*(3), 100–104.

Barger-Anderson, R., Isherwood, R., & Merhaut, J. (2010, February). *The Co-Design Model: A collaborative approach to inclusive education.* Paper presented at the 47th Annual International Conference of the Learning Disabilities Association of America, Baltimore, MD.

Bryant, D.P., Smith, D.D., & Bryant, B.R. (2008). *Teaching students with special needs in inclusive classrooms.* Boston, MA: Allyn & Bacon.

Friend, M. (2011). *Special education: Contemporary perspectives for school professionals* (3rd ed.). Boston, MA: Pearson.

Gately, S.E., & Gately, F.J. (2001). Understanding co-teaching components. *Teaching Exceptional Children, 33,* 40–47.

Halvorsen, A., & Neary, T. (2001). *Building inclusive schools: Tools and strategies for success.* Needham Heights, MA: Allyn & Bacon.

Hawbaker, B.W., Balong, M., Buckwalter, S., & Runyon, S. (2001). Building a strong base of support for all students through coplanning. *Teaching Exceptional Children, 33*(4), 24–30.

Isherwood, R., Barger-Anderson, R., Merhaut, J., Badgett, R., & Katsafanas, J. (2011). First year co-teaching: Disclosed through focus group and individual interviews. *Learning Disabilities: A Multidisciplinary Journal, 17*(3), 113–122.

Santoli, S.P., Sachs, J., Romey, E.A., & McClurg, S. (2008). A successful formula for middle school inclusion: Collaboration, time, and administrative support. *Research in Middle Level Education Online, 32*(2). Retrieved from http://www.amle.org/Publications/RMLEOnline/Articles/Vol32No2/tabid/1780/Default.aspx

Shade, R.A., & Stewart, R. (2001). General education and special education preservice teachers' attitudes toward inclusion. *Preventing School Failure, 46*(1), 37–41.

Simmons, R.J., & Magiera, K. (2007). Evaluation of co-teaching in three high schools in one school district: How do you know when you are truly co-teaching? *Teaching Exceptional Children Plus, 3*(3), 1–12.

Villa, R.A., Thousand, J.S., & Nevin, A.I. (2004). *A guide to co-teaching: Practical tips for facilitating student learning.* Thousand Oaks, CA: Sage Publications.

Worrell, J.L. (2008). How secondary schools can avoid the seven deadly "sins" of inclusion. *American Secondary Education, 36*(2), 43–56.

Zigmond, N., & Magiera, K. (2001). A focus on co-teaching (use caution). *Current Practice Alerts from the Division for Learning Disabilities and Division for Research of the Council for Exceptional Children, 6,* 1–4. Retrieved from the "Use Caution" section of http://www.dldcec.org/alerts/

CHAPTER **13**

Co-Teaching

Four years of attending classes and field experiences of working with students with varying abilities and teaching various subjects and grade levels...now I could finally see the light at the end of the tunnel. Student teaching! The first day of student teaching finally arrived as my body was overwhelmed with a variety of emotions. I was utterly excited to be teaching fourth-graders, nervous to enter an unfamiliar school in Las Vegas, Nevada, yet anxious to meet my host teacher and students. Monday morning, I ventured down to Room 19 to meet an upbeat, welcoming lady by the name of Mrs. Paxman. Not only does she teach more than 30 fourth-graders of varying abilities, but she also co-teaches with Mrs. Galvin, a special educator, for math and reading. I was extremely excited to have the opportunity to co-teach, because this practice has become an area of focus in the field of education. However, many questions filled my mind. "Will our personalities or teaching styles clash?" "Will I become comfortable in learning and teaching an unfamiliar curriculum?"

I finally met Mrs. Galvin, my co-teaching partner. We spent a great amount of time getting to know each other and discussing our teaching styles. Mrs. Galvin provided helpful insight about our roles, instructional strategies, and responsibilities in co-teaching. After a few days of observing Mrs. Paxman and Mrs. Galvin co-teaching, it was my turn to implement co-teaching. Although I felt nervous about co-teaching, I also felt at ease because I had two experienced teachers to provide guidance and support. As time went by, Mrs. Galvin and I become more solid and integrated as a team. As we all know, students do not learn the same way. Co-teaching allowed for skills to be presented and modeled in a variety of ways. Students had a choice of a variety of strategies that facilitated the understanding and application of specific skills. Co-teaching allowed Mrs. Galvin and me to share the responsibility of managing student behaviors, planning, providing enrichment and remediation, and facilitating small-group instruction.

Throughout the short 3-month student-teaching experience, I learned a tremendous amount about co-teaching and its effectiveness. I became a believer in the power of co-teaching in that it extends out to more students to ensure they are grasping the content or able to demonstrate the skills being taught. Personally, co-teaching has taught me the importance of collaboration and made it clear that two heads are better than one. I realize that one teacher does not always connect with every student and now appreciate that all teachers have different fortes and challenges.

By Kaleigh Hoover, Slippery Rock University alumna
and behavior and learning support teacher in the Baltimore County Public Schools system

Because of legislation and litigation, schools across the United States are mandated to include children of all abilities together, thereby forcing a surge in collaboration among professionals in the classroom (Friend, 2011). The 2004 reauthorization of the Individuals with Disabilities Education Act, the No Child Left Behind Act of 2001, and other special education laws and decisions specific to individual states and certain circuits are moving school districts toward a more inclusive environment for the education of all students (Werts, Culatta, & Tompkins, 2007). Because of increased inclusive practices and the evolving composition of classrooms, teachers must collaborate to address the diverse needs of students. In this chapter, models of co-teaching are described as one pathway to support this collaboration within the Co-Design Model.

In the older model, general and special education services were provided in separate rooms. In the contemporary movement, education is provided to all students within the general education classroom, when the IEP team members determine that the general classroom is the LRE. Even though this movement is not a change with LRE and the law, it does mark a change in the way many schools have conducted placement decisions to determine the LRE. When inclusive practices are used, instruction may be provided via collaboration between two or more professionals within the general education classroom (Friend, 2011; Werts et al., 2007). Collaboration involves respecting each professional's talents and skills. Collaboration also means sharing in "designing, implementing, and monitoring" for all students, both those with and without disabilities (Friend, 2011, p. 102). Co-teaching by a general education and a special education teacher is a model for delivering instruction in the inclusive classroom (Friend, 2011; Villa, Thousand, & Nevin, 2004).

MODELS OF CO-TEACHING

Several definitions for co-teaching exist. However, for implementation of the Co-Design Model, the authors have chosen the definition provided by Marilyn Friend (2007). Co-teaching is a way for two professionals to provide specially designed instruction to students with disabilities. It affords access to the general education curriculum in the LRE with appropriate supplemental aids and services. Both professionals share the physical space of the classroom, take ownership of sharing all students, and are respectful of each other's skill sets and training (Cook & Friend, 1996; Friend, 2011).

Professionals who may be assigned to co-teaching include general education teachers; special education teachers; special teachers such as librarians; physical education, computer, art, and music teachers; reading specialists; literacy and math coaches; and therapists (e.g., speech-language, physical, and occupational therapists). Note that paraprofessionals are not in this list. Although the role of the paraprofessional is quite important in today's classroom, the affiliation between the paraprofessional and the teacher is not one of co-teaching. The role of the paraeducator is addressed later in this chapter.

We define the practice of co-teaching as shared collaborative educational practices between two or more professionals (Barger-Anderson, Isherwood, & Merhaut, 2010). For this pathway to be used successfully, teachers and paraprofessionals must receive training about co-teaching models and about the district's expectations. It is also important for partners in the collaborative environment to realize that co-teaching will be supported through resources other than a "one-shot" training experience. Chapter 17 discusses training and professional development more thoroughly.

Marilyn Friend recognizes six models in her research. In the Co-Design Model the authors advocate the use of five of these models (Friend, 2007):

1. One teach/one assist

2. Stations

3. Parallel

4. Alternative

5. Team

Table 13.1 is an overview and visual depiction of the five models of co-teaching promoted in the Co-Design Model. (Friend's sixth model is one teach/one observe.)

A CLOSER LOOK AT THE FIVE MODELS

The five models of co-teaching offered by Friend (2005, 2007) provide teachers with a systematic approach for implementing shared instructional practices. To assist with the implementation of successful co-teaching, Keystone Educational Consulting

Table 13.1. Overview of co-teaching models

Model	Definition	Visual depiction
One teach/ one assist	One professional serves as the main facilitator/provider of knowledge, while the other professional serves as the assistant. The assistant may help promote on-task behavior, answer individual questions posed by students, assist with housekeeping duties, implement behavior plans, and so forth. There are a variety of ways to use the professional serving as the assistant in a meaningful manner.	X O O O O O O O O O O O O O O O O X
Stations	The classroom is divided into student groups of three or more. Each professional is responsible for the learning that occurs at one of the stations, while one or more of the stations are devised to run independently of a teacher. A paraprofessional may assist with a station as long as no direct instruction is being provided. The students may rotate through the stations within the class period.	O O O X O O O O O O O O O O X O O
Parallel	The class is divided into two equal parts. Once the class has been divided, each professional is responsible for instruction for one group. Each teacher is providing the same content to each group of students. The benefit of this model is the decrease in student–teacher ratio.	X O O O O O O O O X O O O O O O O O
Alternative	Professionals are encouraged to "think outside the box" for this model. The alternative model promotes large-group instruction for the majority of the class, while a small group of students receives instruction in an alternative location (either within the classroom or outside the classroom). Teachers are encouraged to trade responsibility for teaching the large group and to keep the composition of the small group flexible.	X O O O O O O O O O O O O X O O O O
Team	In team teaching, both teachers share the stage. Team teaching is a collaborative effort between two professionals to provide or facilitate instruction to a whole group of students. Given time, this model may be very rewarding. Trust must be established between the two teachers before the team model yields the greatest benefits.	X X O O O O O O O O O O O O O O O O

Sources: Friend (2005, 2007).

Key: X, teacher; O, student.

Group has created a Co-Teach Lesson Plan form. (A reproducible version of the form is provided in the appendix.) This lesson plan form allows teachers to designate which model of co-teaching will be implemented and helps them assign roles to promote active participation of both teachers. The remainder of this section describes the five models and provides a sample lesson plan for each.

1. In the one teach/one assist model, one professional serves as the main facilitator or provider of knowledge; the other professional serves as the assistant (Figure 13.1). The assistant may help promote on-task behavior, answer individual questions posed by students, assist with housekeeping duties, implement behavior plans, and prompt and cue as necessary. There are a variety of ways to use the professional serving as the assistant in a meaningful manner. However, repeated use of this model of co-teaching rarely results in productive use of the other professional. Many times, overimplementation of this model results directly in the deprofessionalization of the other teacher.

2. In the stations model, the classroom is divided into groups of three or more students. Each professional is responsible for the planning, implementation, and assessment of learning that occurs at one of the stations, while one or more of the stations are devised by the co-teachers to run independently of a facilitator (Figure 13.2). A paraprofessional may assist with a station as long as no direct instruction of new content is being provided. (Again, the role of paraprofessionals in relation to co-teaching is addressed later in this chapter.) The students rotate from station to station throughout the class period. If behavior or concerns with student transitions from station to station cause trepidation, the teachers may move while the students remain in place. A benefit of this model is a lower student–teacher ratio. Also, different learning modalities may be addressed at each of the stations. Use of this model increases engagement time of students within each station.

3. In the parallel model, the class is divided into two equal parts. Once the class has been divided, each professional is responsible for instruction of one group (Figure 13.3). A paraprofessional may be responsible for a group if new content is not being presented and the teacher has made the decisions for the content of the lesson. Each teacher is providing the same or similar content to each group of students. As in the stations model, one of the benefits of this model is the decrease in student–teacher ratio. A common complaint about this model is the increase in noise from two teachers speaking at the same time in one classroom. It is common for co-teachers to *not* succeed during the first trial of parallel co-teaching. Barger-Anderson, Isherwood, and Merhaut (2010) recommend trying this model at least two times before abandoning it. Other benefits from the use of this model include increased engaged time of students, the option to address various learning styles, and flexibility in grouping students.

4. In the alternative model, professionals are encouraged to "think outside the box." The alternative model promotes large-group instruction for the majority of the class, while a small group of students receives instruction in an alternative location (either within or outside the classroom). Teachers are encouraged to switch roles, trading responsibility for teaching the large group (Figure 13.4). The composition of the small group should remain flexible. Some days the small group may comprise students needing enrichment and another day those needing remediation. It may even comprise the students who were absent the day before. It is important to keep an open mind for this model and be creative with the use

Co-Teach Lesson Plan

Co-teachers: Ms. Lime and Ms. Barbosa	Date: Jan. 11	Room: 204	Day: Tuesday	Grade: 5	Time/period: 3rd period	Subject: Language Arts

Co-teaching model: _X_ One teach/one assist __Parallel __ Stations __ Alternative __ Team __ Other	Co-plan time: 1/6 10:15–11:15 a.m.

State standard	Short-term objectives	Evaluation
1.2.5 D	**1.** Using a Know-want-learn (KWL) chart, the students will identify what they already Know, what they want to Know, and what they have learned about the Chinese zodiac during this lesson. Each column will have a minimum of three entries. **Modifications:**	Completed KWL chart
1.6.5 D	**2.** While being read a story aloud, students will participate in oral questioning while listening to the story. Each student must answer at least one time when called upon. **Modifications:** Students may ask a peer for assistance when answering the questions.	Observation and checklist
1.6.5 C	**3.** Using the packet of materials provided, the students will orally identify their zodiac sign and complete an animal outline with at least three accurate facts. **Modifications:**	Observation and completed animal outline
	4. Given time in class, students must orally present their animal to the class and share at least two reasons why or why not the animal is a good descriptor of them. **Modifications:** Students may practice what they are going to share with the class with a teacher before presenting to the class.	Observation and checklist
Materials: The Animals of the Chinese Zodiac, KWL chart, Chinese zodiac packets, markers, book, pencils		Other:
Introduction: *Teacher responsible:* Ms. Lime	Teacher will introduce a KWL chart. Together teacher and students will complete the K (Know) section of the chart with prior Knowledge about the Chinese zodiac and the W (what they Want to learn) section of the chart with what they would like to Know about the Chinese zodiac.	
Lesson sequence: *Teacher responsible:* Ms. Barbosa	Read the book The Animals of the Chinese Zodiac by Susan Whitfield to the class. Teacher will provide packets to the students with information on the zodiac and explain how to identify the animal that matches their date and year of birth. Students will work in pairs to locate the animal that matches their birth date and year. They will be given an outline of their animal and write at least three descriptors of the animal inside the outline.	
Closing: *Teacher responsible:* Ms. Lime	Students will each share their Chinese zodiac animal with the class. They will share whether they think the animal's description is a good description of themselves. The students must share why or why not. Students will complete the L (what they Learned) section of the KWL chart.	
Homework: *Teacher responsible to assign:* Ms. Lime *Teacher responsible to correct:* Ms. Lime	The students will find the Chinese zodiac sign of at least three family members or friends.	
Reflections:		

Co-Teach Lesson Plan

Co-teachers: Mr. Sparrow Ms. Bea	Date: Feb. 5	Room: 13	Day: Tuesday	Grade: 5	Time/period: 2nd period	Subject: Social Studies & Reading

Co-teaching model: __ One teach/one assist __ Parallel X Stations __ Team __ Alternative __ Other	Co-plan time: 1/29 1:45–2:45 p.m.

State standard	Short-term objectives	Evaluation
1.3.5. Standard A	**1.** Using the packet of materials provided, students will guess and identify their animal in the Chinese zodiac. **Modifications:** Read material to students. Display a few characteristics of each animal on a PowerPoint slide show, to limit the amount of material the student needs to read. Teacher assistance to ensure accuracy.	Checklist
1.4.5 Standard D	**2.** Individually, the students will complete a graphic organizer that compares/contrasts at least two zodiac animals. **Modifications:** Students may complete the graphic organizer in pairs.	Completed graphic organizer
1.6.5 Standard D	**3.** While being read a story aloud, students will participate in oral questioning while listening to the story. Each student must answer at least one time when called upon. **Modifications:** Students may ask a peer for assistance.	Observation and checklist
	4. **Modifications:**	

Materials: The Animals of the Chinese Zodiac, Chinese zodiac packets, story, graphic organizers, PowerPoint slide show, timer, pencils	Other:

Introduction: *Teacher responsible:* Ms. Bea	The students are asked to think about what animals they like best. The Chinese zodiac will be introduced. The students will guess which animal they think they are. The students will be divided into three groups and given directions and transition information for the station activities. When they hear the timer ring, it is time to switch stations.
Lesson sequence: *Teacher responsible:* Ms. Bea Mr. Sparrow will facilitate both stations 2 and 3.	Station 1: Read the book The Animals of the Chinese Zodiac by Susan Whitfield and orally discuss the contents throughout the reading and at conclusion. Bea will either read the book aloud or select a student(s) to read aloud. Station 2: Students will be provided with Chinese zodiac animal descriptions and select the animal that fits them the most characteristically. Once students have selected the animal, they must check their birth year and date with the Chinese zodiac to see if their prediction aligned with the correct animal. The teacher will show a PowerPoint slide show to help present the information if needed. Station 3: Students will be given a graphic organizer to complete. The students must select at least two animals to compare/contrast using the graphic organizer. The students may work individually at the station or in pairs.
Closing: *Teacher responsible:* Mr. Sparrow	The students will come together as a whole class for the closing. The teacher will ask the entire class a few questions about the activities from the stations: Recall questions about the book in station 1. How did you react when you found the actual animal that matched your date and year of birth? Did you guess correctly? What are your thoughts about the Chinese zodiac?
Homework: *Teacher responsible to assign:* Ms. Bea *Teacher responsible to correct:* Mr. Sparrow	Students will find the Chinese zodiac sign of at least three family members or friends.
Reflections:	

Figure 13.2. Co-teaching example: stations model. (Copyright © 2013 by Keystone Educational Consulting Group. http://www.keystone-educational.com. Reprinted by permission.)

Co-Teach Lesson Plan

Co-teachers: Mrs. Fletcher and Mr. Perry	Date: Jan. 25	Room: 13	Day: Monday	Grade: 5	Time/period: 12:30–1:30 p.m.	Subject: Social studies, Reading & Language Arts

Co-teaching model: __ One teach/one assist X Parallel __ Stations __ Team __ Alternative __ Other	Co-plan time: 1/11 3:30–4:30 p.m.

State standard	Short-term objectives	Evaluation
World language and culture 2.1	**1.** While being read a story aloud, students will participate in oral questioning while listening to the story. Each student must answer at least one time when called upon. **Modifications:** Students may ask a peer for assistance if needed.	Observation and checklist
Reading, writing, listening, speaking 1.4 Types of writing	**2.** Given Chinese zodiac packets, students will orally identify their Chinese zodiac sign. **Modifications:** Teacher assistance if needed.	Observation
Reading, writing, listening, speaking 1.5 Quality of writing 1.6 Speaking and listening	**3.** Given the Chinese zodiac packets, students will write three complete sentences about their Chinese zodiac sign. **Modifications:** Students will work in groups and will be able to revise their sentences with assistance from the teacher.	Sentences
2.5.5 Standard C	**4.** Given a bar graph and pieces of paper with their name, students will place their name in the correct space on the zodiac bar graph. **Modifications:** Teacher or peer assistance if needed.	Bar graph
Materials: _Celebrating Chinese New Year_ (2 copies), Chinese zodiac packets, papers with names for bar graph, bar graph, paper to write sentences, pencils		Other:
Introduction: *Teacher responsible:* Both teachers	The teacher will divide students into two equal-sized groups based on their ability levels. Each teacher will follow the steps in the Introduction, Lesson Sequence, and Closing with his or her group of students. Teacher will introduce Chinese culture by reading the book _Celebrating Chinese New Year_ by Diane Hoyt-Goldsmith. The teacher will ask questions throughout the story to check for reading comprehension. The teacher will explain to students that they are going to find and learn about their Chinese zodiac sign.	
Lesson sequence: *Teacher responsible:* Both teachers	Each student will review the Chinese zodiac packet to find his or her zodiac sign. Once each child determines his or her sign, the child will write at least three sentences about the characteristics for his or her sign on notebook paper. Students will share their sentences with their peers in their group to make grammatical corrections.	
Closing: *Teacher responsible:* Both teachers	The teacher will tell students that a zodiac sign bar graph for the class has been created in the classroom. Each student will be given a piece of paper with his or her name on it. On their way out of class, they are to place their name in the appropriate zodiac sign category. The class will start the next day by looking at the results of the bar graph.	
Homework: *Teacher responsible to assign:* *Teach responsible to correct:*	There will be no homework assigned for this lesson and activity.	
Reflections:		

Figure 13.3. Co-teaching example: parallel model. (Copyright © 2013 by Keystone Educational Consulting Group. http://www.keystone-educational.com. Reprinted by permission.)

Co-Teach Lesson Plan

Co-teachers: Mr. Findley Ms. Brady	Date: Feb. 17	Room: 205	Day: Monday	Grade: 5	Time/period: 9-10 a.m.	Subject: Language Arts
Co-teaching model: __ One teach/one assist __ Parallel __ Stations __ Team X Alternative __ Other					Co-plan time: 2/8 2:15-3:15 p.m.	

State standard	Short-term objectives	Evaluation
1.2.5	**1.** While being read a story aloud, students will participate in oral questioning while listening to the story. Each student must answer at least one time when called upon. **Modifications:** Students may ask a peer for assistance if needed.	Observation and checklist
1.5.5	**2.** Using the packet of materials provided, students will guess and identify their animal in the Chinese zodiac. **Modifications:** Read material to students. Display a few characteristics of each animal on a PowerPoint slide show, to limit the amount of material the student needs to read. Teacher assistance if needed to ensure accuracy.	Checklist
	3. Individually, the students will complete a graphic organizer that compares/contrasts at least two zodiac animals. **Modifications:** Students may work in pairs.	Graphic organizer
	4. **Modifications:**	

Materials: The Animals of the Chinese Zodiac, Chinese zodiac packets, book (2 copies), graphic organizers, PowerPoint slide show, pencils	Other:

Introduction: *Teacher responsible:* Ms. Brady	Read the book The Animals of the Chinese Zodiac by Susan Whitfield to the class. The students are asked to think about what animals they like best. The students will guess which animal they think they are.
Lesson sequence: *Teacher responsible:* Both teachers	Teachers will divide the students into two groups, one small and one large based on results of previously collected data. Ms. Brady will keep the large group of students, while Mr. Findley takes the small group of students to a work area at the side of the room. Both teachers will follow the steps in the Introduction, Lesson Sequence, and Closing with their group of students. All students will be provided with Chinese zodiac animal descriptions and select the animal that fits them the most characteristically. The teacher will show a PowerPoint slide show to help present the information if needed. Once students have selected their animal, they must check their birth year and date with the Chinese zodiac to see if their prediction aligned with their correct animal. Students will be given a graphic organizer to complete. The students must select at least two animals to compare/contrast using the graphic organizer. The students may work individually or in pairs.
Closing: *Teacher responsible:* Both teachers	The teachers will orally present the class a few questions: Recall questions about the book. How did you react when you found the actual animal that matched your date and year of birth? Did you guess correctly? What are your thoughts about the Chinese zodiac?
Homework: *Teacher responsible to assign:* Both teachers *Teacher responsible to correct:* Both teachers	Students will find the Chinese zodiac signs of at least three family members or friends.
Reflections:	

Figure 13.4. Co-teaching example: alternative model. (Copyright © 2013 by Keystone Educational Consulting Group. http://www.keystone-educational.com. Reprinted by permission.)

of student groupings. This model does not promote pulling the same students or routinely moving the students with an IEP to the back or side of the room to work only with the special education teacher. As in all the models, purposeful and data-driven decisions should determine the composition of the groups and the teacher responsible for the instruction.

5. Team teaching is equal sharing of the stage. Team teaching is a collaborative effort between two or more professionals to provide or facilitate instruction to a whole group of students (Figure 13.5). Given time, this model may be very rewarding. Trust must be established between the two teachers before the model can yields the greatest benefits. At the start, it may even help for the co-teachers to script questions to ask each other in front of the class. The back-and-forth between teachers may be a bit "clunky" at first; taking turns may be almost as formal as passing a baton. Over time, however, the goal is to achieve a seamless transition from teacher to teacher.

APPLICATION TO THE SHARED CLASSROOM

When considering co-teaching models, the collaborative partners need to first select which model to implement for which lesson and then, when necessary, decide how to group the students.

It is important for pairs to avoid overuse of the one teach/one assist model. Too often, this model is viewed as the "default" model. True, it is easy to implement and requires little planning time. Also, for the teacher playing the role of assistant, little curriculum knowledge is necessary. As stressed throughout this book, though, both teachers must be viewed by each other and by the students as equal contributors in the classroom. They must be seen as equal in behavior management, instruction, clerical duties, and more. If a co-teaching pair routinely implements one teach/one assist with the general education teacher acting as the lead, equality between the teachers will not be realized.

Co-teaching partners should use their common planning time to identify which of the five co-teaching models will be best suited for which lessons. It is recommended in the Co-Design Model to include a healthy diet of all five models. The particular model implemented should be determined according to student needs, curriculum knowledge of teachers, and if necessary, grouping decisions.

Students are placed in groups in the parallel, stations, and alternative models. Grouping decisions should be the responsibility of both teachers. Groups should be flexible and determined according to needs and abilities of students. Types of grouping include purposeful grouping and random grouping. Purposeful grouping simply means grouping students according to data and teacher input. This may include heterogeneous or homogeneous ability groupings, behavior groupings, or some combination of both.

THE ROLE OF THE PARAPROFESSIONAL
IN A COLLABORATIVE ENVIRONMENT

Friend (2005) states that co-teaching does not include the collaboration between a paraeducator and a professional. This is not to say that the role of the paraprofessional is insignificant. Quite the contrary. Paraprofessionals are integral to efforts to support and promote the education of all students. However, we caution educators to consider

Co-Teach Lesson Plan

Co-teachers: Mr. Titan Mr. Gibbs	Date: Feb. 13	Room: 107	Day: Friday	Grade: 5	Time/period: 40 minutes	Subject: English & Social Studies

Co-teaching model: __ One teach/one assist __Parallel __ Stations X Team __ Alternative __ Other	Co-plan time: 2/7 8:15–9:30 a.m.

State standard	Short-term objectives	Evaluation
	1. While being read a story aloud, students will participate in oral questioning while listening to the story. Each student must answer at least one time when called upon. **Modifications:** Students may ask a peer for assistance when answering the questions.	Observation and checklist
1.4.3	**2.** Given packets on the zodiac signs, students will orally identify their Chinese zodiac sign. **Modifications:** Teacher assistance if necessary to ensure accuracy.	Observation
1.5.3	**3.** After identification of their sign, students will write three complete sentences about their Chinese zodiac sign. **Modifications:** Students may work in groups and will be able to revise their sentences with assistance from the teacher.	Sentences
2.5.5. Standard C	**4.** Given a bar graph and pieces of paper with their name, students will place their name in the correct space on the zodiac bar graph. **Modifications:**	Bar graph
Materials: Book: Celebrating Chinese New Year, Chinese zodiac packets, paper with names for bar graph, bar graph, paper to write sentences, pencils		Other:

Introduction: *Teacher responsible:* Both teachers	Teachers will introduce Chinese culture by reading the children's book Celebrating Chinese New Year by Diane Hoyt-Goldsmith. The teachers will ask questions throughout the story to check for reading comprehension. The teachers will explain to students that they are going to find and learn about their Chinese zodiac sign.
Lesson sequence: *Teacher responsible:* Both teachers	Teachers review the Chinese zodiac packet to find the student zodiac signs. Once each child determines his or her sign, the child will write at least three sentences about the characteristics for his or her sign on lined paper. Students will share their sentences with their peers in their group to make grammatical corrections before submitting the sentences to the teacher.
Closing: *Teacher responsible:* Both teachers	Teachers will tell students that a zodiac sign bar graph for the class has been created in the classroom. Each student will be given a piece of paper with his or her name on it. On their way out of class, they are to place their name in the appropriate zodiac sign category. The class will start the next day by looking at the results of the bar graph.
Homework: *Teacher responsible to assign:* Both teachers *Teacher responsible to correct:* Both teachers	Students will find the Chinese zodiac sign of at least three family members or friends.
Reflections:	

the proper use of the paraprofessional in the inclusive classroom. Bryant, Smith, and Bryant (2008) strongly recommend that teachers and paraeducators make clear the roles and responsibilities of each participant. This step ensures clarity of expectations for both the teacher and the paraprofessional.

Teachers are responsible for the actions of paraeducators who are under their supervision. Duties of the paraprofessional may include

- Proctoring and grading exams

- Progress monitoring for behavior and academic success

- Reteaching or remediation of a topic

- Clerical duties

- Attendance at necessary meetings

- Attending to individual student needs (Bryant, Smith, & Bryant, 2008)

Barger-Anderson and et al. (2010) promote use of the paraeducator with teacher-planned activities for preteaching and for enrichment as well. Riggs (2005) cautions new teachers to be informed about the paraprofessional's background and experience but stresses the importance of recognizing the paraeducator as a worthy associate.

Blalock (1991) stresses the importance of proper training for paraprofessionals. We often provide for paraprofessional training within school districts. Training achieves the best results when conducted over several training sessions with topics generated by the school district. The Co-Design Model promotes paraprofessional training on topics such as collaboration, behavior management, and crisis prevention programs; their role and expectations in a collaborative classroom; and strategies and tactics to assist with remediation and practice of academic objectives.

CONCLUSION

It is important to note that successful co-teaching typically does not occur after a "one-shot" training session. Co-teaching tactics take time to develop via successful collaborative teacher interactions, training, and support. Collaborative co-teaching relationships should promote sharing of classroom duties. These aspects include establishing a common belief system for classroom management, common planning, accommodations and modifications for students with instruction, physical organization of the classroom, and accordance for assessments (Barger-Anderson et al., 2010; Gately & Gately, 2001; Isherwood & Barger-Anderson, 2007). Zigmond and Magiera (2001) conclude that successful co-teaching results from careful planning, ongoing co-planning, enthusiastic pairs of teachers compatible in philosophy (as well as temperament and personality), and strong administrative support. Paraprofessionals can also be important partners in co-teaching approaches, if care is taken to delineate roles and provide appropriate training.

Murawski and Dieker (2004) imply that the method of co-teaching for collaborative instruction may increase learning outcomes for all students in the general education setting, while ensuring that students with disabilities receive necessary modifications and instruction by a content expert. Rice and Zigmond (2000) also conclude that well-implemented co-teaching could be beneficial for all students, both with and without disabilities.

REFERENCES

Barger-Anderson, R., Isherwood, R., & Merhaut, J. (2010, February). *The Co-Design Model: A collaborative approach to inclusive education.* Paper presented at the 47th Annual International Conference of the Learning Disabilities Association of America, Baltimore, MD.

Blalock, G. (1991). Paraprofessionals: Critical team members in our special education programs. *Intervention in School and Clinic, 26*(4), 200–214.

Bryant, D.P., Smith, D.D., & Bryant, B.R. (2008). *Teaching students with special needs in inclusive classrooms.* Boston, MA: Allyn & Bacon.

Cook, L., & Friend, M. (1996). Co-teaching: Guidelines for creating effective practices. *Focus on Exceptional Children, 28,* 1–16.

Friend, M. (2005). *The power of 2* (2nd ed.). Port Chester, NY: National Professional Resources.

Friend, M. (2007). *Co-teaching defined.* Retrieved from http://www.marilynfriend.com/basics.htm

Friend, M. (2011). *Special education: Contemporary perspectives for school professionals* (3rd ed.). Boston, MA: Pearson.

Gately, S.E., & Gately, F.J. (2001). Understanding co-teaching components. *Teaching Exceptional Children, 33,* 40–47.

Hoyt-Goldsmith, D. (1998). *Celebrating Chinese new year.* New York, NY: Holiday House. Individuals with Disabilities Education Improvement Act (IDEA) of 2004, PL 108-146, 20 U.S.C. §§ 1400 *et seq.*

Isherwood, R.S., & Barger-Anderson, R. (2007). Factors affecting the adoption of co-teaching models in inclusive classrooms: One school's journey from mainstreaming to inclusion. *Journal of Ethnographic and Qualitative Research, 2,* 121–128.

Murawski, W.W., & Dieker, L.A. (2004). Tips and strategies for co-teaching at the secondary level. *Teaching Exceptional Children, 36,* 52–58.

No Child Left Behind Act of 2001, PL 107-110, 115 Stat. 1425, 20 U.S.C. §§ 6301 *et seq.*

Rice, D., & Zigmond, N. (2000). Co-teaching in secondary schools: Teacher reports of developments in Australian and American classrooms. *Learning Disabilities Research and Practice, 15*(4), 190–197.

Riggs, C.G. (2005). To teachers: What paraeducators want you to know. *Teaching Exceptional Children, 36*(5), 8–12.

Villa, R.A., Thousand, J.S., & Nevin, A.I. (2004). *A guide to co-teaching: Practical tips for facilitating student learning.* Thousand Oaks, CA: Sage Publications.

Werts, M.G., Culatta, R.A., & Tompkins, J.R. (2007). *Fundamentals of special education: What every teacher needs to know* (3rd ed.). Upper Saddle River, NJ: Pearson.

Whitfield, S. (1998). *Animals of the Chinese zodiac.* Northampton, MA: Interlink.

Zigmond, N., & Magiera, K. (2001). A focus on co-teaching (use caution). *Current Practice Alerts from the Division for Learning Disabilities and Division for Research of the Council for Exceptional Children, 6,* 1–4. Retrieved from the "Use Caution" section of http://www.dldcec.org/alerts/

CHAPTER 14

Differentiated Instruction

Robert C. Snyder

Imagine sitting in a traditional fifth-grade classroom. It is time for a social studies lesson on Colonial America and the teacher has each of the students reading one paragraph out loud to the class as each turn passes to the next student in the row. You see several students not paying attention. One student is tapping a beat lightly on his desk; another is watching the lawn mower cutting away outside the window. A third student is disassembling a mechanical pencil inside her desk. Still another is secretly writing a note to a friend. Several others are counting ahead to find and practice their assigned paragraph to avoid embarrassment should they stumble while reading aloud. And we wonder why our students fall behind students in other countries when they are compared on international tests.

Now imagine a second fifth-grade classroom. It is also time for social studies, but this time, students are arranged in desk clusters of four students. Colonial-era music is softly playing in the background while the teacher walks from group to group, facilitating activities and interacting with each of the students. One group is using the textbook information to collaboratively write a song with lyrics pertaining to the lesson topic. Another group is using four laptop computers to explore a teacher-designed WebQuest on the topic. Several students are working in their group on individual posters that will explain facts and concepts about the topic. Another group is in the back of the room developing a role-play skit to share with the class at the end of the work sessions. Another group is standing at the SMART Board in the front of the room, creating a poem in the cinquain form on Colonial American daily life. All of the students are engaged and no one is watching another group; they are aware that they will all get a chance to pick any three stations they wish to work at over the next 3 days.

So what is the difference, besides student engagement? The second classroom involves student choice in learning the lesson content based on a student's own learning style preferences. The student who was disassembling the mechanical pencil is a tactile student who is now able to manipulate the computer WebQuest. The student looking out the window may be a visual learner who is now able to work on creating a poster. The student tapping a beat is an auditory learner who can now tap out a beat to go with the song lyrics the group is creating. The student social

Robert C. Snyder, Ph.D., is an associate professor at Slippery Rock University in Pennsylvania. His experience includes teaching fifth- and sixth-grade science for 10 years. For the last 11 years he has worked at Slippery Rock University, where he teaches preservice teachers in the Elementary Education/Early Childhood Department.

butterfly writing the note no longer has a need to do so, now that he has the opportunity to work with group members. On the other hand, students who work better alone (intrapersonal learners) have the option to create their own posters. Last, the group role play allows kinesthetic learners an opportunity to express the content with action. The major difference is that the second teacher harnesses the power of learning styles, learning modalities, and multiple intelligences. In which classroom would you rather be learning? In which would you rather be teaching? The change agent in moving from the first classroom scenario to the second is the teacher and how he or she uses learning style theory to affect teaching practice.

By Robert Snyder, Ph.D., Associate Professor of Education at Slippery Rock University

Differentiating instruction is a multifaceted concept that supports the universal design for learning process. Specifically, universal design is defined as "a blueprint for creating instructional goals, methods, materials, and assessments that work for everyone—not a single, one-size-fits-all solution but rather flexible approaches that can be customized and adjusted for individual needs." (National Center on Universal Design for Learning, 2009, n.p.). Target audiences who benefit directly from universal design include 1) students with disabilities and 2) teachers whose teaching style is inconsistent with particular students' preferred learning styles (National Center on Universal Design for Learning, 2009). This chapter focuses on collaborative efforts for modifying how material is presented to students with disabilities to promote understanding and individual success. Differentiated instruction is supported as a pathway for success in the Co-Design Model.

Tomlinson (1999, p. 2) defines differentiated classrooms as those in which "teachers provide specific ways for each individual to learn as deeply as possible with the understanding that every student's road map for learning is different from everyone else's." In this model, teachers begin instruction where the students are, rather than from the front of the curriculum guide. They also understand that they must engage students in instruction through different learning modalities, by appealing to differing interests, and by using varied rates of instruction and degrees of complexity. In addition, three main areas are often differentiated: namely, content, process, and product (Tomlinson, 1999). Most teachers adjust the level of content depth with ease for struggling learners. Thus, this chapter focuses primarily on the area of process differentiation, with some discussion of applications to differentiating products or assessments.

DIFFERENTIATION AND GARDNER'S MULTIPLE INTELLIGENCES

With regard to process, most teachers understand the importance of differentiating based on learning style. Often, this differentiation occurs through engagement of visual, auditory, and kinesthetic learners. The problem with implementing differentiation within lesson plans is that these three categories are too broad in nature to provide specific goals for differentiation. A better lens through which to view such differentiation is the paradigm of Howard Gardner's multiple intelligence theory (Gardner, 1983). This theory outlines avenues or intelligences of learning. A detailed explanation of how each of these intelligences interweave with Tomlinson's differentiated instruction concept is presented in the following section. Then, examples of how to apply differentiation by multiple intelligences to content-area lessons are given.

The *visual-spatial intelligence* represents those students who learn best by visual icons. Immediately artistic students come to mind, but many other students also use visual-spatial intelligence. For example, students who are able to read maps, blueprints, graphs, and so forth are visual-spatial. Consider navigation, for example. Some people are able to use a map to find their way from one location to another. Other people may not be able to do so and prefer written, step-by-step directions. Still others may rely on the auditory support of a global positioning system. Students who end up working as architects, engineers, or military officers are generally strong in the visual-spatial category. Another segment of the work force that uses visual-spatial abilities is students who go on to work for moving companies because of their valuable ability to visualize where every coffee table and corner cabinet will go.

Verbal-linguistic learners are the traditional "good students." Students who read, write, and process lectures well are verbal-linguistic. Because most of high school content is delivered through verbal-linguistic methods, these students excel and typically are the ones who go on to college, where, again, strong reading, writing, and lecture processing is a must.

One common misconception worth addressing before moving further concerns words projected on a screen, as in a PowerPoint presentation. Many teachers consider this kind of projection a visual-spatial technique. However, if only words are shown, it is still a verbal-linguistic mode of communication. It is the same words that would be handed out in a paper form if they were not projected. To capitalize on visual-spatial delivery, the slide needs to include icons or pictures that go along with and represent the words. Consider the difference in the two PowerPoint sample slides in Figure 14.1: Slide A, even when projected on the screen, is still delivered in a verbal-linguistic mode, while Slide B appeals to both verbal-linguistic and visual-spatial learners, allowing both learning styles the opportunity to process and make sense of the information.

The third pathway is *musical-rhythm intelligence*. These students are the ones who, during times when they are supposed to be working silently, are tapping a beat with a pencil or foot or in some cases even humming softly. Why? Musically intelligent students process information by associating it with beats and rhythms that allow them to make sense of the data and store it in the brain. This connection may not make sense to those who are not musically intelligent; however, everyone has glimpses of what this is like. For example, imagine driving down the road in a car, while flipping through the radio stations. Suddenly, an old song is located, one that has not been heard in years. What happens? This experience tends to make people recall friends or places associated with that song, usually with amazingly vivid detail that would have otherwise never been recalled to short-term memory. All of this information was triggered by the song associated with that person, place, or event. This is how musically intelligent students process the information they receive on a daily basis. These students really do learn best when they put on their headphones to study!

Logical-mathematical intelligence refers to those students who are good at mathematics understanding. However, this pathway includes more than just "number crunching." Students who are linear thinkers are also logical-mathematical. Consider various teaching styles for a moment. Some teachers need to lay out everything required for a lesson, such as handouts, materials, and demos, somewhere in the room so that all the lesson items are arranged in linear order, which is used as a way to keep track of what comes next in the lesson sequence. Teachers may do this to ensure that they do not skip anything or present something out of order from the way they

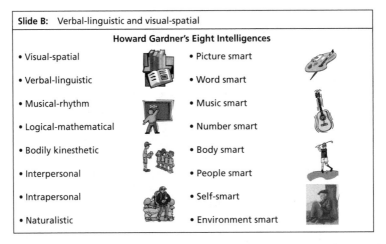

Figure 14.1. A comparison of information presented by verbal-linguistic versus combined verbal-linguistic and visual-spatial pathways. (*Source:* Gardner, 1999.)

had planned. These teachers are relying on their logical-mathematical intelligence. In contrast, other teachers may have no problem picking up certain lesson segments with a linear sequence as the lesson progresses. These teachers do not rely upon a logical-mathematical intelligence to function. In the classroom, logical-mathematical students need order and systematic directions or steps in order to process the content.

Students who are very good athletes or who have fine motor skills are typically *bodily kinesthetic* learners. Such students benefit from hands-on learning activities. This pathway ties in well with Piaget's concrete operational stage of development, which posits that abstract learning cannot be processed until concrete understanding is developed (Inhelder & Piaget, 1958). However, bodily kinesthetic learners tend to favor this concrete or tactile process much more than do their peers in the other intelligence areas. Indeed, they tend to make a living out of being skilled with their hands. Imagine an auto mechanic, surgeon, or bomb disposal specialist to understand the importance of highly skilled individuals in this intelligence area.

For *interpersonally intelligent* individuals, socializing with others is not only emotionally stimulating but also a necessity for processing information. These students truly do learn better by reading each other test questions or practicing flashcards. Brainstorming as a group helps interpersonal students process information and understand concepts.

In contrast, *intrapersonal* learners process best by working alone in quiet solitude. Working with groups tends to be distracting and inhibits their ability to process and make sense of content. This tendency creates a dilemma in the classroom because the needs or strengths of interpersonal and intrapersonal learners are opposite. So what is a teacher to do? For a start, teachers can use both cooperative learning and independent activities equally. Often, the best approach is to allow students a choice of working with a partner or working alone. Again, consider the teaching profession: Imagine a teacher in-service training day and the administration asks each teacher for something important, such as curriculum revision documents, and it has to be turned in before the end of the day! Many teachers would immediately want to just go to their rooms and work quietly without distraction to get it done, However, other teachers may want to meet with a group to discuss and brainstorm what needs to be accomplished and perhaps divide up the work. The first would be intrapersonal processing, whereas the latter is an example of interpersonal processing.

Naturalistic intelligence is the eighth intelligence and a more recent addition to the original seven intelligences proposed by Gardner (1999). This category represents students who gravitate toward natural patterns and who gain brain stimulation when in a natural, outdoor environment. These are the students who come to the classroom from the bus stop carrying every leaf, rock, insect, and injured chipmunk they find! In the classroom, these are the students who may be off task within 10 minutes if they are supposed to read two chapters of a novel silently. Yet on a nice day, if the same class goes outside to read silently while sitting in the outdoor classroom or propped up against a tree in the recess yard, these naturalistic students may remain engaged for the duration of the lesson. Just the sight, sounds, and smells of the outdoors allow these learners to become actively engaged and better able to process the verbal-linguistic task of reading a novel.

It is worth pointing out that Gardner (1999) has also proposed a ninth intelligence called *existentialist*. This category represents those students who are "deep thinkers" or "big picture" people. For instance, imagine someone teaching a lesson on the eight planets of the solar system, when a student raises his or her hand and begins asking questions about dark matter or black holes. All the teacher wants to accomplish is the objective of identifying the eight planets and their order in the solar system, yet now this teacher has a student who is apparently trying to distract the class. Instead of getting frustrated, this teacher could embrace the distraction for the betterment of society. This teacher might just have the next Socrates, Plato, or Einstein sitting in the class. Those famous individuals are considered to have possessed a strong existential intelligence.

The importance of these intelligence areas cannot be overlooked when trying to initiate student engagement. By opening up student brain activity via simulation of the student's preferred learning intelligence, the teacher can create active processing in the other learning areas. For example, if a teacher begins a lesson with the statement "open up your textbook to page 52," the students who are not verbal-linguistic learners will immediately tune out, maybe even before they hear the page number. However, if the teacher finds a way to begin the lesson in a manner that appeals to many different intelligences, that teacher now has active brain engagement among the students. If the teacher incorporates verbal-linguistic information at this junction, the students with other learning styles are now more easily able to process such information because they have received some of the information via their preferred style, and the lesson will make more sense.

APPLICATION TO THE CLASSROOM

The goal in applying Gardner's intelligences to fruitful differentiated instruction is to use activities that stimulate as many of the learning intelligences as possible in addition to other adaptations made for students with IEPs. It is not, for instance, about singing an entire lecture to benefit musically intelligent students one day and showing a slide presentation on another to benefit the visual learners. Rather, it is tapping into as many styles as possible through short little activities. It is not about teaching more but teaching smarter. This section features examples from content areas that demonstrate this teach-smarter concept with respect to activating multiple learning styles at one time.

To start, here is one way a teacher could introduce the math concept of box and whisker plots during the first 5–10 minutes of class. The teacher hands out 11 index cards with numbers to some of the students. Say the numbers are 12, 15, 16, 18, 19, 22, 23, 24, 27, 30, and 31. The students are to line up in order facing the class and holding up the cards, with the lowest number on the left side of the class and the highest on the right side. Next, the students are to identify the lower extreme (12) and the upper extreme (31) of the range of numbers. The teacher has the student holding the number 12 hold a piece of yarn as the teacher run the yarn from the lower extreme to the person with number 31, who will hold the other end of the yarn. There is now a line running the length of the range of numbers. Now the students identify the median (number 22 in this example). Once accomplished, the teacher lays down a meter stick perpendicularly between the student's feet identifying 22 as the median. Now the class looks at the lower half (12, 15, 16, 18, 19) and identifies the new "median," or lower quartile. Once 16 is identified, the teacher places a meter stick perpendicularly beneath the feet of that student. The teacher uses additional meter sticks to connect back to the median, so that a box is now formed from 16 to 22. The process is repeated for the upper quartile. The students now see a life-size version of the box and whisker plot in Figure 14.2.

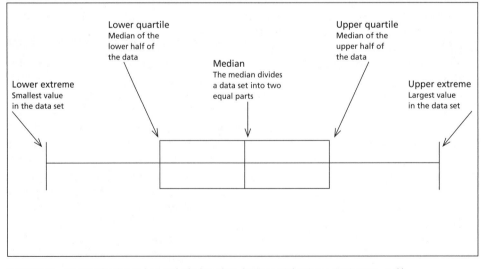

Figure 14.2. An introduction to box and whisker plots. (*Source:* HighPoints Learning Inc., n.d.)

At this point, the teacher would have the students return to their seats and begin a more traditional mode of instruction. The difference now is that more student brain activity is engaged. The activity helps students who are visual-spatial (they see the yarn line and meter-stick box), kinesthetic (they are up and moving around to create this human box and whisker plot), interpersonal (they interact with each other as they line up and create the model), and logical-mathematical (they develop the linear range, identify the median, and so forth). The end result is that they all have a conceptual understanding, filtered through their own learning style, of what a median, upper quartile, and lower quartile are. They are now receptive to learning via a verbal-linguistic model. So this investment of 5–10 minutes of time accessing four different intelligences now has the potential to save many minutes or hours of reteaching the concept to students who were disengaged or unable to comprehend the concept from the traditional verbal-linguistic mode.

Similar activities can be used for review. As an illustration, suppose one is teaching history and plans to give a test on the American Civil War. On the test is a time line where the students will have to place the major events of the Civil War in chronological order. As a 15-minute review activity, the teacher could hand out index cards with the events, such as Fredericksburg, Antietam, Cold Harbor, Gettysburg, Shiloh, and so forth. The teacher could also play Civil War–era music in the background and have the students place themselves in order. The group that will benefit the most are the visual-spatial learners, because once they see where their friends and classmates are standing and what they are holding, this arrangement will become a mnemonic device that they can recall during the test. Their thought process would look like this: "Okay, I was holding Fredericksburg and Sally was next to me (on the right) and she had Antietam. My friend Billy was on the other side of me holding Chancellorsville, and Rita was beside him holding Gettysburg…." But visual-spatial students are not the only ones to benefit from this activity. Other intelligences engaged with this activity include kinesthetic (up moving around and getting into a life-size time line), interpersonal (communicating and debating about who stands where, even referring to notes or the textbook when proof is needed), musical-rhythm (the Civil War–era music in the background), logical-mathematical (creating a chronological line), and verbal-linguistic (reviewing notes and textbook for accuracy in the lineup of events). Again the payoff comes from activating brain stimulation for five different learning styles in a single 15-minute activity—in other words, "teaching smarter" with regard to various intelligences.

The key element is often simplicity and initial engagement of the learning style. For example, suppose a teacher has a social studies class and wants to pair the students to work on a study guide relating to Colonial American history in order to engage interpersonal learners. The teacher could assign the students to partners. Or the teacher could let the students choose their own partners. Both have pitfalls: Students may not like the partners assigned, or the teacher may have to intervene in an argument when several students want to be partners with the same person. But there is a third way that has several benefits. In this case, the teacher could distribute pairs of index cards with exactly the same song titles for patriotic songs such as "America," "Yankee Doodle," and "Star-Spangled Banner." (Lyrics could be included on both cards as well for ease of recognition of the song.) Then the teacher would tell the students they have to find their partner but that they can only hum their song (or a line or refrain). Once the students find their match, they begin working on the study guide (primarily a verbal-linguistic activity). The difference now is in brain stimulation of other intelligences, not only musical-rhythm but also kinesthetic, interpersonal, and intrapersonal. For example, an intrapersonal learner might be assessing how she feels about humming and might approach the task by either humming really loud, humming quietly, or not humming but hoping her partner is really loud. An additional benefit is that the teacher can make the distribution look random but behind the scenes he or she can purposely ensure that two students do not get matching cards if they cannot work well together. The teacher could also keep the random appearance but ensure that a high-functioning student is paired with a learning-support student (or other struggling student) to allow peer tutoring or coaching to develop. However, this goal will remain invisible to the students.

So far this chapter has reviewed characteristics for each of the multiple intelligences and some content-area examples of how to stimulate learning with various intelligences. Now the discussion explores the many other differentiated instruction practices that can be used to stimulate various intelligences. Tomlinson (1999) recognizes several instructional activities for differentiating instruction. These include but are not limited to stations, centers, tiered activities, learning contracts, and choice boards. Other strategies include anchor activities, concept walls, concept maps, graphic organizers, learning menus, and think dots (Tomlinson, 2003). This list is not exhaustive but represents a selection of strategies that can be used to incorporate multiple intelligences. Table 14.1 shows how the two principles of multiple intelligences and differentiated instruction overlay each other.

Table 14.1.   Matrix of multiple intelligences and differentiated instruction strategies

Intelligence	Choice boards	Cubing/think dots	Learning menus	Role, audience, format, and topic (RAFT)	Graphic organizers/concept maps	Anchor activities	Learning contracts	Tiered lessons
Visual-spatial	✳	✳	✳		✳	✳		✳
Verbal-linguistic	✳	✳	✳	✳		✳	✳	✳
Musical-rhythm	✳		✳					✳
Logical-mathematical	✳	✳	✳	✳	✳	✳	✳	✳
Bodily kinesthetic	✳	✳	✳					✳
Interpersonal	✳	✳	✳	✳		✳		✳
Intrapersonal	✳	✳	✳			✳	✳	
Naturalistic								✳
Existentialist							✳	✳

Sources: Tomlinson (2003); Gardner (1999).

WHAT DIFFERENTIATED INSTRUCTION
MIGHT LOOK LIKE IN THE SHARED ENVIRONMENT

Every teacher has a different mastery of and comfort level with each of the intelligence areas. The advantage of the Co-Design Model is that each teacher can bring his or her strengths with regard to multiple intelligences to each lesson. This strategy requires communication and planning regarding each teacher's role with each of the implemented intelligences. For instance, in a parallel lesson, one teacher may incorporate music by creating and sharing a rap song about the water cycle, and the other teacher may use visual-spatial techniques, such as a graphic organizer that prompts the students to draw the water cycle. After 20 minutes, the teachers switch groups. This type of parallel lesson allows both teachers to work with a smaller group of students, thereby increasing student–teacher interaction in the activities.

In another example, the teachers may design station work based on specific intelligences that they want to incorporate for the particular inclusion learners they have in the class. Thus, each station may be set up with different intelligences in mind. The teachers might divide responsibility of creating and facilitating each station based on their own preferences in the intelligence areas. Therefore, one teacher might develop a station that uses kinesthetic and interpersonal intelligences. At this station, students would use fraction manipulatives to solve equivalent fraction problems with a partner. The second teacher might develop a station that uses logical-mathematical, verbal-linguistic, and intrapersonal intelligences. In this case, students would work individually in a given scenario, such as creating a friendly letter for a new student that explains the steps of how to find equivalent fractions. A third station might be set up as an independent station in which students use interpersonal and visual-spatial intelligences. This could be directions for a game, in which one team gives the name of a fraction and the other team has to draw a diagram showing three equivalent fractions for the fraction given.

The key to maximizing use of multiple intelligences in the Co-Design Model is to have each teacher take an intelligence inventory to identify their strengths, communicate the results with each other, and use such strengths to identify what co-teaching model is best applied in light of the lesson objectives and intelligence areas needed for differentiating the instruction based on the learners in that classroom. This self-evaluation can be very enlightening to teaching partners.

WEB RESOURCES FOR DIFFERENTIATED INSTRUCTION

The following are some web sites that illustrate the kinds of tools and approaches available for differentiated instruction.

- Dare to Differentiate—a resource-sharing site for teachers that provides examples and templates for choice-board, RAFT (role-audience-format-topic), think-dot, center, and learning-menu strategies
  http://daretodifferentiate.wikispaces.com

- Multiple intelligences site of the Birmingham [United Kingdom] Grid for Learning—online multiple intelligence survey
  http://www.bgfl.org/bgfl/custom/resources_ftp/client_ftp/ks1/ict/multiple_int/index.htm

- Everything DI!—examples of applying multiple intelligence
  http://www.everythingdi.net/mitech/mi_tech.htm

- New Horizons for Learning, Johns Hopkins University School of Education—
  multiple intelligence overview and resources
  http://www.newhorizons.org/strategies/mi/front_mi.htm

- Learning Disabilities Association of Iowa, Multiple Intelligences Assessment Menu
  2010—examples of assessment options for each of the multiple intelligences
  http://www.lda-ia.org/Multiple%20Intelligences%20Assessment%20Menu%20
  2010.doc

Table 14.2. Strategies for differentiating assessment via multiple intelligences

Verbal-linguistic menu

Use storytelling to explain __
Set up a debate to discuss __
Write a poem, myth, legend, short
  play, or news article about __
Relate a short story or novel to __
Give a presentation on __
Lead a class discussion on __
Write journal entries on __

Logical-mathematical menu

Create a time line of __
Design and conduct an experiment on __
Make a strategy game that includes __
Make a calendar of __
Categorize facts and information on __
Use inductive or deductive reasoning to __
Select and use technology to __

Musical-rhythm menu

Write song lyrics for __
Sing a rap or song that explains __
Indicate the rhythmical patterns in __
Give a presentation with appropriate
  musical accompaniment on __
Explain how the music of a song is
  similar to __
Collect and present songs about __

Visual-spatial menu

Create a chart, map, cluster, or graph of __
Create a slide show, videotape, or photo
  album of __
Design a poster, bulletin board, or mural of __
Use a memory system to learn __
Create a piece of art that demonstrates __
Develop a set of architectural drawings that __
Color-code the process of __
Illustrate, draw, paint, or sketch __

Naturalistic menu

Identify the natural pattern __
Create an analogy using the animal
  kingdom for __
If stranded on an island, explain how
  you would approach this task __
Describe the effects on __

Interpersonal menu

Create and implement group rules for __
Conduct a class meeting to address __
Organize or participate in a group that will __
Generate a variety of multiple perspectives on
  the topic of __

Intrapersonal menu

Create a personal analogy for __
Set a goal to accomplish __
Describe how you feel about __
Explain your personal philosophy about __
Explain your intuitive hunches about __
Self-assess your work in __

Bodily kinesthetic menu

Role-play or simulate __
Create a movement or sequence of
  movements to explain __
Choreograph a dance of __
Invent a board or floor game of __
Make task or puzzle cards of __
Build or construct a __

*Adapted from CAMPBELL, LINDA C.; CAMPBELL, BRUCE; DICKINSON, DEE, TEACHING AND LEARNING THROUGH
MULTIPLE INTELLIGENCES, 1st Edition, © 1996. Reprinted by permission of Pearson Education, Inc., Upper Saddle
River, NJ.*

CONCLUSION

Once differentiated instruction is in place, teachers can use the various intelligences to allow student choice in demonstrating their knowledge or mastery of content. For example, if the students have just learned about the rock cycle, the teacher can create a general rubric of what content the students should know, such as metamorphic rock, igneous rock, and so forth. Once the rubric is created, the teacher can provide several options for students to demonstrate their knowledge. For example, one student may choose to write a story about a rock as it journeys through the rock cycle. Another may choose to write song lyrics, another may choose to create a poster, and another might decide to make a model. With the general-content rubric developed in advance and made clear to the students, it does not matter whether they hand in a poster, song lyrics, or poem; the teacher can easily assess whether they have the content included and accurately developed. Ideas for offering assessment options based on multiple intelligences are widely available. The web site resources in the previous section provides many examples. Table 14.2 illustrates how these assessments fit each of the intelligence areas.

In summary, the use of Gardner's multiple intelligences can have a major influence on how a teacher decides to differentiate instruction. As with application of any new strategy, it takes a great deal of work and many modifications after each attempt, but the payoff is high with respect to student learning. The best advice is to start small, with one lesson or one activity, and grow from there. Once improvement in student engagement and understanding is observed, it becomes easier to develop into future lessons.

REFERENCES

Campbell, L., Campbell, B., & Dickenson, D. (1996). *Teaching and learning through multiple intelligences*. Needham Heights, MA: Allyn & Bacon.

Gardner, H. (1983). *Frames of mind: The theory of multiple intelligences.* New York, NY: Basic Books.

Gardner, H. (1999). *Intelligence reframed: Multiple intelligences for the 21st century.* New York, NY: Basic Books.

HighPoints Learning Inc. (n.d.). *Quartiles.* Retrieved from http://www.northstarmath.com/SiteMap/Quartiles.html

Inhelder, B., & Piaget, J. (1958). *The growth of logical thinking from childhood to adolescence.* New York, NY: Basic Books.

National Center on Universal Design for Learning. (2009). *About UDL.* Retrieved from http://www.udlcenter.org/aboutudl/whatisudl

Tomlinson, C.A. (1999). *The differentiated classroom: Responding to the needs of all learners.* Alexandria, VA: Association for Supervision and Curriculum Development.

Tomlinson, C.A. (2003). *Fulfilling the promise of the differentiated classroom.* Alexandria, VA: Association for Supervision and Curriculum Development.

CHAPTER **15**

Technology

Rapid developments in technology are quickly reshaping the way people engage the world. Through the power of the Internet, information is no longer something only the expert possesses but something the public can easily gain access to, consume, or create. Personal and professional relationships can now be formed and sustained beyond one's backyard through large, web-based social networks. Virtual communities allow the individual to connect with others, globally, based on a common set of friends, common interests, or common aspirations. Its influence can be neither ignored nor avoided. Job applications and face-to-face interviews are now being handled entirely online. Digital pictures are taken and uploaded to the Internet using mobile phones. Mobile computing and touch screens are here, as the keyboard and mouse quickly drift off into the history books. This is our world, and in many ways one's level of engagement with it determines his or her level of relevance.

A segment of society that understands this dynamic and has begun to rally behind these advancements in technology is public education. Many educators are now using Web 2.0 tools to create dynamic, content-rich learning activities that really engage the students where they are. These web-based tools are cost effective (and often free); they are accessible 24/7 on the Internet; and they are media-rich, making them capable of presenting information in multiple formats that engage multiple (and often all) modalities. And perhaps one of the greatest strengths of these new media is their ability to create learning spaces that are student centered and promote active learning (Hsu, Ching, & Grabowski, 2009).

Wikis are a good example of this concept. A wiki is a web-based collaborative writing tool that has a seemingly limitless number of applications within educational settings. As a presentation tool, a wiki can be used to quickly serve up new information that is dynamic, interactive, and accessible 24/7. Although a wiki page can be used to communicate new information to learners using straight text, interactive components, such as audio recordings, streaming video, and illustrations, can be added in just a few clicks. As a social and constructivist tool, authorship of the wiki can be turned over to the students, who can then use the wiki to work together on creating a common knowledge base. That knowledge base could be a simple bulleted list or a comprehensive collaborative writing project. Ultimately, the wiki provides a learning space that engages the students socially, allows them to create something new from what they know, and accommodates diverse styles of learning and learning needs.

However, wikis are only one example of how advances in technology are being leveraged by some educators to create meaningful learning experiences for students: A quick Internet search on "Web 2.0 tools for teachers" will return millions of results. Blogs, social bookmarking, cloud computing, screencasting, webcasting, and mashups are just a few of the most common examples at this moment. The real challenge, however, is not the availability of tools but simply trying to keep up with them all. As mentioned, wikis can be wonderful learning tools, but often student access to these web sites is blocked in the classroom. Students are able to do more and more with mobile computing, but mobile phones are often prohibited in schools. Prensky points out in "Digital Natives, Digital Immigrants" that "our students have radically changed. Today's students are no longer the people our education system was designed to teach" (2001, p. 1). And this article was written in 2001! Clearly, advances in technology are quickly changing the way people engage with the world. In order to ensure that schools are creating learning experiences for students that are relevant and leverage all that technology has to offer, three main questions need to be addressed:

- Who are the students?
- How can teaching methodologies be reshaped to reflect the reshaping world?
- And how do teachers bring that world into the classroom?

By Brian Danielson, Director of the Center for
Technology and Design at Slippery Rock University

In 2001, the software designer, educational consultant, and writer Mark Prensky coined the term *digital native* to describe the generation of students born after 1990 (Prensky, 2001). He used this term because this is the first generation to grow up completely under the influence of computers and digital technology. According to Prensky, it is likely that students will spend 10,000 hours playing video games, 20,000 hours watching television, and fewer than 5,000 hours reading before they graduate from high school. E-mail, the Internet, digital music downloads, cell phones, and text and video messaging are all a part of the Digital Age in which students are growing up and all are an important part of their lives. For these reasons, as well as more presented within this chapter, technology in the collaborative classroom is included as a pathway for achieving success via the Co-Design Model.

Many educational leaders are looking to technology as a centerpiece in creating a student-centered, constructivist pedagogical paradigm shift that can create more effective and engaging classrooms. However, effective integration of technology is the result of many factors, with the most important factor being the teacher's competence and ability to shape instructional technology activities to meet students' needs. Many of the teachers leading classrooms across the United States completed their own formal education well before the Digital Age. These *digital immigrants* (as Prensky calls them) often know less about technology than do their students. As a result, we see technology avoidance in many of the classrooms we visit in the course of our work.

As schools continue to develop more inclusive classroom settings, it is essential that technology be used as part of daily classroom instruction. Many students with various types of disabilities (as well as their peers without disabilities who struggle with academic work) do not respond to the traditional "stand and deliver" style of instruction. Often, these students cannot cope neurologically with this type of instruction because they have receptive and expressive language problems and cannot process information when it is delivered solely in an auditory or lecture mode. The use of various types of technology in the classroom has the potential to remedy this problem because it may increase the engagement level of students and address their preferred mode of learning.

Few, if any, educators question the idea that technology is essential to creating an environment that fosters student engagement and helps increase academic achievement. But integrating technology into classroom instruction is a complex process that requires teachers to first learn the technology and then use it in a way that enhances the learning process. In particular, in the inclusive classroom technology should be used to support active engagement, provide multimodal experiences, foster participation in groups, allow alternative ways to demonstrate proficiency (assessment), promote critical thinking, and help make connections to the outside world. All of these basic principles for technology use in a classroom integrate nicely with a differentiated philosophy for teaching and can be used to promote inclusive school environments.

When teachers think about using technology to differentiate instruction for students, a good place to begin is to first examine the content being taught, the products students are expected to create, and the process of instructional delivery and then determine how technology can be used by both the teacher and the student to enhance the teaching and learning process. Consider that multimedia and digital applications and tools can combine video, sound, text, animation, and graphics to address various learning styles in the inclusive classroom, as well as foster student strengths as demonstrated through multiple intelligences (see Chapter 14). The following are some of the benefits of using technology in daily lessons to address learner needs:

1.   Digital technology and multimedia reach a variety of senses and can provide a multimodal experience. This allows the teacher to be sure that all types of learning styles and preferences are being considered.

2.   The use of technology allows students to produce products of their own choice and design. This increases active participation in the curriculum and leads to a deeper understanding of the content. It also fosters ownership of the learning.

3.   Technology allows the teacher to provide choices for students to demonstrate proficiency. This is part of a differentiated assessment philosophy that is essential for an inclusive school environment.

4.   Technology can help promote critical thinking in a classroom through project-based experiences that require students to do research, analyze the content of web sites, and apply mastery in the synthesis of new products using technology.

5.   Technology can be used to promote communication among students, as well as between students and teachers, through such options as wiki spaces, blogs, Twitter, WebQuests, and other forms of technology. Students and teachers can discuss content, organization of content, presentation of material, interpretation of text and other information, and insights and opinions that foster new attitudes and ideas in the classroom.

Teachers have a responsibility to provide students with different avenues for acquiring content and constructing and making sense of new ideas and concepts. Marrying differentiated instruction with technology empowers teachers with opportunities for creating classroom content that fits the needs of diverse learners in countless ways. The rest of this chapter is devoted to specific examples of how technology can be used to differentiate classroom instruction. Table 15.1 summarizes many excellent web sites that provide great ideas for differentiating instruction.

USING WEBQUESTS AS AN INSTRUCTIONAL TOOL

In our experience as educational consultants, one of the best but most underused technology tools available to classroom teachers to help differentiate instruction is the WebQuest. The WebQuest model was developed by Bernie Dodge in the mid-1990s

Table 15.1. Selected web sites for integrating technology into instruction

Web site	Curriculum area	Description
WebQuests* http://WebQuest.org http://www.questgarden.com	Multiple areas	Existing WebQuests
Game show templates* http://jc-schools.net/tutorials/PPT-games/	Multiple areas	PowerPoint games
JeopardyLabs http://jeopardylabs.com	Multiple areas	Game-show format with reusable hyperlink
Funbrain* http://www.funbrain.com/teachers/	Multiple areas	Comprehensive elementary web site with games and activities
SuperTeacherTools http://www.superteachertools.com	Multiple areas	Flash games and other tech tools for teachers
Thinks.com http://www.thinks.com	Multiple areas	Database of brain teasers, digital chess, other fun games
Freeology http://www.freeology.com/graphicorgs/	Multiple areas	Database of graphic organizers and other teacher tools
Mr. Nussbaum http://www.mrnussbaum.com	Multiple areas	Interactive web site that covers all areas of the curriculum
National Library of Virtual Manipulatives* http://nlvm.usu.edu/en/nav/vlibrary.html	Math	Library of virtual math manipulatives
Illuminations (National Council for Teachers of Mathematics)* http://illuminations.nctm.org	Math	Hundreds of activities, lessons, and recommended web links
AplusMath http://www.aplusmath.com	Math	Comprehensive math web site
Exploratorium http://www.exploratorium.edu/explore/handson.html	Science	Database of hands-on science activities
WebElements http://www.webelements.com	Science	Interactive periodic table of elements
Edheads http://www.edheads.com	Science/health	Science and health virtual activities on topics such as knee replacement
HyperHistory Online http://www.hyperhistory.com/online_n2/History_n2/a.html	History	Interactive time line
Famous trials (University of Missouri–Kansas City School of Law) http://www.law.umkc.edu/faculty/projects/ftrials/ftrials.htm	History	Detailed web site of all the great trials in history, with diagrams, transcripts, images, and so forth
Starfall* http://www.starfall.com	Literacy	Interactive, graphic-rich auditory experiences for all levels of literacy development
Kurzweil text-to-speech tools* http://www.kurzweiledu.com	Literacy	Accessibility tools for text
Online dictionaries* http://dictionary.reference.com	Phonics	Dictionary words pronounced aloud
VocabularySpellingCity http://www.spellingcity.com	Spelling	Comprehensive web site of spelling games, activities, and test giver
Grammar Bytes http://www.chompchomp.com	English	Interactive grammar activities
Web English Teacher http://www.webenglishteacher.com	English	Comprehensive web site of lesson plans and activities for English

Note: Asterisk designates a site discussed in this chapter.

and continues to be an excellent and easy method to integrate technology into instruction. A WebQuest is an inquiry-oriented activity in which the learners interact with resources on the Internet to learn information and complete a task that often results in some form of product being produced (Dodge, 1995). The process of completing a WebQuest involves following step-by-step directions provided by the teacher and accessing preestablished web sites that support the learning activity. Some of the best WebQuests include web documents, video clips, virtual experiences, and access to experts. According to Dodge (1995), a well-designed WebQuest will involve the student in the process of analysis, synthesis, and evaluation. Critical components of a WebQuest follow:

1. An introduction

2. A research-oriented task

3. A process in which all of the supporting web sites are listed

4. Clearly defined steps for researching the task

5. Directions for creating a product or products

6. An evaluation rubric

7. A list of references and credits

WebQuests can vary in length, ranging from a 1- to 3-day activity to a 3-week experience that includes the expectation that the learner will produce multiple products. The WebQuest should not be an isolated assignment but should be connected to the subject curriculum, state and national standards, and previous material learned in the classroom (Skylar, Higgins, & Boone, 2007).

Bernie Dodge, the developer and creator of the WebQuest model, maintains two robust databases of existing WebQuests. The sites, http://WebQuest.org and http://www.questgarden.com, are filled with thousands of these teacher-made activities, organized by grade level and subject matter. Before using an existing WebQuest, however, the teachers should give some careful consideration to the availability of computers for student use, the readability of the content of the web sites that support the learning, the vocabulary being used within the web pages, the age appropriateness of the task, and whether the WebQuest can be completed independently or is more appropriate as a group activity. A well-designed WebQuest provides students with an efficient tool to conduct research, think critically, examine relevant topics, experience learning in multimodal ways, engage the curriculum in ways not allowed by traditional methods of teaching, and work collaboratively. Researchers Kortecamp and Bartoshesky (2003) found strong evidence that WebQuests foster collaboration among students and that a majority of students perceived a benefit to this kind of collaboration.

For students with disabilities, WebQuests are an ideal activity for at least two reasons. First, because WebQuests are a tool that is accessed primarily via the Internet, modifications are much easier. Digitized text is easily modified to make it more accessible for students with a variety of needs. Text can instantly be made larger, it can be highlighted or underlined, definitions can be easily and quickly attained, and screen-reader software enables nonreaders or poor readers to listen via synthesized speech. Second, research-based strategies such as advanced organizers, study guides, and graphic organizers can be developed in conjunction with the WebQuest to assist the students with comprehension (Skylar et al., 2007).

WebQuests can easily be incorporated into the co-taught classroom to support meeting the needs of all learners. Teachers may consider using a WebQuest for students identified as gifted and talented. The alternative co-teaching model could be used to provide enrichment for these students, as one co-teacher works exclusively with a small group of students on a WebQuest while the other co-teacher instructs a larger group of students in content more appropriate for their level of proficiency and understanding. In this scenario, the needs of the gifted students are being met by using the WebQuest as specially designed instruction while the other students are also having their needs met in an appropriate way.

An additional way a WebQuest can be used in the inclusive classroom is as an alternative assessment on a differentiated menu or choice board. Students with an interest in technology might choose to complete a WebQuest as an assignment to demonstrate their level of understanding of a concept or unit of instruction, or they might even be given an opportunity to construct a WebQuest for other students to complete. Both of these examples demonstrate the use of WebQuests to support student learning in a differentiated manner.

ILLUMINATIONS AND OTHER MATH WEB SITES

A helpful web site for educators that supports math instruction is the Illuminations site developed by the National Council for Teachers of Mathematics. This site (http://illuminations.nctm.org) contains a database of hundreds of differentiated lesson plans and supporting materials arranged by math topic and grade; a list of web links that support math instruction in areas such as geometry, computation, algebra, measurement, and so forth; and 105 online activities designed to be graphic representation of various concepts taught in typical math classes. This web site not only provides teachers with ideas for lesson planning but also gives them tools to differentiate content. The Illuminations site is a great resource because it provides interactive visual representations of math concepts ranging from simple number identification to more complex algebraic concepts. Examples include an interactive fractal tool, a graph creator, a box plotter, and a compound interest simulator. Illuminations support the teaching of mathematics using the Concrete-Representational-Abstract (CRA) Model of instruction. Researchers and professional organizations suggest the importance of teaching through concrete objects (Devlin, 2000) and visual representations of important math concepts to help students better understand the abstractions that are ubiquitous in mathematics (National Council of Teachers of Mathematics, 2000). The CRA Model is based on sequential instruction that begins by providing students with concrete examples of math concepts, followed by visual representations, followed finally by more abstract examples. In our work as consultants, teachers have remarked on the difficulty of obtaining concrete manipulatives and representations of math concepts as math gets more and more developmentally complex. The Illuminations web site is effective in that it provides activities that students can manipulate but that also present students with a visual representation of the concept.

Illuminations can be used in the inclusive co-taught classroom to help differentiate math instruction in a variety of ways. First, it can be used in a stations teaching model as one of three stations students must visit in a math class period. Co-teachers could be responsible for facilitating two of the stations by providing direct, explicit instruction, whereas the third station could be a technology station in which students must complete an independent activity on the Illuminations web site. All three stations would be developed to support the learning of a single math concept, but students would be exposed to three different methods of teaching it.

Another way in which Illuminations can be used is as an instructional tool during a lesson in which the team-teaching model is being used. Teachers can work together to provide explicit instruction in math and support the instruction by projecting tools found on the web site. One teacher might demonstrate solving a complex math formula on the whiteboard, and then his or her co-teacher might use one of the activities found on the Illumination web site to reinforce the learning and provide an interactive representation of the problem. These are only two examples of how Illuminations can be used in an inclusive classroom. There are countless more ways this resource can be used to support a differentiated philosophy.

A second web site that math educators will find useful in classroom instruction is the National Library of Virtual Manipulatives (NLVM) found at http://nlvm.usu.edu. This web site was developed and is maintained by the National Science Foundation and Utah State University. It is a library of uniquely interactive, web-based, virtual manipulatives or concept tutorials, mostly in the form of Java applets, for mathematics instruction with a K–12 emphasis. The premise behind the development of the site is that learning and understanding math at every level requires active engagement. Too much instruction fails to actively involve students. One way to address the problem is through the use of manipulatives, which are physical objects that help students to visualize relationships and applications (Utah State University, n.d.).

When visiting the NLVM, educators will quickly notice that the web site contains an index of the five big areas of math instruction: numbers and operations, algebra, geometry, measurement, and data analysis and probability. Once on the site, teachers are able to access several hundred interactive manipulatives and tools in any of these five areas. Examples include bar charts, base blocks, a chip abacus, geoboards, money, analog and digital clocks, tangrams, and more. Tools are easy to use for both teachers and students: Detailed instructions are provided on each activity, and the national standards addressed by each activity are specified.

Using the NLVM web site allows educators to differentiate instruction for students in various ways. Student learning styles could be considered when planning a math lesson, as students who are primarily visual learners and need concrete objects and visual representations could benefit greatly from the use of this web site during instruction. Co-teachers in an inclusive classroom could use the parallel teaching model, with one teacher instructing half the students in the class using the NLVM web site while his or her co-teacher provides an alternative method of instruction to the other half of the class using music or song as the primary method of instructional delivery.

SUPPORTING LITERACY INSTRUCTION THROUGH TECHNOLOGY

A favorite web site to support literacy development in the primary grades is the Starfall web site developed by Starfall Education (http://www.starfall.com). This site contains interactive, graphic-rich auditory experiences for all levels of literacy development, beginning with letter and sound identification and going all the way through activities to support comprehension. The systematic phonics approach at the core of the activities on the web site, in conjunction with phonemic awareness practice, is perfect for preschool, kindergarten, first grade, second grade, special education, home schooling, and English language development (supporting English language learners and students with English as a second language). We often see this web site being used in co-taught inclusive classrooms as part of the stations teaching model.

Using technology such as Starfall to support literacy development can be beneficial in a number of different ways. First, computers can present any type of auditory or visual materials—including speech, text, music, animations, photographs, or videos—alone or in different combinations. This technology can link different types of representations, such as pictures with sounds, oral readings with written text, videos with subtitles, or any other combinations that might reinforce teaching and learning. It can also provide enormous flexibility, allowing the user to set the speed of speech, decide whether written text is also read aloud, choose the language presented in text and speech, or decide whether to repeat the presentation. This flexibility can be valuable in presenting educational tasks—such as phonemic awareness practice, phonics lessons and drills, fluency practice, vocabulary instruction, and opportunities to learn and apply text-comprehension strategies—to students. The company Kurzweil Educational Systems has developed a text-to-speech tool that is a good example of this and can be used as assistive technology to help make content accessible to students with the cognitive ability but who lack literacy skills (see http://www.kurzweiledu.com).

Second, computers can accept a variety of inputs from students, ranging from mouse clicks to written text to spoken words. (A wide variety of special input devices, such as touch screens, special keyboards, and single-switch devices are also available for young children and students with special needs.) Computers can be programmed to check a child's work to determine whether he or she selected the correct word or picture, typed a correct word, said the correct word, or, with recent advances in computerized speech recognition, read a passage fluently.

Computers are also capable of recording and organizing information and reporting that information in multiple formats. Computers can record the responses of all students in a class to a set of letter–sound matching problems and then immediately report to the teacher the errors made by each student and the most common errors made by the entire class. (Some examples of audience response systems are shown on the web site of Padgett Communications [http://www.pcipro.com/play/]). In more complex tasks involving oral reading or text comprehension, computers can serve as convenient recording and reporting devices for teachers, helping them track student progress far more conveniently than other means of data collection. This capability can be used to inform teachers' instructional decisions and to make documenting students' progress more efficient.

Finally, computers can provide powerful scaffolds or "training wheels" for children's reading by presenting information flexibly, assessing students' work, and responding to students. For example, a student with limited phonics skills or vocabulary can benefit from scaffolding in the form of an online dictionary (e.g., http://dictionary.reference.com) that, at the click of a mouse, can speak the word and display its meaning. Similarly, students who have difficulty chunking sentences into meaningful phrases—a critical component of fluent reading—can have the computer highlight text in meaningful chunks to provide models of how words are grouped for fluent reading. Or a child weak in comprehension strategies can be guided by the computer to pose and answer questions, create concept maps, or check his or her own understanding while reading on-screen text. New technologies enable computers to provide immediate help when children need it in oral reading. The role of the computer is to make individualized, responsive scaffolds available for each child, thereby providing, as closely as possible, what a teacher would provide when working individually with a student. Scaffolding is addressed as a pathway for success in the Co-Design Model (Chapter 16).

WEB GAMES AND WEB 2.0 TOOLS TO SUPPORT INSTRUCTION

Although reading is a skill that can be supported by technology in multiple and obvious ways, many other curriculum areas can also be supported through the use of technology that allows teachers to differentiate instruction along the way. Take, for example, the integration of PowerPoint games with Bloom's Taxonomy to create leveled questions during a social studies lesson that includes technology to increase learner interest. The game-show format can be very effective as well. The site http://jc-schools.net/tutorials/PPT-games/ allows the user to download visually rich templates, complete with authentic sound, to a hard drive. The drive can then be used in a stations teaching model as an opportunity to review learned material, in a team-teaching model to review for a midterm exam, or in an alternative teaching model to provide an enrichment activity for advanced learners. Other teacher-friendly game sites include http://jeopardylabs.com (a site that allows the teacher to construct a game-show template and assign it a hyperlink so that it can be used repeatedly), http://www.puzz.com/stickelsframegames.html (a site containing frame games that can be used as bell ringers and brain teasers at the beginning or end of a class period), and http://www.funbrain.com/teachers/, which is a comprehensive K–8 web site that presents games designed to primarily support reading and math.

Another consideration for teachers is how they can use technology in the presentation of material to differentiate the process of learning for students. Kathy Schrock, the Director of Technology for Nauset Public Schools in Cape Cod, Massachusetts, and an adjunct professor at Wilkes University and Arcadia University, has developed a tremendous resource for teachers on her web site, called Kathy Schrock's Guide for Educators (http://school.discoveryeducation.com/schrockguide/). This page refers to a comprehensive list of Web 2.0 tools (http://www.go2web20.net) that teachers can use in almost any subject area. Web 2.0 tools are second-generation web applications that facilitate interactive information sharing, interoperability, user-centered designs, and collaboration on the World Wide Web. Examples of these tools include wiki spaces, blogs, audio and video file-sharing web sites, and social bookmarking. A few of our favorites include Viddler (http://www.viddler.com), which is a friendly video platform that can be used to post videos (students can interact with the video through tagging on the time line built into the program); Prezi (http://www.prezi.com), which can help to create astonishing presentations live and on the web; and Xtranormal (http://www.xtranormal.com), which is a movie-maker site that allows users to create animated movie clips of important information through character dialogue. These tools can also be used to support differentiated assessment because they provide students with opportunities to use the technology to create extraordinary projects representing their understanding of concepts and content being taught. The use of Web 2.0 tools allows the student to share their work not only with their teacher and classmates but also with people all over the world.

WHAT TECHNOLOGY LOOKS LIKE IN THE CO-TAUGHT CLASSROOM

There should be little doubt that one of the most effective techniques for improving student achievement, if it is implemented with fidelity, is co-teaching (Scruggs, Mastropieri, & McDuffie, 2007). Consider, for example, the benefits of two teachers in a classroom. Under the best of circumstances, two teachers can reduce the student–teacher ratio in half. When both teachers are fully used, then both teachers are more available to assist individual students (Mason, 2010).

Now consider the unlimited possibilities if technology is added to the co-teaching partnership. Technology could be added to each of the models of co-teaching in the following ways:

- Mobile technology computer carts could be used in a stations teaching model as a single station.

- Individual computers or laptops could be used by students during an alternative teaching model to allow students access to web sites for enrichment.

- SMART Boards could be used during a parallel teaching lesson by one of the co-teachers to provide instruction to half of the students in a classroom.

- Differentiated assessment strategies, such as choice boards, could include options that require students to use Web 2.0 tools such as Prezi, GoAnimate, Xtranormal, and VoiceThread to create products that reflect their learning.

- Co-teachers could use wiki spaces to post assignments, communicate with parents, or provide instructional videos for students to access outside school. Both co-teachers can have a presence in the wiki space.

- Kindles, Nooks, or other electronic book devices could be used as assistive technology in an alternative teaching model as one co-teacher instructs students in a large group while the other co-teacher provides instruction using these devices in a smaller group.

- Multimedia presentations can be given by co-teachers using a team teaching model. Some of the technology used might include PowerPoint, Prezi, RealPlayer or YouTube video clips, and music downloads.

The preceding list includes only a few ways technology can be integrated into the inclusive classroom and used by co-teaching teams. In each of these examples, technology can be used to increase student engagement, provide alternative ways for students to be assessed, and provide a multimodal instructional experience.

CONCLUSION

Given that today's students have grown up using technology in their day-to-day lives, educators have an obligation to find ways to integrate technology into the classroom. Considering the diversity found in classrooms as a result of the inclusion movement and the changing demographics of the United States, it almost seems impossible to continue teaching without the use of technology. Classroom teachers need to embrace a philosophy of differentiated instruction and technology integration with the idea that these are components of creating the type of brain-friendly classrooms of the future. Schools must train teachers to use technology and support them with the necessary equipment, infrastructure, and professional development to become more knowledgeable and competent than the students they teach. Table 15.1 serves as a starting place where teachers can begin exploring web sites and online instructional tools. Many of these sites have been recommended by teachers as proven tools of the trade.

REFERENCES

Devlin, K. (2000, September 29). Finding your inner mathematician. *Chronicle of Higher Education,* p. B5.

Dodge, B. (1995). WebQuests: A technique for Internet-based learning. *Distance Educator, 1*(2), 10–13.

Hsu, Y.-C., Chung, Y.-H., & Grabowski, B. (2009). Web 2.0 technologies as cognitive tools of the new media age. In L.T.W. Hin & R. Subramaniam (Eds.), *Handbook of research on new media literacy at the K–12 level: Issues and challenges* (pp. 353–371). New York, NY: Information Science Reference.

Kortecamp, K., & Bartoshesky, A. (2003, March). *WebQuests: An instructional tool that engages adult learners, promotes higher level thinking, and deepens content knowledge.* Paper presented at the Society for Information Technology and Teacher Education International Conference, Albuquerque, NM.

Mason, C. (2010, September 30). Co-teaching with technology [Blog post]. *EducationNow Blog, Center for Educational Improvement.* Retrieved from http://www.edimprovement. org/ 2010/09/co-teaching-with-technology/

National Council of Teachers of Mathematics. (2000). *Principles and standards for school mathematics.* Reston, VA: Author.

Prensky, M. (2001). Digital natives, digital immigrants. *On the Horizon, 9*(5), 1–6.

Scruggs T., Mastropieri M., & McDuffie K. (2007). Co-teaching in inclusive classrooms: A metasynthesis of qualitative research. *Exceptional Children, 73*(4), 392–416.

Skylar A., Higgins K., & Boone R. (2007). Strategies for adopting a WebQuest for students with a learning disability. *Intervention in School and Clinic, 43*(1), 20–28.

Utah State University. (n.d.). *National Library of Virtual Manipulatives site information.* Retrieved from http://nlvm.usu.edu/en/nav/siteinfo.html

CHAPTER **16**

Scaffolding

Joe Grushecky—teacher by day, guitarist by night—is a Pittsburgh, Pennsylvania, icon. Grushecky teaches emotional support at the secondary level at Sto-Rox High School. This school district is located just west of Pittsburgh. It is an urban district located in an economically distressed area. Grushecky uses his music to connect with his students. His guitar is seen sitting on his desk. Instead of a name plate outside his classroom, there is a picture of him and Bruce Springsteen playing guitar together. Grushecky has found a way to include music in his teaching style, connect with students, and make a difference with youth by scaffolding music to make connections with prior knowledge and experiences. In an interview, Grushecky said,

> I believe music has the ability to change lives. You never forget the lyrics to your favorite song, but you will forget the 22nd president of the United States. Being a professional musician, I see music affect lives both positive[ly] and negative[ly]. I use music for the emotional end of it. Music helps to see the world in a different light. It helps explain to kids that music is reflective of the times. The 1950s with Elvis, at other times in history with the outrage felt…, the trajectory of the country with today's rap and the choices to be made along the way.… You can listen to anything but what you gravitate to…opens you up. Understanding the basis and foundation of music is important. For example, heavy metal comes from the blues. Black History Month, sharecroppers, and moving north are frameworks of the blues. History, music, and the arts are a fabric of the country.
>
> Joe Grushecky, interview with Richael Barger-Anderson, July 22, 2010

Scaffolding is the final pathway included in the Co-Design Model as a recommended practice in collaborative classrooms. *Scaffolding* is defined as an instructional approach to assist with the acquisition of new skills or novel information. Via scaffolding, support is provided to the student at their current level of comprehension. Scaffolding is then removed as the student attains mastery of the new skill and becomes independent (Carter, Prater, & Dyches, 2008). Scaffolding is also defined as "differentiated instruction by providing assistance and supports by modeling and practice of multistepped skill or content areas and gradually removing the supports until accurate, independent performance is achieved" (Carter, Prater, & Dyches, 2008, p. 357) In other words, support is provided during the initial introduction of a skill, and as the student achieves mastery, the supports are removed (Smith & Tyler, 2010).

The metaphor of scaffolding and the implementation of the approach in the educational arena have gained popularity and support through research since the early 1990s. The metaphor of scaffolding is often used to explain the involvement of the *more knowledgeable other (MKO)* in the learning process and *the zone of proximal development,* terms introduced by Lev Vygotsky (1978). The MKO may be an adult or a more advanced peer who helps a student learn (Daniels, 2001; Hammond, 2002; Stone, 1998; Wells, 1999). The zone of proximal development is defined as the difference of what a learner can do with help and cannot do without help. The learner masters a skill through the teacher or peer providing modeling and assistance. Eventually, the learner is able to complete the task independently (Vygotsky, 1978).

SCAFFOLDING AS A RECOMMENDED PRACTICE

Scaffolding is a strategy that is supported by evidence-based research. Studies supporting the conceptual metaphor for the involvement of either adults or more knowledgeable peers in the acquisition of new material has been documented since the 1980s (Bodrova & Leong, 2007; Hammond, 2002; Wells, 1999). Scaffolding techniques have been used in many content areas of learning such as reading, writing, science, and social studies (Beers, 2003; Bodrova & Leong, 2007; Smith & Tyler, 2010). For example, Bodrova and Leong support the use of scaffolding in a writing technique called scaffolded writing. This technique promotes internalizing concepts of words as well as writing each separate word with the help of a teacher or MKO in the beginning. As learning progresses, the help being provided by the MKO is minimized until it is no longer needed by the learner.

Beers (2003) promotes scaffolding with the use of statements to help master the concept of how to make inferences. Again, the learner is provided support by the MKO. As time progresses and mastery of learning is achieved, the MKO's support is faded out. Scaffolding has been documented as beneficial for use with many educational techniques. Other examples include studies that support scaffolding with the use of differentiating instruction, graphic organizers, and helping students to complete guided notes (Smith & Tyler, 2010).

As stated previously, research supports scaffolding in various subject areas and grade levels (Donovan & Smolkin, 2002; Hammond, 2002; McDevitt & Ormrod, 2002; Pennsylvania Department of Education [PDE], 2009). Scaffolding provides support as needed when a student is learning a new skill, ultimately creating independent learners. Scaffolding promotes the mastery of new skills along with supports in place that are differentiated based on the individual needs of each learner (PDE, 2009; Hammond, 2002).

Smith and Tyler (2010) delineate the seven steps to accomplish scaffolding: 1) decide the type of support needed, 2) model or demonstrate the desired skill to be mastered, 3) allow for independent or group practice, 4) model again if needed, 5) encourage the student to continue practicing the skill until mastery is achieved, 6) make certain the student can complete the skill independently, and 7) allow opportunities for the student to successfully complete the skill without support.

WHAT SCAFFOLDING MIGHT LOOK LIKE IN THE SHARED ENVIRONMENT

Scaffolding in a collaborative environment combines the use of two recommended practices: co-teaching and scaffolding. When scaffolding is implemented, whether in the co-taught classroom or in a classroom with one teacher, it may look different with different pairs of learners. For example, the MKO (either adult or peer) may be more active with a less advanced learner. As the learner becomes more confident and knowledgeable with the material, the learner will become more active. On the contrary, the MKO may play a more passive role if the learner is already more advanced. The roles of the MKO and learner will vary depending on the players, the topic, and the skill (Lloyd & Fernyhough, 1999).

Having two teachers in the room to assist students and serve as MKOs should promote the strategy even more effectively. Two professionals can combine talents and implement this strategy to achieve success. In this situation, the co-teaching models discussed in Chapter 13 should be considered. The collaboration established through the co-teaching models will enable the teachers to plan for the effective use of scaffolding in the shared classroom.

Illustration of a Scaffolded Lesson

Figure 16.1 shows a sample lesson plan that demonstrates a collaborative approach to teaching the days of the week in Spanish with the use of scaffolding. (A reproducible version of this form, Co-Teach Lesson Plan, is provided in the appendix.) In this lesson, the stations model of co-teaching is implemented. Within the lesson, various ways to meet diverse learning styles are addressed (see Chapter 14). Use of visuals, opportunities for oral responses, creation of musical verses, and written assignments are ways to meet a variety of learner styles. The stations model of co-teaching is a good fit for this lesson because scaffolding not only requires the acquisition of the new skill but also provides for practice of the new skill. This lesson allows for two of the stations to have teacher facilitation while one station runs independently. This arrangement allows scaffolding to be implemented correctly through teacher assistance and practice opportunities.

Figure 16.2 provides an example of a graphic organizer that can be used within the lesson plan presented in Figure 16.1 for teaching the days of the week in Spanish. Graphic organizers are excellent for meeting the needs of visual learners as well as providing the practice needed for the technique of scaffolding.

Another example of the integration of a graphic organizer into a lesson with the technique of scaffolding is with a variation of a T chart with use of visuals. Visual depictions may be an additional way to help connect prior knowledge to new knowledge. For example, a picture of a moon has been inserted next to *lunes*. *Lunes* may trigger the thought of the more familiar word of lunar or moon, which in turn may help the student think of "Moonday" or Monday. Connecting prior knowledge to new knowledge is an excellent way for the MKO to scaffold the content being mastered.

It is important for students to help create their own graphic organizers because each person has his or her own prior knowledge. A common graphic depiction teachers use to help scaffold *martes* as Tuesday is the picture of the donuts for representation of Fat Tuesday or Mardi Gras, which sounds similar to *martes*. A picture of the candy Smarties may be inserted next to Tuesday. Some students may think *martes* sounds like "Smarties." They may connect their prior knowledge of Smarties with the word *martes* by thinking about eating Smarties to help "get smart" for a test on Tuesday.

A picture of a dove may be inserted next to Wednesday because *miércoles* sounds similar to "miracle." To some people, a dove is representative of a miracle. Students may connect prior knowledge with this because they may think it is a miracle that the week is half over. A picture of a hand is found next to *jueves* (Thursday). *Jueves* sounds like "waves" and a hand could be a symbol for waving hello. Because

Co-Teach Lesson Plan

Co-teachers: Ms. Carmel Mr. Carter	Date: Jan. 16	Room: 078	Day: Monday	Grade: 6	Time/period: 3rd period	Subject: Language Arts

Co-teaching model: __ One teach/one assist __Parallel
        X Stations   X Team
        __ Alternative   __ Other
	Co-plan time:
	7th period on Tuesday

State standard	Short-term objectives	Evaluation
Speaking and Listening 1.6.6.A	**1.** Using the materials, the student will create flashcards with 100% accuracy in spelling the days of the week. **Modifications:** If needed, student will be provided with a model, provided teacher assistance, and/or provided with premade flashcards to ensure 100% accuracy.	Completed flashcards
Speaking and Listening 1.6.6.A	**2.** Using the materials, the student will orally practice all flashcards with a peer and/or teacher at least three times. **Modifications:** Student may be provided with extended time to practice.	Observation of practice
Quality of Writing 1.5.6.F	**3.** Using a writing instrument, the student will complete each graphic organizer within 12 minutes. **Modifications:** Student may be provided with premade components for each of the areas needed to complete the graphic organizers.	Completed graphic organizers
Speaking and Listening 1.6.6.B	**4.** Given a blank calendar page, the student will complete the calendar page by including the days of the week in Spanish with accuracy for at least five of seven days. **Modifications:** Teacher assistance provided if needed.	Completed calendar page
Materials: Display of days of the week in Spanish and English, flashcards, handout of the days of the week in Spanish and English, T charts, wheel charts, copy of song "I Gotta Feeling," CD player, blank calendar pages		Other
Introduction *Teacher responsible:* Team-teach model—both teachers are responsible.	Teachers tell the students that everyone is going to learn the days of the week in Spanish. Teachers tell the students to close their eyes and say the days of the week in Spanish together. Teachers model the days of the week while students attempt to say along. Teachers ask to try again together and then one more time together (choral responding). Teachers ask the students to open their eyes and look at the words on the board. Teachers have displayed the days of the week in Spanish with the corresponding English day of the week below. With teacher prompting and pointing, the students choral respond the days of the week again in Spanish. This is repeated until the majority of the class is speaking aloud.	

Figure 16.1. Lesson plan with use of scaffolding. (Copyright © Keystone Educational Consulting Group. http://keystone-educational.com. Reprinted by permission.)

Co-Teach Lesson Plan (*continued*)

Lesson sequence *Teacher responsible:* Stations model—Ms. Carmel facilitates Station 1; Mr. Carter facilitates Station 2; Station 3 will run independently.	Teachers provide all students with a handout of the days of the week in English and Spanish. Teachers tell the students they are going to be divided into three groups. Each group will have 12 minutes at a station. Each station will have a different activity to practice learning the days of the week in Spanish. The directions for each station will be given or provided at each station. Teachers break the students into three groups and make the transition into the stations. Ms. Carmel will ring the bell, as an indicator to move stations. Station 1 will move to 2, 2 to 3, 3 to 1, and so forth until all students have participated in all stations. Teachers move to their perspective stations along with the students. Station 1: Each student will make a set of flashcards with English on one side and Spanish on the other side. (See objectives for possible adaptations.) Once the flashcards are complete, students will take turns practicing with one another and the teacher. Station 2: Each student will create a T chart graphic organizer. On one side of the T chart will be the words in English; the other side will have Spanish. The students will then work with one another and the teacher to draw a graphic depiction for each day of the week to help them remember. For example, a moon might be drawn next to lunes (lunar) to help remember Monday (Moonday). Station 3: Each student will create a wheel graphic organizer. This station will run independently without a teacher. The students may help each other or create independently. A list of the days of the week in English and Spanish will be provided to ensure accuracy of the content for the graphic organizer. As an anchor activity for any group that finishes a station early: Students will listen to the song, "I Gotta Feeling" by the Black Eyed Peas. This song incorporates the days of the week into the song. Students will then create a musical or rhythmic beat to integrate the days of the week in Spanish (e.g., The Addams Family theme song; "Row, Row, Row Your Boat").
Closing *Teacher responsible:* Team-teach model—both teachers are responsible.	Return together as whole class. Teachers ask the students to choral respond the days of the week in Spanish as a whole class. Teachers ask the students to place the flashcards on their desk. Teachers take turns saying the days of the week in English while the students hold up the corresponding flashcard in Spanish. Teachers ask if any student would like to say the days of the week aloud. Teachers ask if any groups or individuals would like to share the graphic depictions from the T chart graphic organizer. Teachers ask if any groups would like to share a song created in the anchor activity time. Teachers tell the students the final activity will be to complete a calendar page for the current or upcoming month. The students will finish the calendar by including the days of the week in Spanish. Each student will present the completed calendar page to the whole class, small group, or teacher.
Homework *Teacher responsible to assign:* Ms. Carmel *Teacher responsible to correct:* Mr. Carter	Students will have 5 days to complete the final calendar page activity. See objectives for possible adaptations.
Reflections:	To be completed after completion of the lesson.

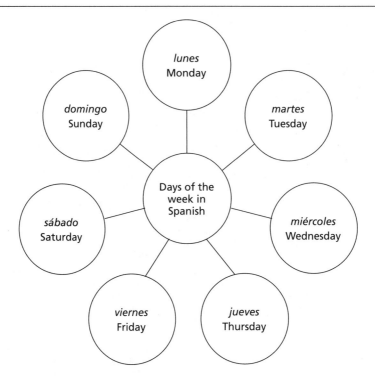

Figure 16.2   Graphic organizer for use with scaffolding.

there is only one more day left in the week, they are soon able to wave hello to the weekend.

A picture of mayonnaise may be inserted next to Friday. Some people think the word *viernes* sounds like "mayonnaise." They remember *viernes* by thinking about eating a sandwich with mayonnaise on Friday. Some families eat easy-to-fix meals on Friday (a sandwich) because they are tired after finishing the week. Saturday is often a person's favorite day of the week. Some students relax and enjoy playing video games on Saturday, or in Spanish, *sábado*. A student may connect prior knowledge with playing a video on *sábado* because both words have similar endings.

Finally, the last day of the week in Spanish is *domingo*. First, you may consider a picture of a flamingo next to *domingo*. Students may think of flamingo because it rhymes with *domingo*. The connection, or scaffold, to their prior knowledge is that they often take a vacation, or rest, on Sunday. When they think of sunny places to rest on Sunday, they may imagine seeing a flamingo. A bingo card has also been inserted next to *domingo*. A student may have relatives who like to play bingo on Sunday. Thus, they remember bingo on *domingo*. And last but not least, it might be a student's experience that their family does not like to cook on Sunday. On Sundays, the family orders pizza from Domino's. Thus, they think Domino's on *domingo* (pizza on Sunday). A picture that helps one student may not help another if their prior knowledge or experiences are not the same.

In another approach, guided notes are helpful to integrate into a lesson with scaffolding. Table 16.1 provides guided notes that outline the process of successfully incorporating the use of scaffolding with this lesson. Finally, some helpful tips are provided in Table 16.2.

Table 16.1. Guided notes for scaffolding

Steps	Application	Comments
1. Imitation without understanding	Say the days of the week with eyes closed Choral responding	Introduction of the new skill via modeling from the teacher
2. Self-guidance	Practice with a partner Use of flashcards Use of graphic organizers Create a song or poem (e.g., to the tune of "I Gotta Feeling" by the Black Eyed Peas, *The Addams Family* theme song, or "Row, Row, Row Your Boat")	Opportunity for practice with group or by self
3. Internalization	Say aloud to class, small group, or teacher Share poem or song with class Publish page of calendar	Opportunity for student to demonstrate skill can be performed independently and successfully

Source: Smith and Tyler (2010).

Possibilities for Sharing Instruction in Scaffolded Lessons

In the beginning of a collaborative relationship, two professionals who are sharing instructional responsibilities often begin by using the one teach/one assist model of co-teaching. To implement the example of learning the days of the week in Spanish by using the one teach/one assist model, one teacher would take the primary lead of the lesson for introducing the days of the week in Spanish, while the other teacher would assist with the lesson. Assisting the students may entail prompting and cueing as necessary, helping students to stay on task, and possibly classroom management tasks such helping students get materials, signing students in and out for restroom passes, and sharpening pencils.

As both teachers evolve in the Co-Design Model, they should become more fluent in the other co-teaching models (Chapter 13). As in the sample lesson plan, both teachers may plan for and facilitate learning in the stations model while implementing the technique of scaffolding. As described in the lesson plan, three stations would be used. At one station, the objective is to complete flashcards of the days of the week. At the other two stations, the objective is to complete graphic organizers. All three of these stations promote scaffolding.

The parallel model of co-teaching can also support scaffolding for this particular lesson. One teacher may be responsible for helping half of the class complete a graphic organizer along with participating in choral responding. The other teacher leads the other students in completing flashcards and guided notes. The initial groups would continue for approximately half of the class time, and then the groups would switch for the remainder of the period.

Once the teachers have reached a collaborative level in their relationship within the Co-Design Model, they will be able to model scaffolding to the students within the team-teaching model of co-teaching. For this model, the instructors "share the stage" during a lesson. In this example, one teacher may introduce the days of the week in Spanish. As this teacher introduces each new word, the other teacher "bounces" out ideas and makes connections with his or her prior knowledge for the students to hear. In this way, the two teachers are modeling scaffolding. The students are

Table 16.2.   Helpful tips for scaffolding

Scaffold in groups or with partners.
>   Work in small groups or with partners promotes social interactions.
>   Social interaction is important for internalizing information.

Organize students into heterogeneous groups.
>   Heterogeneous groups provide a mix of ability for academic and behavioral needs within each small group of students.
>   More knowledgeable peers will help to advance the learning of others in the group.
>   Modeling of appropriate behavior in the groups by majority of members is a positive experience for students with behavioral needs.
>   Students should be grouped on the basis of existing data on academic and behavioral needs.

Allow for teacher prompting.
>   Teacher facilitation should be available to all groups.

Provide guided notes for students.
>   Guided notes assist the students in processing the steps of scaffolding their learning.

Monitor progress.
>   Progress monitoring ensures that all group members are learning.

Build on prior knowledge.
>   All students have differing prior experiences and thus different prior knowledge.
>   Making connections to student' prior knowledge will help them acquire and retain the new skills.

Sources: Hammond (2002); Pennsylvania Department of Education (2009); and Smith and Tyler (2010).

then encouraged to participate in this oral scaffolding to help network, through social interactions, to make their own connections of new knowledge with prior knowledge.

As with all lessons, some students may finish the activity early. It is suggested that teachers provide anchor activities to allow for a productive use of time for even those students who complete the tasks with time to spare. Additional practice of a skill is a component of successful scaffolding. For this example, music could be integrated into the lesson via an anchor activity. The lyrics of the song "I Gotta Feeling" by the Black Eyed Peas contain the days of the week. This song could be played for the students as an example of incorporating the content into the song. The students would then be challenged to incorporate the days of the week in Spanish into either that song or another song that is familiar to them. A popular choice is using the theme song from the *The Addams Family* television show to learn the days of the week in Spanish.

CONCLUSION

Scaffolding is a widely recognized recommended practice (IRIS Center for Training Advancements, n.d.; PDE, 2009; Reid & Lienemann, 2006; Smith & Tyler, 2010). Scaffolding is proven as a technique to offer supports to learners while helping them become independent learners. Scaffolding promotes mastery of learning by building on prior knowledge. The strategy also encourages learning via socialization between peers and through teacher prompting (Hammond, 2002; PDE, 2009; Smith & Tyler, 2010).

We advocate use of scaffolding because it may be used to integrate many research-based recommended practices as well as being a recommended practice in itself. It also lends itself well to co-teaching in a collaborative environment, as discussed in this chapter. Instructional strategies promoted via scaffolding include writing through scaffolded writing, making inferences, differentiated instruction, graphic organizers, and guided notes (PDE, 2009; Smith & Tyler, 2010). Carter, Prater, and Dyches (2008) state that scaffolding advances the likelihood for success in meeting learning objectives. Scaffolding techniques are useful for many content areas, including reading, writing, science, social studies, and more (Beers, 2003; Bodrova & Leong, 2007). For these reasons, scaffolding is endorsed as a pathway to achieve success with the Co-Design Model.

REFERENCES

Beers, K. (2003). *When kids can't read: What teachers can do—A guide for teachers 6–12.* Portsmouth, NH: Heinemann.

Bodrova, E., & Leong, D.J. (2007). *Tools of the mind: The Vygotskian approach to early childhood education* (2nd ed.). Upper Saddle River, NJ: Merrill.

Carter, N., Prater, M.A., & Dyches, T.T. (2008). *What every teacher should know about: Making adaptations and accommodations for students with mild to moderate disabilities.* Upper Saddle River, NJ: Pearson Education.

Daniels, H. (2001). *Vygotsky and Pedagogy.* New York, NY: Routledge/Falmer.

Donovan, C., & Smolkin, L. (2002). Children's genre knowledge: An examination of K–5 students' performance on multiple tasks providing differing levels of scaffolding. *Reading Research Quarterly , 37*(4), 428–465.

Hammond, J. (Ed.). (2002). *Scaffolding teaching and learning in language and literacy education .* Newtown, Australia: Primary English Teacher Association.

IRIS Center for Training Advancements. (n.d.). *STAR legacy module: Providing instructional supports: Facilitating mastery of new skills.* Nashville, TN: Vanderbilt University. Retrieved from http://iris.peabody.vanderbilt.edu/sca/chalcycle.htm

Lloyd, P., & Fernyhough, C. (Eds.). (1999). *Lev Vygotsky: Critical assessments.* New York, NY: Routledge.

McDevitt, T.M., & Ormrod, J.E. (2002). *Child development and education.* Upper Saddle River, NJ: Merrill Prentice Hall.

Pennsylvania Department of Education. (2009). *Teaching matters.* Retrieved from http://www.learningport.us/resource/?course_id=682

Reid, R., & Lienemann, T.O. (2006). Strategy instruction for students with learning disabilities. In D.D. Smith & N.C. Tyler (Eds.), *Introduction to special education: Making a difference* (7th ed.). Upper Saddle River, NJ: Pearson.

Smith, D.D., & Tyler, N.C. (2010). *Introduction to special education: Making a difference* (7th ed.). Upper Saddle River, NJ: Merrill.

Stone, A. (1998). The metaphor of scaffolding: Its utility for the field of learning disabilities. *Journal of Learning Disabilities, 3*(4), 344–364.

Vygotsky, L.S. (1978). *Mind in society: The development of higher psychological processes* (M. Cole, V. John-Steiner, S. Scribner, & E. Souberman, Eds.). Cambridge, MA: Harvard University Press.

Wells, G. (1999). *Dialogic inquiry: Towards a sociocultural practice and theory of education.* New York, NY: Cambridge University Press.

SECTION **III**

Conclusion

CHAPTER **17**

Training and Professional Development

The task of leadership is not to put greatness into humanity, but to elicit it, for the greatness is already there.

John Buchan, 1st Baron Tweedsmuir (1930)

The challenges and responsibilities facing teachers and administrators are greater today than ever before. Yet the noble task of educating America's youth remains the same. A successful educational leader is one who must face the responsibility to prepare our children and educators to meet the challenges of tomorrow. This quest for excellence cannot be conquered alone. It takes collaboration, support, and the constant training of the community, parents, students, and quality educators to achieve a school district's inspired mission.

Creating a framework for professional development that is consistent and supports the needs of your teachers and students instills the confidence they require to be successful. Within my 2 years at Sto-Rox serving as Supervisor of Special Education, developing and maintaining a successful professional development program have been at the top of my list to ensure that our students receive quality services and education. The programs and collaborating professionals have instilled self-confidence, a sense of belonging, and positive rapport, particularly with our paraprofessionals and special education teachers. Professional development instills best practices and continued education to allow individuals to become better at what they do. I believe Atul Gawande, author of the book *Better: A Surgeon's Notes on Performance* (2007), captures the importance of professional development, teamwork, and collaboration best by stating, "Success is difficult to measure, even harder to achieve, and is almost always a team effort, requiring 'a hundred small steps to go right.' But we must always try. Because only then will we all do better" (p. 21).

By Erin Grimm, IDEA Training and Consultation Coordinator,
Allegheny Intermediate Unit, and former Special Education Supervisor of
Sto-Rox School District, serving Stowe Township and McKees Rocks, Pennsylvania

This portion of the book addresses the importance of training and ongoing support via professional development, measuring success and data collection, and concluding thoughts. This chapter discusses training at the preservice level as well as professional development, which includes both training and support, for teachers in the field.

159

Professional development is also necessary for administrators and paraprofessionals. Professional development that has been prepared with teachers' input and assistance is more likely to influence the instruction occurring in the classroom (McClesky & Waldron, 2002). In accordance with this finding, the No Child Left Behind Act of 2001 calls for teacher assistance while planning professional development (Billingsley, 2005). This step helps to alleviate the attitude of nonenthusiasm many teachers bring to in-service days (Sergiovanni & Starratt, 2002). Also, the ongoing professional development of teachers must be taken into account (Jenkins & Yoshimura, 2010). Finally, there are many other factors for successful professional development that should be planned for, such as administration involvement, inclusion of paraprofessionals, peer networking, administrative support, use of outside consultants, web-based support, access to professional resources, and funding concerns.

TRAINING FOR PRESERVICE TEACHERS AND PROFESSIONAL DEVELOPMENT FOR ACTIVE TEACHERS, ADMINISTRATORS, AND STAFF

For inclusion to be successful, it is essential that both preservice teachers and teachers in the field receive training in the rationale behind co-teaching and strategies for implementation. Teachers must be informed about why they are being scheduled to co-teach, and their questions, concerns, and fears must be addressed (Villa, Thousand, & Nevin, 2004). One common source of concern is lack of knowledge on the part of general education teachers about teaching students with disabilities (Cook, 2000; Kavale & Forness, 2000), which can lead to negative attitudes toward inclusive classrooms (Silverman, 2007). Given such lack of knowledge, one must ask whether the students with disabilities in these inclusive classrooms are receiving appropriate instruction to meet their individual needs.

If additional training is provided to teachers in the area of instructing students in special education, teachers may be more willing and more positive and effective in the approach to inclusive and collaborative education. Currently, additional training in the area of special education is not a requirement of teachers in the field. Therefore, attitudes may *not* change (Shade & Stewart, 2001). This is an important reason why the Co-Design Model needs to be implemented within educational systems.

Two additional concerns identified by teachers regarding inclusion are 1) the possibility that inclusive practices may negatively affect general education students in the class (Kavale & Forness, 2000) and 2) that inclusion will result in more work for the instructors. Teachers already maintain a busy schedule. A concern is that more inclusive and collaborative practices will equal more time and energy. It was found that with training and support, these feelings will subside (Barger-Anderson, Isherwood, & Merhaut, 2010; Isherwood & Barger-Anderson, 2007).

O'Rourke, Main, and Cooper (2008) found that preservice teachers in grades K–12 had, overall, a positive outlook toward inclusive classrooms. In some states, all teacher candidates, regardless of content area, are now being required to take a certain amount of special education, English language learner coursework, or both (e.g., PDE, 2010).

The Co-Design Model promotes training in the area of collaborative and inclusive practices that will support preservice teachers and teachers in the field. This includes training, via professional development, for general and special educators at levels from preschool through secondary, speech and language therapists, reading specialists, and all other professionals in the classroom. Professional development is also recommended for paraprofessionals and administrators. The Co-Design Model holds that a one-time training session with participants is not enough. Jenkins and Yoshimura concur that training needs to be more than a "one shot in-service" (2010, p. 36). It is necessary to provide follow-up training and ongoing support to faculty, staff, and administration involved in collaborative and inclusive practices (Barger-Anderson et al., 2010; Isherwood & Barger-Anderson, 2007).

Avramidis, Bayliss, and Burden (2000) found that general educators with more professional development in the area of inclusion were more likely to have positive attitudes toward the inclusion of students with special needs. The next section of the chapter considers factors that promote ongoing, administration-supported development for faculty and staff in the area of inclusion and collaborative instruction.

ONGOING SUPPORT VIA PROFESSIONAL DEVELOPMENT

Teacher attitudes toward inclusive classrooms are connected to levels of training, knowledge, and experience in working with students with disabilities. The more training and knowledge obtained by the teachers in the area of special education, the less negative the attitudes toward promotion for inclusion (Van Reusen, Shoho, & Barker, 2000). Leatherman and Niemeyer (2005) concur that more training and knowledge is helpful in attaining a positive approach to inclusive and collaborative education. These authors found that previous experience with inclusion also played a role in the acceptance of inclusive practices. The factors highlighted as important by these authors include preservice training, support from administrators, and support via collaboration with resource staff.

Ongoing support (maintenance) within a professional development program is an indispensable step to promote success (Jenkins & Yoshimura, 2010). The Co-Design Model promotes ongoing support via professional development activities in five areas: administration, outside consultants, web-based support, professional resources, and peer networking. The Co-Design Model promotes using any or all of these avenues to support teachers, staff, administrators, and preservice teachers. When possible, it is best for all parties (or as many as possible) to receive the same professional development experiences to help ensure that colleagues working within the same collaborative environment and expectations are working from the same training framework. This professional development may be completed in small groups; in large groups; in a heterogeneous group of participants that includes administration, teachers, and paraprofessionals; or in homogenous groups. Figures 17.1 and 17.2 present the models for training and ongoing support within the Co-Design Model (Barger-Anderson et al., 2010).

Administration and Outside Consultants

When examining co-teaching relationships and the importance of ongoing training and support, Isherwood and Barger-Anderson (2007) found that teachers respond favorably to frequent observations in the classroom by their administrators. Such observations validate the teachers' efforts and energy and send a message that the initiative of collaborative practices is embraced at the administrative level. This study found a connection between success and feedback and number of visits by administrators with the faculty and staff.

The use of outside consultants is another option for providing feedback via observations. The Co-Design Model promotes the use of outside consultants only if school districts have the monetary funds to support such assistance. Outside consultants who provide training and conduct follow-up observations in the classrooms

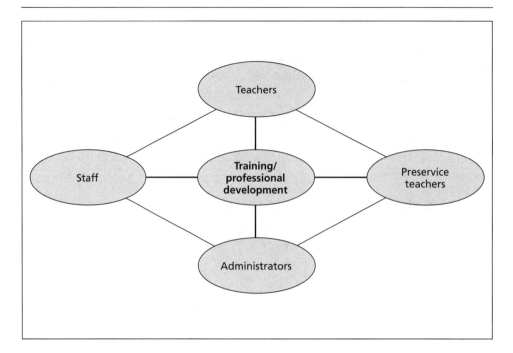

Figure 17.1.   Training and professional development. (From Barger-Anderson, R., Isherwood, R., & Merhaut, J. [2010, February]. *The Co-Design Model: A collaborative approach to inclusive education.* Paper presented at the 47th Annual International Conference of the Learning Disabilities Association of America, Baltimore, MD; adapted by permission.)

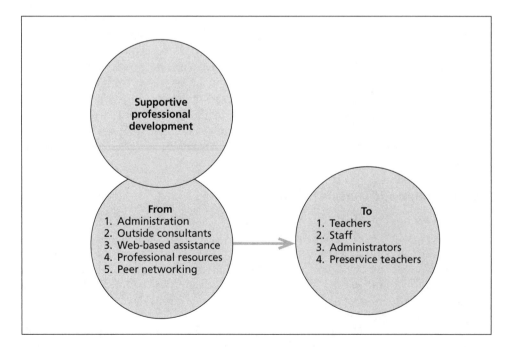

Figure 17.2.   Professional development: ongoing support. (From Barger-Anderson, R., Isherwood, R., & Merhaut, J. [2010, February]. *The Co-Design Model: A collaborative approach to inclusive education.* Paper presented at the 47th Annual International Conference of the Learning Disabilities Association of America, Baltimore, MD; adapted by permission.)

build rapport and trust with the collaborative partners. Time for pre- and postobservation conferences between the observees and the observers is always recommended (Barger-Anderson et al., 2010).

Consultants can provide large-group professional development training as well as small-group training. These training sessions should be tailored to provide resources specific for district needs. Small-group training and classroom visitations may consider individual teacher needs, classroom needs, and individual student needs before and after observations (McClesky & Waldron, 2002). Outside consultants may serve as a liaison among the teachers, staff, and administration and provide ongoing support for administration (Barger-Anderson et al., 2010). Figures 17.3 and 17.4 present examples of a completed Co-Teaching Observation form and Co-Teaching Postobservation Conference form that report on the collaborative environment created by two teachers. (Reproducible versions of these forms are provided in the appendix.) This particular observation was completed by an outside consultant. The two teachers, Denise Heiligenstein and Michael Henry, are faculty members of the Seneca Valley Area School District at the intermediate level. This school district is located in the southern region of Butler County, Pennsylvania. Mr. Henry is a general education teacher, and Ms. Heiligenstein serves as a learning support teacher. These observation forms may be used by administrators, outside consultants, peers, and preservice teachers when conducting observations of co-teaching.

Web-Based Support, Professional Resources, and Peer Networking

As with many school reform initiatives, implementing collaborative practices is a complex process. With change come challenges to the initiative that can determine success or failure. School administrators and faculty members can be proactive in trying to prevent the roadblocks and avoid failure if they spend time reviewing the research on co-teaching and listening to the experiences of schools that have already implemented this strategy (Isherwood, Barger-Anderson, Merhaut, Badgett, & Katsafanas, 2011; Jenkins & Yoshimura, 2010). In addition to using the support provided by administration and outside consultants, administrators, teachers, staff, and preservice teachers are encouraged to find knowledge, guidance, and support through three other sources: 1) web-based support, 2) professional resources, and 3) peer networking.

When using the Internet for web-based support, various teacher-generated web sites, such as TeacherTube (http://www.teachertube.com), and other professional sites, such as that of the Council for Exceptional Children (http://www.cec.sped.org) may be advantageous. Chapter 15 gives many resources for using technology within the Co-Design Model.

Professional resources may include access to professional journals, either online or by subscriptions mailed to the school districts (Barger-Anderson et al., 2010). A trend in some school districts is to have a "book of the year" that the district purchases for teachers to read. The teachers then meet once a month to conduct literature circles to discuss and digest the content (M. Miller, personal communication with Richael Barger-Anderson, August 16, 2010). Administrators may find it especially helpful to review the chapters in this book on leadership, curriculum knowledge, personality types, and co-design time (Chapters 4, 6, 11, and 12, respectively) when troubleshooting some of the frequent concerns encountered with establishing collaborative environments in a school setting. These chapters highlight some of the research available and address areas of the Co-Design Model that can help educational leaders address collaborative issues. Some of these research areas include the creation of supportive environments, pairing teachers according to curriculum knowledge and personality

Co-Teaching Observation Form

General education teacher: Mr Henry

Co-teacher: Ms. Heiligenstein

Viewer name: Dr. Richael Barger-Anderson

Subject: History   Grade: 10th

Date of observation: April 7   Time: 3rd pd.

Directions: *Check "Y" if the behavior is observed and "N" if it is not observed during the lesson.*

I. Professionalism

1. Both teachers were present at the beginning of the period.   Y_X___   N_____
2. Both teachers appear to have positive rapport with all students.   Y_X___   N_____
3. Both teachers managed some aspect of the instruction.   Y_X___   N_____
4. Both teachers communicated in a positive manner with each other.   Y_X___   N_____
5. There were equal spaces for both co-teachers in the classroom.   Y_X___   N_____
6. The names of both co-teachers appear on important class documents.   Y_X___   N_____

II. Instruction

1. Both teachers provided instruction to some or all of the students.   Y_X___   N_____
2. There was evidence that at least one co-teaching model was used.   Y_X___   N_____
   (Circle model[s] used: parallel, alternative, stations, (team,) one teach/one assist)
3. Evidence of differentiated instruction was observed.   Y_X___   N_____
4. Students were organized for instruction based on needs.   Y_X___   N_____
5. Lesson was delivered utilizing more than one modality.   Y_X___   N_____
6. Co-teachers implemented instruction through group work or in pairs.   Y_X___   N_____
7. Both teachers used questioning strategies to engage students.   Y_X___   N_____
8. Both teachers provided scaffolding during learning opportunities.   Y_X___   N_____
9. Teachers modeled intellectual discussion with each other during lesson.   Y_X___   N_____
10. Students asked both teachers for assistance or clarification.   Y_X___   N_____

III. Assessment

1. Both teachers checked students for understanding during the lesson.   Y_X___   N_____
2. Adaptations were made to assessments based on students' needs.   Y_X___   N_____
3. Assessment data were used to group students for instruction.   Y_X___   N_____
4. Both teachers were responsible for grading student work.   Y_X___   N_____
5. Both teachers were responsible for evaluating all students.   Y_X___   N_____

IV. Classroom management

1. Both teachers actively and consistently reinforced rules.   Y_X___   N_____
2. Both teachers implemented behavior plans for individual students.   Y_X___   N_____
3. Both teachers redirected off-task behavior when observed.   Y_X___   N_____
4. Both teachers handled some aspect of the housekeeping duties.   Y_X___   N_____

Directions: *Provide narrative feedback of the observation in this section. Results should be shared with the teacher(s), either individually or as a team.*

Teacher communication   *(level of verbal and nonverbal communication between both co-teachers and between co-teachers and students):*

A shared environment in the classroom was clear and evident. Both teachers display a confidence and sense of ownership in the classroom.

Verbal and nonverbal communications were positive.

Both teachers are creating a nurturing, student-friendly classroom.

Figure 17.3.   Example of completed Co-Teaching Observation Form. (Copyright © 2013 by Keystone Educational Consulting Group. http://www.keystone-educational.com. Reprinted by permission.)

Co-Teaching Observation Form (*continued*)

Physical organization   *(evidence that the room is shared between co-teachers, two teacher desks, and so on):*

Through posting of both names outside the classroom, within the classroom and on class documents, a collaborative environment is promoted.

Materials were readily available.

Objectives, procedure, materials, and homework clearly posted in front of room.

Classroom management   *(establishment of rules, explanation of rules to students, enforcement of rules and consequences, parent contacts, establishing a sense of shared teaching as equals to the students and the parents):*

High levels of engagement promoted for all students throughout the lesson.

Music played at the start of class that connects with the objectives for the day. This really helps to create an environment that promotes learning and connects knowledge to their learning style.

Rapport and respect are shared among the teachers and students.

Impressive!

Entrance slips at start of class help to use every minute of class for instructional time.

Lesson/assessment planning   *(establishment of scope and sequence, identification of type of co-teach model[s], state standards addressed, shared creation of materials):*

We can discuss this during the debriefing time.

It is obvious that some planning time is either available or being "found" by this co-teaching team.

Adaptations/modifications   *(adjustments made to curriculum materials, allowance for additional time, physical space adjustments to allow for full participation, subtlety of arrangements, success of all students, and so on):*

Music

Visuals via technology

Questioning techniques by both teachers

Opportunities for student questions and engagement

Use of scaffolding to connect content to student experiences

Voice level

Word bank for whiteboard activity

Video clip

Choral responding

Instructional presentation   *(implementation of a co-teach model, variety of learning modalities addressed, differentiated instruction, active student participation, small-group work or pairs utilized, students address both teachers, and so on):*

Super! What a terrific and effective use of the co-teaching model. Both teachers are using skill sets the entire time. Both teachers are sharing the responsibilities of the classroom equally.

This is an example of co-teaching at the collaborative stage.

I would classify this lesson as a form of the team-teaching model.

I had a hard time writing this observation report because I wanted to participate in the lesson ☺.

Variety of learning modalities via visuals, music, whiteboards, entrance slips, artifacts to show students (bread, sawdust, hard tack), movie trailer.

Excellent use of questions and activities to promote higher levels of learning (application, evaluation,...)

Choral responding is a great strategy—nice job.

Nice idea to share and suggest current movies on the topics.

Whiteboard activity with map. Useful as a form of assessment and review.

Please be sure to check out our web site at www.keystone-educational.com for more information and ideas on use of the co-teach models, anchor activities, differentiated instruction, and more.

I will email some information on question cubes that you might find helpful.

Assessment   *(variety of forms, authentic, both co-teachers grade assignments and create and grade assessments, and so on):*

Variety of assessment forms in lesson: observation, entrance slips, checklists

Co-Teaching Postobservation Conference Form

General education teacher: _Mr Henry_

Co-teacher: _Ms. Heiligenstein_

Viewer name: _Dr. Richael Barger-Anderson_

Subject: _History_   Grade: _10th_

Date of observation: _April 7_   Time: _3rd pd._

Directions: *Provide narrative feedback on the observation. Results should be shared with the teacher(s) either individually or as a team.*

Overall strengths of the view:

– Knowledge of content

– Ability to bring content to life

– High expectations for students to perform

– Positive attitude of teachers

– Rapport established with the students by both teachers

Keep up the great work! I hope I am able to visit your classroom again. Please invite other co-teaching teams from the district to observe your lessons.

Target areas for the next view (*identify what needs improvement*):

Continue to address multiple learning styles.

Continue to make learning environment welcoming and inviting.

Continue to use the 5 models of co-teaching.

Continue to maximize the learning potential via excellent use of time and classroom management skills.

Action for improvement (*discuss strategies for improvement*):

Continue to look for available times to meet for co-designing of the lessons. It is always difficult to have enough time for planning.

Thank you! I look forward to my next visit.

Figure 17.4. Example of completed Co-Teaching Postobservation Conference feedback form. (Copyright © 2013 by Keystone Educational Consulting Group. http://www.keystone-educational.com. Reprinted by permission.)

compatibility, and scheduling common planning time to give teachers the chance to design collaborative lessons and collaborative learning environments.

The third source of support for collaborative and inclusive efforts is peer networking. The Co-Design Model advocates peer networking both within and between school systems. Peers may share helpful tips on scheduling, creative ways to find common planning time, and useful web-based sources and professional resources. Teachers may observe each other for modeling of teaching techniques and strategies and ideas for classroom management and arrangement of the physical space. It is suggested that peers visit one another's classroom within the same district and in neighboring districts. Administrators can support these actions by arranging for coverage for teachers to conduct these observations, by providing transportation for visits to neighboring districts, and by attending the visits themselves. Administrators may find it beneficial to conduct roundtable discussions with other administrators and teachers during such site visits (Barger-Anderson et al., 2010).

FUNDING CONCERNS

Outside consultants are not necessary to the implementation of the Co-Design Model, but for schools pursuing such assistance, there is the critical question of availability of funds. Entering into a long-term relationship with outside consultants may seem expensive. Possible funding sources including external grants, federal monies earmarked for special education initiatives, and other legitimate transfers of allocated funds within the budget.

Establishing train-the-trainer models within the school system is an economical route for provision of professional development, both training and ongoing support. In such models, the district funds only a small number of the faculty and staff to be trained by experts from outside the district. This training may occur at conferences, remote sites, or on site. The trained faculty and staff are then responsible for training and supporting others in the district (Poplin, 2003). By contrast, the Co-Design Model advocates that all participants receive professional development firsthand. That is, the faculty, paraprofessionals, and administrators involved in inclusive instruction should attend professional development sessions and receive the follow-up assistance. Train-the-trainer models are suggested here only because they offer a cost-effective way to ensure that some professional development, both training and support, does occur if funds are not available for large-group training, site visitation, and ongoing support from consultants.

CONCLUSION

When schools implement inclusive classrooms, it is necessary to reduce fear, provide support, and offer professional development to all parties involved—teachers, administrators, and staff. These items are critical in establishing a positive attitude toward collaboration and inclusive classrooms on the part of all participants. Reducing fear and replacing concerns with knowledge and support will promote learning and collaborative practices not only for students with disabilities but also for students in general education. General educators who embrace beliefs and contribute actions to support collaboration represent a substantial portion of teachers finding success in the special education process (Kavale & Forness, 2000).

Training, via professional development, at both the preservice level and for practicing teachers, staff, and administrators, is important, as is ongoing support (Avramidis et al., 2000; Shade & Stewart, 2001; Villa, Thousand, & Nevin, 2004), though teachers often fear they are losing too much of their valuable time (Jenkins & Yoshimura, 2010). Ongoing support may be realized in various ways. Possible ongoing support may be found through administrative support via provisions for outside consultants, web-based assistance, professional resources, and peer networking. The type and level of support is often determined by funding concerns. Because the funds allocated for professional development and support will vary widely, the Co-Design Model will look different from district to district.

In conclusion, the following quote from a graduate student in special education illustrates well the need for and benefits of training and support for collaboration:

> I love the concept of co-teaching because I feel that it does have the potential to help all students, but couldn't agree more with the concerns presented by Dr. Barger-Anderson; I have felt all of them. When I worked at the high school level as a special education teacher, I was in many different classrooms throughout the day. I have felt like I was intruding in some classrooms, like I didn't have enough content knowledge of the subject in other classes, and like a teaching aide in others. I was fortunate enough, however, to be a part of the team-teaching model for co-teaching with one teacher. We were able to mesh our teaching styles to not only provide a great experience for the students, but for us as teachers as well. This was an example of two teachers who were open to the idea of co-teaching and the students really benefited.

Co-teaching does take practice. In another class I co-taught in, I would describe the co-teaching method as one teach/one assist. It took several months for the teacher and me to develop a system that really worked for the students. I did not find the one teach/one assist approach as rewarding for me, but the students did benefit from having another teacher in the room. Even though the district I work in has provided many in-service training sessions on co-teaching I think the concept has a long way to come. Due to the benefits I personally witnessed in some of the classes I was involved in, I hope the concept of co-teaching continues to be focused upon and that ongoing training and administrative support is provided so that teachers continue to develop an understanding of it and realize that it is not going away. (Needham, 2010)

REFERENCES

Avramidis, E., Bayliss, P., & Burden, R. (2000). Student teachers' attitudes towards the inclusion of children with special educational needs in the ordinary school. *Teaching and Teacher Education, 16*(3), 277–293.

Barger-Anderson, R., Isherwood, R., & Merhaut, J. (2010, February). *The Co-Design Model: A collaborative approach to inclusive education.* Paper presented at the 47th Annual International Conference of the Learning Disabilities Association of America, Baltimore, MD.

Billingsley, B.S. (2005). *Designing effective professional development in cultivating and keeping committed special education teachers: What principals and district leaders can do.* Thousand Oaks, CA: Corwin Press and Council for Exceptional Children.

Buchan, J. (1930). *Montrose and leadership.* London, United Kingdom: Oxford University Press.

Cook, B.G. (2000). Teachers' attitudes toward their included students with disabilities. *Exceptional Children, 67*(1), 115–135.

Gwande, A. (2007). *Better: A surgeon's notes on performance.* New York, NY: Henry Holt.

Isherwood, R.S., & Barger-Anderson, R. (2007). Factors affecting the adoption of co-teaching models in inclusive classrooms: One school's journey from mainstreaming to inclusion. *Journal of Ethnographic and Qualitative Research, 2,* 121–128.

Isherwood, R., Barger-Anderson, R., Merhaut, J., Badgett, R., & Katsafanas, J. (2011). First year co-teaching: Disclosed through focus group and individual interviews. *Learning Disabilities: A Multidisciplinary Journal, 17*(3), 113–122.

Jenkins, A.A., & Yoshimura, J. (2010). Not another in-service! Meeting the special education professional development needs of elementary general educators. *Teaching Exceptional Children, 42*(5), 36–43.

Kavale, K.A., & Forness, S.R. (2000). History, rhetoric, and reality: Analysis of the inclusion debate. *Remedial and Special Education, 21*(5), 279–296.

Leatherman, J.M., & Niemeyer, J.A. (2005). Teachers' attitudes toward inclusion: Factors affecting classroom practices. *Journal of Early Childhood Teacher Education, 26,* 23–36.

McClesky, J., & Waldron, N.L. (2002). Professional development and inclusion schools: Reflections on effective practice. *The Teacher Educator, 37,* 159–173.

Needham, A. (2010, July 15). *Re: Co-teaching is wonderful* [Online forum comment]. Retrieved from http://sru.desire2learn.com/d2l/1ms/discussions/messageLists/frame.d2l?isShared=tid=1420599&ou=63230

No Child Left Behind Act of 2001, PL 107-110, 115 Stat. 1425, 20 U.S.C. §§ 6301 *et seq.*

O'Rourke, J., Main, S., & Cooper, M. (2008). Secondary v. K–7: Preservice teachers' attitudes toward inclusion. *The International Journal of Learning, 15*(7), 97–104.

Pennsylvania Department of Education. (2010). *Chapter 49 web site.* Retrieved from http://www.portal.state.pa.us/portal/server.pt/community/chapter_49

Poplin, C. (2003). Models of professional development. *T.H.E. Journal, 30*(11), 38–40.

Sergiovanni, T.J., & Starratt, R.J. (2002). Supervision as professional development and renewal. In T.J. Sergiovanni & R.J. Starratt (Eds.), *Supervision: A redefinition* (7th ed.) (pp. 205–220). Boston: MA: McGraw Hill.

Shade, R.A., & Stewart, R. (2001). General education and special education preservice teachers' attitudes toward inclusion. *Preventing School Failure, 46*(1), 37–41.

Silverman, J.C. (2007). Epistemological beliefs and attitudes toward inclusion in preservice teachers. *Teacher Education and Special Education, 30*(1), 42–51.

Van Reusen, A.K., Shoho, A.R., & Barker, K.S. (2000). High school teacher attitudes toward inclusion. *The High School Journal, 84*(2), 7–20.

Villa, R.A., Thousand, J.S., & Nevin, A.I. (2004). *A guide to co-teaching: Practical tips for facilitating student learning.* Thousand Oaks, CA: Sage Publications.

CHAPTER 18

Measuring Success and Closing Thoughts

It is almost a given these days that kids will go to preschool to gain socialization and beginning academic skills before heading into the official start of their schooling in kindergarten. And as young parents some years ago, that is also what we wanted for our children—*all* our children. Our older daughter Stephanie had been enrolled in a large, thriving, well-established program that offered a wide variety of both preschool and private kindergarten classes. She had graduated from that program and was already fully immersed in the second grade at our local public school when it was time for us to consider preschool options for our 3-year-old twins, Alek and Sarah. We had been quite happy with Stephanie's experience at the large, well-known program and decided with little hesitation to enroll our twins there as well. But to our surprise, they turned us away. You see, Alek has Down syndrome, and the director of the preschool program informed us that they were not equipped to handle a child with "special" needs. Mind you, at this age his "needs" were not that "special" in comparison with other 3-year-olds. He was toilet trained but needed help to remember to wash his hands. He loved music and loud group activities but needed a lot of help redirecting his attention during quiet times. He enjoyed being around other kids but needed help learning how to share the toys.

Knowing a bit about the laws and our legal rights, we knew we could probably hire a lawyer (or even ask the local chapter of the American Civil Liberties Union to supply one) to fight for Alek's right to equal educational opportunities. But when it came to our child's education, we really wanted him to be in a place where he would be accepted willingly, rather than insisting he attend school in a place that was "forced" to accommodate him. So we looked elsewhere in town and ended up finding a small, fledgling program that looked like it might be a good fit. When we discussed the possibility of the new, small preschool accommodating Alek's "special" needs, the director of the program indicated that they did not have much experience with nontypical kids but were willing to work with us on a trial basis to see if they could provide necessary supports for Alek. It was January and we would reassess the situation at the end of the school year in May. Over the next few months, with the addition of a classroom aide and a few parent/teacher meetings, things seemed to be going smoothly. When discussions started in May about placements for the following fall, we hesitantly broached the subject of whether or not Alek would return the following year. The teacher and director were surprised by the question. "Why wouldn't we take him back?" was their immediate reply. The thought of turning him away had never crossed their minds. This small program, with far fewer resources than the large, established preschool, had learned how to adjust and adapt their program in ways that ended up benefiting all the kids in the program, not just Alek.

Fast-forward 13 years…. A friend of ours from Boy Scouts, who knows Alek well, recently took a position teaching at the large, established preschool that Stephanie had attended and was surprised to hear from us that Alek had been turned away. According to our friend, this preschool is now absolutely dedicated to serving *all* children who wish to attend, so much so that they have even established a scholarship to annually support tuition for a child with special needs. And during a recent local Down Syndrome Society gathering we relayed the story of our preschool experience to a family whose 3-year-old is currently enrolled in that same large preschool. We indicated that we were glad the school had changed its policies since turning Alek away 13 years earlier. The family was surprised and couldn't wait to tell us the impact this event had had on the preschool. The mom had recently been talking with the director of the large, established preschool about their open policy toward special needs children. The director recounted to the mom that years ago, when she was a new director at the school, a family with a special needs son had inquired about enrollment, and she had turned them away, fearing that her facility did not have the knowledge or the resources to accommodate his needs. But after that moment, regretting the decision she had made, she vowed to change her program so they would not have to turn away another child. In the end, the large, established program had also changed for the better.

The take-away message from our story is this: When you are a teacher or a principal or even a preschool director, whether your program is small and new and short on resources or large and established with abundant resources, never be afraid to adapt and change. Through collaboration, it is possible to adapt and change to make education a more rewarding experience for everyone.

By Chris and Rob Masters, proud parents of Alek, Sarah, Stephanie, and Bart

The purpose of the final chapter of this book is to reemphasize the message that has been featured in every chapter: the importance of collaboration. Collaboration between special and general educators is growing in today's schools, to the point that it is no longer considered unusual. This change is gradual but nonetheless occurring (Cullen, 2007). Friend and Cook (2010) state that many times a teacher's ability to work well with others is as important to achieving success as is the teacher's skill set and training. To reap the maximum rewards of collaboration between professionals, the individuals must recognize each other's strengths and, many times, differing areas of expertise (Kloo & Zigmond, 2008; Little & Dieker, 2009). With this chapter, we want to motivate readers to work to increase meaningful inclusive education in a shared environment.

BENEFITS TO VARIED TYPES OF LEARNERS

First, this chapter examines the impact of inclusive and collaborative practices not only for children who qualify to receive services in special education, but also for students who are gifted and talented, students considered "at risk," and English language learners.

Students Identified for Special Education and "Typical" Learners

Is a co-teaching classroom more beneficial for students identified with disabilities than solo-taught classrooms? Even though research to answer this question is inconclusive, studies have been conducted to identify factors that promote successful co-teaching. Magiera and Zigmond (2005) studied co-teaching in a middle school. They found that teachers may need training and common planning time to ensure that both teachers are committed and active in delivery of instruction. Specifically, it was found that when the special education co-teacher was present, the general education teacher spent considerably less time with the students identified with a disability. The general education teacher focused more on the "typical" learners. Also, the special education teacher spent more one-on-one time with students with disabilities. With proper training and common planning, co-teaching may take a dynamic form in which both parties are actively engaged in instruction of all students. When this occurs, learning by both the "typical" learner and the student identified with a disability will be positively impacted.

Murawski (2006) concurs with the findings of Magiera and Zigmond (2005). Her research findings suggest little to no benefit in co-teaching unless proper training, respect for one's co-teaching partners' skill set (parity), and common planning time occur. The results from this study clearly show that without administration support and professional development, no matter how willing the co-teaching partners are to share the classroom space and responsibilities, use of two professionals in the classroom will not be maximized.

Students Identified as Gifted and Talented

Gifted education has experienced a movement toward increased collaborative educational practices as well, with more instruction taking place in the inclusive classroom (Reis, 2003; Rogers, 2007). IDEA does not address "giftedness." For this reason, no single definition of the category is accepted (Johnsen, 2009; Zirkel, 2009). In 1972, the first definition for this category was presented in a report to Congress. This report was entitled "Education of the Gifted" (Marland, 1972). The No Child Left Behind Act of 2001 includes the following definition of *giftedness*:

> Students, children, or youth who give evidence of high achievement capability in areas such as intellectual, creative, artistic, or leadership capacity, or in specific academic fields, and who need services and activities not ordinarily provided by the school in order to fully develop those capabilities. (Title IX, Part A, Section 9101 [22])

Unfortunately, a misconception of the gifted and talented population is that they will be "okay" on their own; they will succeed with or without effective teaching. This is not the case. It is estimated that 10%–20% of all underachieving members of this category drop out of school (Heward, 2009). Another concern about this category is the possible underrepresentation of minority groups and females (Ford, 1998; Friend, 2011; Grant & Grant, 2000). Many articles report that African-American students are overrepresented in all categories of special education except for one, gifted education, where they are severely underrepresented (Cartledge, Gardner, & Ford, 2009; Grant & Barger-Anderson, 2009; Young, Wright, & Laster, 2005).

Heward (2009) reports that most students identified as gifted are receiving their instruction in the general education classroom. Landrum (2002) reports many benefits from the collaborative model for both the general education teacher and the gifted teacher; however, schools often do not have a gifted teacher available for collaboration. Thus, ownership of meeting the needs for this population is placed on the general education teacher. It is widely accepted that students in this category should be educated in an inclusive classroom. However, critics are concerned that general education teachers will not differentiate effectively or successfully meet their diverse needs (Friend, 2011).

"At-Risk" Learners and English Language Learners

Students who make up the "at-risk" category of learners are diverse. Mercer and Mercer note that these students may have "varying characteristics such as disabilities, poverty, limited family support, cultural differences, language differences, ineffective teaching, and lack of educational funding" (2005, p. 4). However, according to Mercer and Mercer, the commonality is that these students are experiencing school failure without any special assistance or support. Fortunately, co-teaching and collaborative general and special education teachers are occurring more often and should promote the learning of all students within the classroom, no matter whether they are "identified" or not (Friend, 2011).

Students whose primary language is not English are identified as English language learners (ELLs). The most common second language in the United States is overwhelmingly Spanish (75%). The second largest language group of ELLs comprises speakers of Asian/Pacific Islander languages (10%). The number of students identified as ELLs is increasing and attracting more attention. The rates of ELLs in classrooms have risen more than 9% from 1979 to 2007, and the estimated number of ELLs in U.S. schools is 20% (National Center for Educational Statistics, 2007). Collaborative teaching has been proven effective for instruction with ELLs (Honigsfeld & Dove, 2008; Waxman & Tellez, 2002; York-Barr, Ghere, & Sommerness, 2007). In one report, student achievement has shown a significant increase since collaborative efforts have been implemented between an ELL teacher and a general education teacher (York-Barr et al., 2007).

STUDIES OF THE CO-DESIGN MODEL

To date, the Co-Design Model has been implemented to some degree in more than 70 public and alternative education programs in Pennsylvania, Iowa, Texas, and the U.S. Virgin Islands. The Co-Design Model has also been presented at more than 15 international, national, state, and local conferences. Because of the promotion of ongoing support from administration and via professional development and classroom observations, the Co-Design Model is more likely to make an impact when implementation of the elements and pathways are consistent and continual (Hoover, Barger-Anderson, Isherwood, & Merhaut, 2010).

As with any type of program and initiative, it is necessary to measure the impact of moving from research and training to implementation and practice. One of the most important features of the Co-Design Model is its adaptability to any educational entity, grade level, culture, or dynamics of faculty and student population. There is no single "silver bullet" to achieve a quick fix in education. However, this is one approach that will respect the individual school culture and create a paradigm shift simultaneously (Hoover et al., 2010).

A GLANCE INTO THE FUTURE

Scruggs, Mastropieri, and McDuffie (2007) conducted a metasynthesis of 32 qualitative studies considering co-teaching within inclusive classrooms. Striking similarities in the results were identified. First, most of the participants reported that co-teaching is supported but only if certain areas of need are addressed. These dimensions include allowance for common planning, administrative support, and professional development.

The Co-Design Model promotes the implementation and allowance of these areas, as well as other necessary elements, such as common philosophies for classroom management, discussion of site assembly, assessment techniques, creation and execution of appropriate adaptations, and curriculum knowledge (Barger-Anderson, Isherwood, & Merhaut, 2010). Because of the ever-changing composition of our heterogeneous classrooms (Friend, 2011; Werts, Culatta, & Tompkins, 2007) and accountability for learning via high-stakes testing (No Child Left Behind Act of 2001), the Co-Design Model looks to embrace qualities of both collaborative practices and recommended strategies for instructional implementation. Participants involved in implementing the Co-Design Model must recognize the value of collaboration with professionals of similar and different skill sets. The Co-Design Model is also applicable for training preservice teachers and for embracing paraprofessional skill sets.

Collaboration as a professional practice is evident and growing in demand. It is necessary for teachers and all participants in the schools to join forces and work toward the common goal: success of all students (Friend, 2011; Isherwood, Barger-Anderson, Merhaut, Badgett, & Katsafanas, 2011). Implementation of the Co-Design Model will promote successful collaborative practices in inclusive settings to benefit various learning styles, abilities, and diversity in classrooms.

REFERENCES

Barger-Anderson, R., Isherwood, R., & Merhaut, J. (2010, February). *The Co-Design Model: A collaborative approach to inclusive education.* Paper presented at the 47th Annual International Conference of the Learning Disabilities Association of America, Baltimore, MD.

Cartledge, G., Gardner, R., III, & Ford, D.Y. (2009). *Diverse learners with exceptionalities: Culturally responsive teaching in the inclusive classroom.* Upper Saddle River, NJ: Pearson Education.

Cullen, M. (2007). Voices of leadership: Stronger together. *Educational Leadership, 65*(10), 90–92.

Ford, D.Y. (1998). The underrepresentation of minority students in gifted education: Problems and promises in recruitment and retention. *The Journal of Special Education, 32*(1), 4–14.

Friend, M. (2011). *Special education: Contemporary perspectives for school professionals* (3rd ed.). Boston, MA: Pearson.

Friend, M., & Cook, L. (2010). *Interactions: Collaboration skills for school professionals* (6th ed.). Boston, MA: Allyn & Bacon.

Grant, P.A., & Barger-Anderson, R. (2009). The misrepresentation of culturally and linguistically diverse students in special education. *Multicultural Learning and Teaching, 4*(2), 70–79.

Grant, P.A., & Grant, P.B. (2000). Teaching students with gifts and talents. In F.E. Obiakor, S.A. Burkhardt, F. Rotatroi, & T. Wahlberg (Eds.), *Intervention techniques for individuals with exceptionalities in inclusive settings: Advances in special education* (pp. 149–172). Stamford, CT: JAI Press.

Heward, W.L. (2009). *Exceptional children: An introduction to special education* (9th ed.). Upper Saddle River, NJ: Pearson Merrill Prentice Hall.

Honigsfeld, A., & Dove, M. (2008). Co-teaching in the ESL classroom. *Delta Kappa Gamma Bulletin, 74*(2), 8–14.

Hoover, K., Barger-Anderson, R., Isherwood, R., & Merhaut, J. (2010). The Co-Design Model: A collaborative approach to inclusive education. *Journal of Scholarly Endeavor, X,* 54.

Individuals with Disabilities Education Improvement Act (IDEA) of 2004, PL 108-446, 20 U.S.C. §§ 1400 *et seq.*

Isherwood, R., Barger-Anderson, R., Merhaut, J., Badgett, R., & Katsafanas, J. (2011). First year co-teaching: Disclosed through focus group and individual interviews. *Learning Disabilities: A Multidisciplinary Journal, 17*(3), 113–122.

Johnsen, S.K. (2009). Identification. In B. Kerr (Ed.), *Encyclopedia of giftedness, creativity, and talent.* Thousand Oaks, CA: Sage Publications.

Kloo, A., & Zigmond, N. (2008). Coteaching revisited: Redrawing the blueprint. *Preventing School Failure, 52,* 12–20.

Landrum, M. (2002). *Consultation in gifted education: Teachers working together to serve students.* Mansfield, CT: Creative Learning.

Little, M.E., & Dieker, L. (2009). Co-teaching: Two are better than one. *Principal Leadership, 9,* 43–46.

Magiera, K., & Zigmond, N. (2005). Co-teaching in middle school classrooms under routine conditions: Does the instructional experience differ for students with disabilities in co-taught and solo-taught classes? *Learning Disabilities Research and Practice, 20*(2), 79–85.

Marland, S.P. (1972). *Education of the gifted and talented—Volume 1: Report to the Congress of the United States by the U.S. Commission of Education.* Washington, DC: U.S. Government Printing Office.

Mercer, C.D., & Mercer, A.R. (2005). *Teaching students with learning problems* (7th ed.). Upper Saddle River, NJ: Prentice Hall.

Murawski, W.W. (2006). Student outcomes in co-taught secondary English classes: How can we improve? *Reading and Writing Quarterly, 22,* 227–246

National Center for Educational Statistics (2007). *Postsecondary education quick information system: Survey of students with disabilities at postsecondary education institutions.* Washington, DC: U.S. Department of Education.

No Child Left Behind Act of 2001, PL 107-110, 115 Stat. 1425, 20 U.S.C. §§ 6301 *et seq.*

Reis, S.M. (2003). Reconsidering regular curriculum for high-achieving students, gifted underachievers, and the relationship between gifted and regular education. In J.H. Borland (Ed.), *Rethinking gifted education* (pp. 186–200). New York, NY: Teachers College Press.

Rogers, K.B. (2007). Lessons learned about educating the gifted and talented: A synthesis of the research on educational practice. *Gifted Child Quarterly, 51,* 382–396.

Scruggs, T.E., Mastropieri, M.A., & McDuffie, K.A. (2007). Co-teaching in inclusive classrooms: A metasynthesis of qualitative research. *Council for Exceptional Children, 73*(4), 392–416.

Waxman, H.C., & Tellez, K. (2002). Effective teaching practices for English language learners. *Spotlight on Success, 705,* 1–2.

Werts, M.G., Culatta, R.A., & Tompkins, J.R. (2007). *Fundamentals of special education: What every teacher needs to know* (3rd ed.). Upper Saddle River, NJ: Pearson.

York-Barr, J., Ghere, G., & Sommerness, J. (2007). Collaborative teaching to increase ELL student learning: A three-year urban elementary case study. *Journal of Education for Students Placed at Risk, 12*(3), 301–335.

Young, C., Wright, J., & Laster, J. (2005). Instructing African American students. *Education, 125*(3), 516–524.

Zirkel, P.A. (2009). What does the law say? *Teaching Exceptional Children, 41*(5), 73–75.

Appendix

Checklist for Assembly of Site

Curriculum Discussion Starters

Developing Common Principles with Your Co-Teaching Partner

Behavior Management Discussion Starter

Matrix of Student Needs

Shared Assessment

Co-Design Time Planning Calendar

Co-Teach Lesson Plan

Co-Teaching Observation Form

Co-Teaching Postobservation Conference Form

Checklist for Assembly of Site

Item	Yes *Discussed together and decided it is needed at this time.*	No *Discussed together and decided it is not needed at this time.*
Two teacher desks		
Both teachers' names displayed in room		
Both teachers' pictures displayed in room		
Both names listed on assignments		
Both names listed on communications sent to parents		
Table in room to provide small-group instruction		
Classroom rules posted and signed by both teachers		
Student desk arrangement (consideration of special needs; do not put all students with an individualized education program in one area)		
Additional area		
Additional area		

In *Strategic Co-Teaching in Your School: Using the Co-Design Model* by Richael Barger-Anderson,
Robert S. Isherwood, & Joseph Merhaut
(2013; Paul H. Brookes Publishing Co., Inc.)

Curriculum Discussion Starters

Curriculum area: _____

Unit	Topic/skills	Responsibility

In *Strategic Co-Teaching in Your School: Using the Co-Design Model* by Richael Barger-Anderson,
Robert S. Isherwood, & Joseph Merhaut
(2013; Paul H. Brookes Publishing Co., Inc.)

Developing Common Principles with Your Co-Teaching Partner

List of principles	My principles	Your principles	Possible solutions

In *Strategic Co-Teaching in Your School: Using the Co-Design Model* by Richael Barger-Anderson,
Robert S. Isherwood, & Joseph Merhaut
(2013; Paul H. Brookes Publishing Co., Inc.)

Behavior Management Discussion Starter

Does anyone have an individualized education program (IEP)?
    Names
    Roles for execution
	Discussion tips: During the planning process, both teachers should discuss this question to determine which students in the classroom have IEPs and what specially designed instruction is required for them.

Class rules
    Expectations
    Who will develop rules?
    How many rules?
    Posting of rules
	Discussion tips: When setting up the behavior management plan, the teachers need to discuss and reach agreement on student expectations. Who will develop the rules for the classroom, or will this be decided together?
	
	How many rules will there be, and how will they be displayed in the classroom?

Consequences
    Positive
    Negative
	Discussion tips: Both positive and negative consequences should be used for behavior management. Both teachers need to discuss exactly how the consequences will be handed down. A positive consequence can be as simple as assigning a percentage of the student's grade for appropriate behavior.
	
	A negative consequence could be as simple as having a behavior grade that starts at 100% and slowly taking points away for inappropriate behavior.

Need for classwide behavior plans
    Types of reinforcers:
        Intrinsic
        Extrinsic
	Discussion tips: Most teachers would agree that intrinsic reinforcement is best. Students need to feel good about doing something good or doing well on an assignment. Praising the student helps to intrinsically reinforce positive actions. Extrinsic reinforcement focuses more on giving the student some type of reward for doing well. In the planning process, the co-teachers need to decide what works best for which students.

In *Strategic Co-Teaching in Your School: Using the Co-Design Model* by Richael Barger-Anderson,
Robert S. Isherwood, & Joseph Merhaut
(2013; Paul H. Brookes Publishing Co., Inc.)

Matrix of Student Needs

Student name	Area identified	Sources for identification	Other

In *Strategic Co-Teaching in Your School: Using the Co-Design Model* by Richael Barger-Anderson,
Robert S. Isherwood, & Joseph Merhaut
(2013; Paul H. Brookes Publishing Co., Inc.)

Shared Assessment

Type of assessment	Adaptations	Responsibility

In *Strategic Co-Teaching in Your School: Using the Co-Design Model* by Richael Barger-Anderson,
Robert S. Isherwood, & Joseph Merhaut
(2013; Paul H. Brookes Publishing Co., Inc.)

Co-Design Time Planning Calendar

Month:

<table>
<tr><td></td><td></td><td></td><td></td><td></td></tr>
<tr><td></td><td></td><td></td><td></td><td></td></tr>
<tr><td></td><td></td><td></td><td></td><td></td></tr>
<tr><td></td><td></td><td></td><td></td><td></td></tr>
<tr><td></td><td></td><td></td><td></td><td></td></tr>
<tr><td></td><td></td><td></td><td></td><td></td></tr>
<tr><td></td><td></td><td></td><td></td><td></td></tr>
</table>

Co-Teach Lesson Plan

Co-teachers:		Date:	Room:	Day:	Grade:	Time/period:	Subject:

Co-teaching model:	__ One teach/one assist __ Parallel __ Stations __ Team __ Alternative __ Other	Co-plan time:

State standard	Short-term objectives	Evaluation
	1. Modifications:	
	2. Modifications:	
	3. Modifications:	
	4. Modifications:	

Materials:	Other:

Introduction: *Teacher responsible:*	
Lesson sequence: *Teacher responsible:*	
Closing: *Teacher responsible:*	
Homework: *Teacher responsible to assign:* *Teacher responsible to correct:*	
Reflections:	

In *Strategic Co-Teaching in Your School: Using the Co-Design Model* by Richael Barger-Anderson,
Robert S. Isherwood, & Joseph Merhaut
(2013; Paul H. Brookes Publishing Co., Inc.)

Co-Teaching Observation Form

General education teacher: _____

Co-teacher: _____

Viewer name: _____

Subject: _____   Grade: _____

Date of observation: _____   Time: _____

Directions: *Check "Y" if the behavior is observed and "N" if it is not observed during the lesson.*

I. Professionalism

1. Both teachers were present at the beginning of the period.   Y_____   N_____
2. Both teachers appear to have positive rapport with all students.   Y_____   N_____
3. Both teachers managed some aspect of the instruction.   Y_____   N_____
4. Both teachers communicated in a positive manner with each other.   Y_____   N_____
5. There were equal spaces for both co-teachers in the classroom.   Y_____   N_____
6. The names of both co-teachers appear on important class documents.   Y_____   N_____

II. Instruction

1. Both teachers provided instruction to some or all of the students.   Y_____   N_____
2. There was evidence that at least one co-teaching model was used.   Y_____   N_____
   (Circle model[s] used: parallel, alternative, stations, team, one teach/one assist)
3. Evidence of differentiated instruction was observed.   Y_____   N_____
4. Students were organized for instruction based on needs.   Y_____   N_____
5. Lesson was delivered utilizing more than one modality.   Y_____   N_____
6. Co-teachers implemented instruction through group work or in pairs.   Y_____   N_____
7. Both teachers used questioning strategies to engage students.   Y_____   N_____
8. Both teachers provided scaffolding during learning opportunities.   Y_____   N_____
9. Teachers modeled intellectual discussion with each other during lesson.   Y_____   N_____
10. Students asked both teachers for assistance or clarification.   Y_____   N_____

III. Assessment

1. Both teachers checked students for understanding during the lesson.   Y_____   N_____
2. Adaptations were made to assessments based on students' needs.   Y_____   N_____
3. Assessment data were used to group students for instruction.   Y_____   N_____
4. Both teachers were responsible for grading student work.   Y_____   N_____
5. Both teachers were responsible for evaluating all students.   Y_____   N_____

IV. Classroom management

1. Both teachers actively and consistently reinforced rules.   Y_____   N_____
2. Both teachers implemented behavior plans for individual students.   Y_____   N_____
3. Both teachers redirected off-task behavior when observed.   Y_____   N_____
4. Both teachers handled some aspect of the housekeeping duties.   Y_____   N_____

Directions: *Provide narrative feedback of the observation in this section. Results should be shared with the teacher(s), either individually or as a team.*

Teacher communication *(level of verbal and nonverbal communication between both co-teachers and between co-teachers and students):*

Co-Teaching Observation Form *(continued)*

Physical organization   *(evidence that the room is shared between co-teachers, two teacher desks, and so on):*

Classroom management   *(establishment of rules, explanation of rules to students, enforcement of rules and consequences, parent contacts, establishing a sense of shared teaching as equals to the students and the parents):*

Lesson/assessment planning   *(establishment of scope and sequence, identification of type of co-teach model[s], state standards addressed, shared creation of materials):*

Adaptations/modifications   *(adjustments made to curriculum materials, allowance for additional time, physical space adjustments to allow for full participation, subtlety of arrangements, success of all students, and so on):*

Instructional presentation   *(implementation of a co-teach model, variety of learning modalities addressed, differentiated instruction, active student participation, small-group work or pairs utilized, students address both teachers, and so on):*

Assessment   *(variety of forms, authentic, both co-teachers grade assignments and create and grade assessments, and so on):*

In *Strategic Co-Teaching in Your School: Using the Co-Design Model* by Richael Barger-Anderson,
Robert S. Isherwood, & Joseph Merhaut
(2013; Paul H. Brookes Publishing Co., Inc.)

Co-Teaching Postobservation Conference Form

General education teacher: _____

Co-teacher: _____

Viewer name: _____

Subject: _____   Grade: _____

Date of observation: _____   Time: _____

Directions: *Provide narrative feedback on the observation. Results should be shared with the teacher(s) either individually or as a team.*

Overall strengths of the view:

Target areas for the next view (*identify what needs improvement*):

Action for improvement (*discuss strategies for improvement*):

Annotated Bibliography

TYPES OF DISABILITIES

The annotated bibliography provides suggested readings on several types of disabilities and other topics. These disabilities include autism, behavior and emotional disorders, gifted with learning disabilities, intellectual disabilities, and specific learning disabilities. Recommended readings for the areas of instructional considerations, assessment, and classroom management are also provided.

Autism

Callahan, K., Skukla-Mehta, S., Magee, S., & Wie, M. (2010). ABA versus TEACCH: The case for defining and validating comprehensive treatment models in autism. *Journal of Autism and Developmental Disorders, 40*(1), 74–88. doi: 10.1007/s10803-009-0834-0

Callahan and colleagues evaluate differences among treatments for students with autism and the implications of such treatments. The article compares applied behavior analysis (ABA) and TEACCH treatment programs in terms of the validity of each treatment program and the results obtained from treatment goals and progress. The article validates that the individual with autism benefits from intense therapy, but it illuminates a bigger concern about the lack of understanding of therapy selection and tolerance among educators, parents, and researchers.

Dorminy, K.P. (2009). Teaching organizational skills to children with high functioning autism and Asperger's syndrome. *Education and Training in Developmental Disabilities, 44*(4), 538–550.

The author examines the importance of organizational skills for students with high-functioning autism and Asperger syndrome. It was concluded that organizational intervention through a file box with a self-monitoring form improved assignment turn-in rates of students with developmental disabilities. With the demands of the No Child Left Behind Act of 2001 (PL 107-110), more students are becoming fully included in mainstream classes; organizational skills need to be taught just as an academic subject is taught in order for students to become independent learners.

Furniss, G. (2009). Art lessons for a young artist with Asperger's syndrome. *Art Education, 62*(3), 18–23.

The author of the article suggests that children who are diagnosed with Asperger syndrome should be encouraged to engage in art. Many children with Asperger syndrome have impressive artistic abilities. This article highlights one student's journey of creating art.

Hines, E., & Simonsen, B. (2008). The effects of picture icons on behavior for a young student with autism. *Beyond Behavior, 18*(1), 9–17.

This article focuses on a strategy developed from a study that used picture icons to aid students with autism in communication and behavior. This study used specific picture icon cards of things that the student wanted, specifically those for which the student displayed disruptive behavior when trying to obtain the items. By having these picture icons easily accessible, disruptive behavior was often eliminated because the student would use the icon to communicate effectively. Taking the time to make appropriate picture icons for a student can be an effective strategy to help eliminate communication problems and ultimately certain associated behavioral issues.

Hume, K. (2007). Visual schedules: How and why to use them in the classroom. *Autism Advocate, 48*, 44–47.

This article discusses the use of visual schedules within a school for students with autism. The author states that students with autism are often visual learners. Therefore, these students will learn the schedule better with a visual aid, as opposed to verbal prompts. Teaching students with visual cues helps them become more independent by using tools available to them. Once students have a schedule mastered, the teacher can vary it according to the students' needs.

Lytle, R., & Todd, T. (2009). Stress and the student with autism spectrum disorder. *Teaching Exceptional Children, 41*(4), 36–42. Retrieved from http://www.cec .sped.org/AM/Template.cfm?Section=Autism_Asperger_s_Syndrome& Template=/TaggedPage/TaggedPageDisplay.cfm&TPLID=37&ContentID=5598

This article focuses on the effects of stress on students with autism spectrum disorders (ASDs). According to Lytle and Todd, students with ASDs have higher levels of hormones and bodily symptoms of stress (anger, anxiety disorders, and sleep disturbances). The article also addresses ways to manage stress effectively in the classroom by reducing distractions, using a routine, and integrating a relaxation corner into the classroom.

Behavior and Emotional Disorders

Fitzpatrick, M., & Knowlton, E. (2009). Bringing evidence-based self-directed intervention practices to the trenches for students with emotional and behavior disorders. *Preventing School Failure, 53*(4), 253–266.

This article discusses the challenges that schools, families, and society have when dealing with children with emotional and behavior disorders. The article also explains how to incorporate effective self-directed intervention strategies into the classroom by way of technology. The authors of this article feel that using technology with students who have social or behavior disorders will increase their academic and social outcomes.

Humphrey, N. (2009). Including students with attention-deficit/hyperactivity disorder in mainstream schools. *British Journal of Special Education, 36*(1), 19–25.

The purpose of this article was to provide an up-to-date overview of evidence-based strategies that can be used by teachers to facilitate the inclusion of students with attention-deficit/hyperactivity disorder (ADHD). These strategies include the need to reframe ADHD; understand the role of medication; minimize distractions; provide predictability, structure, and routine; and apply cognitive and behavioral strategies. It is important for educators to create a classroom environment that accommodates students with ADHD because they have a lower threshold for distraction than other students.

Menzies, H., Lane, K., & Lee, J. (2009). Self-monitoring strategies for use in the classroom: A promising practice to support productive behavior for students with emotional or behavioral disorders. *Beyond Behavior, 18*(2), 27–35. Retrieved from Education Research Complete database.

This article discusses various strategies for a student to monitor his or her own behavior. The main focus is the child's ability to self-monitor the occurrences of a particular behavior. The authors provided the steps on how one should implement the strategy with a child who is capable of doing so. A vignette was also provided for the reader as an example of the assembly in a classroom setting.

Meyer, K., & Kelley, M.L. (2007). Improving homework in adolescents with attention-deficit/hyperactivity disorder: Self vs. parent monitoring of homework behavior and study skills. *Child and Family Behavior Therapy, 29*(4), 25–42. doi:10.1300/J019v29n04_02

This study compares the effectiveness of self-monitored and parent-monitored homework and study skills in reducing homework problems in middle school students with attention-deficit/hyperactivity disorder. The students were taught the strategy known as SQ3R (survey, question, read, write, recite). The authors found both self- and parent monitoring to be effective in improving homework completion and study skills. However, the authors also found some homework problems remained at the time of their follow-up.

Morris Kindzierski, C.M. (2009). "I like it the way it is!": Peer-revision writing strategies for students with emotional and behavior disorders. *Preventing School Failure, 54*(1), 51–59.

The basis of this article and the reason for the study were to compare the effects of independent versus peer revisions. The authors of the study found students' writings were longer and more organized when they were peer revised. The discussion that students engaged in was also positive; it was meaningful and relevant to the topic. Finally, teachers should note that writing needs to be done on a daily basis in order for improvement to take place. Students with and without disabilities can practice effective revision techniques.

Niesyn, M.E. (2009). Strategies for success: Evidence-based instructional practices for students with emotional and behavior disorders. *Preventing School Failure, 53*(4), 227–233. Retrieved from Academic Search Complete database.

This article states that most students with emotional and behavior disorders received the majority of their education inside the general education classroom. Instructional strategies to help these students are crucial. Strategies that have been known to be effective for these students are described, and details are provided. Strategies shared include teacher praise, scaffolding, independent seat work, increased opportunities for correct responses, establishing peer tutoring opportunities, student choice, direct instruction, specific behavior management strategies (token economy), classroom rules and procedures, teacher directives, student self-management strategies, self-monitoring, and self-instruction. Use of these different strategies can promote success of students with emotional and behavior disorders.

Oswald, D., & Sutherland, K. (2005). The relationship between teacher and student behavior in classrooms for students with emotional and behavioral disorders: Transactional process. *Journal of Child and Family Studies, 14,* 1–14. doi:10.1007/s10826-005-1106-z

Discussed in this article were the limitations, challenges, and developmental research completed that considered relationships between teachers and students with emotional and behavior disorders. Perhaps one of the most important points made in this article is that observation of the student and teacher must be done simultaneously. Effective interventions must be implemented if there is a strain on the relationship between teacher and student in the classroom.

Palcic, J.L., Jurbergs, N., & Kelley, M.L. (2009). A comparison of teacher and parent delivered consequences: Improving classroom behavior in low income children with ADHD. *Child and Family Behavior Therapy, 31,* 117–133. doi:10.1080/07317100902910513

This study compares the effectiveness of parent-delivered and teacher-delivered consequences for increasing academic performance and appropriate classroom behavior in students with attention-deficit/hyperactivity disorder. The authors found that both modes of delivering consequences were effective in increasing appropriate classroom behavior. The authors proposed that teacher-delivered consequences would be superior to those delivered by parents because of their immediacy. However, the study showed that parental consequences were superior to teacher consequences, perhaps because parents may deliver more potent consequences than teachers.

Pearce, L. (2009). Helping children with emotional difficulties: A response to intervention investigation. *Rural Educator, 30*(2), 34–46. Retrieved from ERIC database.

The article describes the use of response to intervention for students with emotional and behavior difficulties within the school setting. Response to intervention includes many different interventions, each with different positive and negative aspects. With the interventions, mainly applied behavior analysis and cognitive therapy, teachers and parents reported positive improvements of skill acquisition and retention. The article concludes that with the proper interventions, students developed skills to decrease maladaptive behaviors in the classroom.

Ramsey, M.L., Patterson, D.P., & Kennedy, C. (2010). Using choice to increase time on-task, task completion, and accuracy for students with emotional/behavior disorders in a residential facility. *Education and Treatment of Children, 33*(1), 1–21. doi:10.1177/1098300708330879

Students with emotional and behavioral needs commonly perform one to two grade levels behind their peers academically. The authors argue that teacher emphasis on behavior management diminishes quality and rigor of academic instruction. In the overall results of the authors' study, the students were more academically successful when provided with choices. Students with disabilities are often limited in making choices. Providing choice empowers the students, thus preventing behavior problems.

Stahr, B., Cushing, D., Lane, K., & Fox, J. (2006). Efficacy of a function-based intervention in decreasing off-task behavior exhibited by a student with ADHD. *Journal of Positive Behavior Interventions, 8*(4), 201–211. Retrieved from Education Research Complete database.

This article provides information about the success of functional-based interventions and self-monitoring of students with attention-deficit/hyperactivity disorder who show extreme cases of off-task behaviors. Functional-based interventions focus on the reason for the behavior. Often a student is off task because he or she wants to avoid something. The goal of the study was to replace the inappropriate actions with desired behaviors.

Gifted with Learning Disabilities

Coleman, M.R. (2005). Academic strategies that work for gifted students with learning disabilities. *Teaching Exceptional Children, 38*(1), 28–32.

This article is about the struggles of twice-exceptional students—that is, students who are gifted *and* at the same time experience learning difficulties. This paper talks about how teachers can apply supported learning theories to help children overcome the struggles that hinder their academic success. There are three key principles of learning: Educators must build on the student's knowledge, students must have a deep foundation of factual knowledge in order to develop competence in an area of inquiry, and a metacognitive approach to instruction can help students learn to take control of their own learning.

Eckstein, M. (2009). Enrichment 2.0: Gifted and talented education for the 21st century. *Gifted Child Today, 32,* 59–63.

The authors of this article focus on enrichment clusters as a way to meet the needs of gifted students. Enrichment clusters are groups of students across grade levels who study one topic. The students in the clusters focus on creating a product or service. Students are encouraged to use Internet tools such as podcasts and blogs. The clusters of students then present their final product or service to the selected audience. The authors recommend this model for gifted programs because it promotes collaboration between gifted students and their gifted peers.

Manning, S., Stanford, B., & Reeves, S. (2010). Valuing the advanced learner: Differentiating up. *The Clearing House, 83,* 145–149. doi:10.1080/00098651003774851

This article focuses on the importance of differentiating instruction for gifted learners. Differentiated instruction is often used for struggling learners, but the authors stress the importance of using it for gifted learners as well. The authors suggest finding out what motivates the students and creating an assignment based on those interests. It is also recommended that teachers use the Internet to find activities to challenge gifted learners.

Tretter, T.R. (2010). Systematic and sustained: Powerful approaches for enhancing deep mathematical thinking. *Gifted Child Today, 33,* 16–26.

The author of this article presents four avenues to modify math curriculum for gifted students. The article consists of specific strategies and games, such as Sprouts, that can be used to challenge students who are gifted. The author urges teachers to use these strategies in games across the curriculum in order to challenge gifted students and meet their needs.

Wery, J., & Nietfeld, J. (2010). Supporting self-regulated learning with exceptional children. *Teaching Exceptional Children, 42*(4), 70–78. Retrieved from Education Research Complete database.

This article is about how self-regulated learning is used with children who have exceptional educational needs. The key principles of self-regulated learning are attitudes, beliefs, cognitive strategies, domain knowledge, external supports, and flexibility of strategies. This article discusses a variety of ways teachers can apply these principles in the classroom.

Intellectual Disabilities

Allor, J.H., Mathes, P.G., Jones, F.G., Champlin, T.M., & Cheatham, J.P. (2010). Individualized research-based instruction for students with intellectual disabilities: Success stories. *Teaching Exceptional Children, 42*(3), 6–12.

The authors focus on three students with intellectual disabilities who struggle with reading. The students are involved in a study that seeks to determine whether methods that are successful for the at-risk student with an average IQ are successful for the student with intellectual disabilities. The authors follow the students and their success with a comprehensive reading program. Findings reveal that students made progress with intense, individualized instruction.

Goetz, K., Hulme, C., Brigstocke, S., Carroll, J., Nasir, L., & Snowling, M. (2008). Training reading and phoneme awareness skills in children with Down's syndrome. *Reading and Writing, 21*(4), 395–412. doi:10.1007/s11145-007-9089-3

The authors focused their study on a structured reading intervention focusing on phoneme segmentation and blending skills in the context of learning letter-sounds and reading words in books. Results revealed that students benefited from the initial intervention and the structured literacy program that followed.

Rose, J.L., Dodd, L., & Rose, N. (2008). Individual cognitive behavioral intervention for anger. *Journal of Mental Health Research in Intellectual Disabilities, 1,* 97–108. doi:10.1080/19315860801988368

The focus of this article is reducing inappropriate aggression in people with intellectual disabilities. The authors of the study found that cognitive-behavioral assessments were successful in reducing aggression in people with intellectual disabilities.

Specific Learning Disabilities

Campbell-Whatley, G. (2008). Teaching students about their disabilities: Increasing self-determination skills and self-concept. *International Journal of Special Education, 23*(2), 137–144.

The focus of this article was teaching students with disabilities self-determination skills. Curriculum used to teach students about their disability and coping strategies was implemented. Lessons in this curriculum were designed using the method known by the mnemonic TARGET: In this method teachers target the objectives (T), assess prior knowledge (A), role play (R), generalize to other situations (G), evaluate student attainment (E), and test transfer skills (T). Some of the skills that were taught included understanding what it means to have a learning disability, characteristics related to a learning disability, and knowing individual strengths. The study found that students had a much higher self-concept after completing the course.

Cawley, J., & Parmar, R. (2001). Literacy proficiency and science for students with learning disabilities. *Reading and Writing Quarterly, 17*(2), 105–125. doi:10.1080/105735601300007589

Many science programs require the ability to read. Many students with learning disabilities will likely have problems with this type of science program. This article provided alternatives to the reading-dependent science programs. These alternatives all had one thing in common: hands-on learning. The authors found positive results when comparing learning from a hands-on approach to the learning from a textbook-based approach. Cawley and Parmar reported higher levels of student performance in a hands-on classroom compared to performance of students in the textbook-based classroom.

Crawford, L., & Tindal, G. (2004). Effects of a read-aloud modification on a standardized reading test. *Exceptionality, 12*(2), 89–106. Retrieved from Education Research Complete database.

The authors of this article examined the read-aloud modification in the area of reading. Students in this study completed a standardized reading comprehension assessment under two different administrations. The first was standard, in which they read it themselves. The second type of administration was through video, in which the proctor read it to them. The results revealed that reading a test aloud to students improves scores.

Elksnin, L.K., & Elksnin, N. (2005, October). *Teaching students with LD essential social-emotional skills.* Invited paper presented at the Learning Disabilities Worldwide 14th Annual Congress on Learning Disabilities. Burlington, MA. Retrieved from Education Research Complete database.

The authors discuss the importance of teaching children with learning disabilities social-emotional skills. They argue that children who do not have appropriate social-emotional skills do poorly in school, and children with learning disabilities may have an especially difficult time acquiring these skills. The Elksnins propose that students with a learning disability may not acquire these skills vicariously; rather, such skills may need to be purposely taught to them. Three skills that were suggested for teaching were nonverbal communication, emotional understanding, and social-emotional problem solving. The authors include a breakdown of each skill and examples of how to implement the skills into the curriculum.

Finstein, R., Fei Yao, Y., & Jones, R. (2007). Build organizational skills in students with learning disabilities. *Intervention in School and Clinic, 42*(3), 174–178. Retrieved from Academic Search Complete database.

Organizational skills are essential for everyone; however, students with learning disabilities may struggle in this area. This article provides tips on how to guide these students to obtain the organizational skills that will help them in the future. Some of these tips include posting needed information on a bulletin board, using checklists to track activities, following a daily agenda, using an organizer or planner, pairing with a general education student, using "how-to" cards, posting reminders, and providing help in determining what to carry to school. Teaching students these organizational skills will help them avoid possible frustrations.

Hagaman, J., Luschen, K., & Reid, R. (2010). The "RAP" on reading comprehension. *Teaching Exceptional Children, 43*(1), 22–30.

The article provides bountiful information on reading comprehension. Included is a detailed explanation on the RAP strategy, which requires the students to read a paragraph (R), ask what are the main ideas and details (A), and put information into their own words (P). The stages are broken down and an example is provided.

Montague, M. (2008). Self-regulation strategies to improve mathematical problem solving for students with learning disabilities. *Learning Disability Quarterly, 31*(1), 7–44.

Self-regulation strategies are discussed in order to help improve problem solving by students with learning disabilities. Intensive literature reviews are provided from previous studies. Principles of strategy instruction are given, followed by implications for practice. Considerations for teacher education are discussed, as many teachers may not have the background necessary to properly teach problem-solving skills to students with a learning disability.

Moore, C., & Lo, L. (2008). Reading comprehension strategy: Rainbow dots. *The Journal of International Association of Special Education, 9,* 124–127.

This article focuses on a reading comprehension strategy, Rainbow Dots. The goal of Rainbow Dots is to help students process what they read so they have a clear understanding of the text. Rainbow Dots consists of four strategies: visualization, summarization, inferences, and connections. The teacher teaches minilessons focusing on these four strategies. The authors found this strategy to be effective and strongly recommend it for students with learning disabilities.

Santangelo, T., & Olinghouse, N. (2009). Effective writing instruction for students who have writing difficulties. *Focus on Exceptional Children, 42*(4), 1–20. Retrieved from Education Research Complete database.

Writing can be a daunting task for students and especially those with disabilities. Providing students with drills to improve their skills will benefit the entire classroom. When teachers use a standardized test to determine writing placement, it is vital to look at the skills that are being assessed.

Scruggs, T., Mastropieri, M.A., & Okolo, C. (2008). Science and social studies for students with disabilities. *Focus on Exceptional Children, 41*(2), 1–24.

Science and social studies have primarily been taught by relying on a textbook. The two subjects have not been readily accessible for those with disabilities. Through new research and focus on the subject matter, these subjects can be taught to those with disabilities using various techniques.

Steele, M. (2007). Helping middle school students with learning disabilities pass the federally mandated science tests: science instruction, study skills, and test-taking strategies. *Science Scope, 31*(3), 74–80.

Steele offers many strategies to help students with disabilities improve study skills, work habits, and test taking. Starting with instruction, the teacher should read instructions, organize instruction into themes and concepts, and create study guides. To improve the students' study skills, the teacher should review and allow study time and also introduce study models, visualization, and mnemonics.

Steele, M. (2010). High school students with learning disabilities: Mathematics instruction, study skills, and high stakes tests. *American Secondary Education, 38*(3), 21–28.

This article provides modifications that an instructor can undertake for students who have learning disabilities. The author focuses on subjects such as algebra and geometry. Modifications are explained that can be applied to assessments in these areas, along with study skills that students can develop to better understand mathematical material.

INSTRUCTIONAL CONSIDERATIONS

Bellamy, J.S., & Mativo, J.M. (2010). A different angle for teaching math. *Technology Teacher, 69*(7), 26–28.

This article describes the importance of using real-life situations in the teaching environment. Math and science principles can be abstract when viewed on paper, but when placed in a three-dimensional structure that the student built him- or herself, they become concrete. In summary, this article recalls the Native American proverb, "Tell me and I will forget, show me and I may not remember, involve me and I will understand" (p. 27).

Carolan, J., & Guinn, A. (2007). Differentiation: Lessons from master teachers. *Educational Leadership, 64*(5), 44–47.

According to the authors of this article, the implementation of differentiated instruction in the classroom is not just a response to diversity but also is a way for educators to allow diversity to thrive. Carolan and Guinn discuss the negative response on the part of educators to the idea of implementing differentiated instruction in the classroom, citing limited time, resources, and administrative support as educators' most common concerns. Carolan and Guinn also offer some advice for administrators looking to make training in differentiated instruction a part of their professional development efforts.

Clapper, T.C. (2010). Role play and simulation: Return to teaching for understanding. *The Education Digest, 75*(8), 39–43.

According to Clapper, role play and simulation are not being used to the fullest potential in primary and secondary classrooms. Despite proven success when used in the field of medicine, role play and simulation are overlooked by many primary and secondary educators as a way to actively engage students in learning, as well as improve critical thinking, decision making, and communication skills. The author states that role play and simulation aid students in understanding and appreciating diversity and also in practicing self-reflection. Limited class time and limited resources are noted in this article as the two main barriers to implementing role play and simulation in the classroom.

Cooper-Duffy, K., Szedia, P., & Hyer, G. (2010). Teaching literacy to students with significant cognitive disabilities. *Teaching Exceptional Children, 42*(3), 30–39.

This article provides teachers with strategies that they are able to use within their own classrooms to teach literacy, whether they are special education or general education teachers. The strategies presented give teachers ways not only to keep the students motivated but also to teach lessons to students with significant delays, whether or not they are in a small group with peers who have similar inpairments. The article also provides data demonstrating the effectiveness of the strategies discussed by the authors.

Dalgarno, B., Tinkler, J., & Winzenreid, A. (2010). The interactive whiteboard: A transitional technology supporting diverse teaching practices. *Australian Journal of Educational Technology, 26*(4), 534–552.

This article presents the findings of a study on the impact of interactive white boards. Results revealed that teachers reported a remarkable improvement in student interaction. However, a major caution is that even though teachers should change their methods, they often do not change their teaching styles enough to fully integrate the interactive white boards into the classroom.

Douglas, O., Burton, K., & Reese-Durham, N. (2008). The effects of the multiple intelligence teaching strategy on the academic achievement of eighth grade math students. *Journal of Instructional Psychology, 35*(2), 182–187. Retrieved from Education Research Complete database.

In this study, the authors used a small sample—60 eighth-grade math students—to confirm their hypothesis that using a multiple intelligence approach will lead to higher scores than the direct instruction technique. The authors feel that allowing students to learn using various hands-on activities provides a better understanding and improved behavior.

Gaytan, J. (2010). Instructional strategies to accommodate a team-teaching approach. *Business Communication Quarterly, 73*(1), 82–87. doi:10.1177/1080569909358097

The basis of this article is to make known some of the instructional strategies to facilitate team teaching. The author provides recommendations for developing effective team-teaching environments. Several pedagogical benefits of team teaching are discussed, such as interactive learning environments and the establishment of new research opportunities for faculty.

Geiken, R., Dykstra Van Meeteren, B., & Kato, T. (2009). Putting the cart before the horse: The inquiry-based curriculum. *Childhood Education, 85*(4), 260–263.

The authors of this article consider the differences between two types of classrooms. In one classroom, the teacher may stand in the front of the room lecturing the students on a topic as the students just sit and listen rather than actively participating. Within this environment, the student may be too embarrassed to ask a question for fear of being made fun of by his or her peers. In another classroom, one with an autonomous classroom environment, the students have mutual respect for both each other and the teacher. By fostering this autonomous relationship, the teacher shows the students that he or she has confidence in them to use discussion to be able to view others' perspectives and understand that not all are the same.

Grenawalt, V. (2004). Going beyond the debate: Using technology and instruction for a balanced reading program. *Teacher Librarian, 32*(2), 12–15.

Computerized reading programs have been scrutinized by avid supporters of classwide novel reading. However, programs such as Accelerated Reader and Reading Counts! provide students with individualized reading goals and encourage students to read books of interest to them, rather than something another person (usually the teacher) has chosen. Using a computerized reading program paired with a content area (e.g., history) can be a beneficial way of encouraging reading at each student's individual level while still focusing on the topic.

Hachem, A., Nabhani, M., & Bahous, R. (2008). "We can write!" The writing workshop for young learners. *Education, 36*(4), 325–337. Retrieved from ERIC database.

The article evaluates the use of differentiated instruction and the use of writing workshops to improve writing skills of elementary students. The writing workshop is designed to break the writing process down into pieces that allow teachers to develop skills necessary for on-level writing. Overall, the idea of using writing workshops allows students to express their creativity without putting strict restrictions on topics while also creating a risk-free environment. This workshop allows teachers to embrace differences and teach to the different needs of the students.

Haydon, T., Borders, C., Embury, D., & Clarke, L. (2009). Using effective instructional delivery as a classwide management tool. *Beyond Behavior, 18*(2), 12–17.

This article presents four instructional strategies to increase students' opportunities to respond during classroom instruction. Strategies can be used in any subject or classroom setting. There is a description of each tactic, a reason why one should use it, how to implement it, and potential speed bumps and solutions. A summary of a successful case study is provided for each strategy. The four strategies are choral responding, response cards, errorless learning, and wait time.

Lynch, S.A., & Warner, L. (2008). Creating lesson plans for all learners. *Kappa Delta Pi Record, 45*(1), 10–15.

Lynch and Warner begin their article with discussion of the research-based reasons for implementing differentiated instruction in the classroom, mentioning such topics as Vygotsky's sociocultural theory of learning, brain-based learning, and multiple intelligences. The authors then provide a step-by-step format for planning (and delivering) a differentiated lesson plan, and they even include an example of a lesson plan that follows the format that they developed. This article serves as an introduction to the concept of differentiated instruction and would be useful to the first-time user of differentiated instructional strategies in the primary or secondary classroom.

McIntosh, K., Herman, K., Sanford, A., McGraw, K., & Florence, K. (2004). Teaching transitions: Techniques for promoting success between lessons. *Teaching Exceptional Children, 37*(1), 32–38.

The authors of this article suggest that teachers should not assume children know the rules for transition times. These are skills that some, if not most, children need to be taught and retaught. The article shares how to plan for transitions, techniques for effective transitions, positive supervision techniques, and several examples of transition routines. With training, the children will be more successful during transition times.

Patterson, J.L., Connolly, M.C., & Ritter, S.A. (2009). Restructuring the inclusion classroom to facilitate differentiated instruction. *Middle School Journal, 41*(1), 46–52.

This article describes the use of differentiated instruction to meet the needs of all learners in a mathematics inclusion classroom. Two teachers devised a four-part instructional
model, which resulted in increased student learning. The students were engaged and an
increase in positive attitudes from the students was evident. When differentiated instruction is used, it provides the students with different options for learning the material.

Rock, M., Gregg, M., Ellis, E., & Gable, R. (2008). REACH: A framework for differentiating classroom instruction. *Preventing School Failure, 52*(2), 31–47. Retrieved
from ERIC database.

Differentiated instruction has gained much attention; however, many educators still do not
fully understand the complexity as well as the simplicity that differentiated instruction
can create inside a classroom. When the REACH model (*R*eflect on will and skill, *E*valuate
the curriculum, *A*nalyze the learners, *C*raft research-based lessons, *H*one in on the data)
is followed, differentiated instruction can be simplified, making it easier to implement in
the classroom. Differentiated instruction will allow educators to develop strategies, step-
by-step approaches, and procedures that all students, both those in general education and
those with cognitive disabilities, can use to improve achievement of educational objectives
and outcomes.

Royer, R., & Richards, P. (2008). Digital storytelling. *Learning and Leading
with Technology, 36*(3), 29–31. Retrieved from Education Research Complete
database.

This article outlines 16 recommended strategies in digital storytelling for reading comprehension. The strategies described can foster literacy development and increase reading
comprehension. Digital storytelling can build content knowledge and support struggling
readers by providing reading and writing activities. The stories can range from simple
personal narrative to complex research reports.

Sileo, J.M., & van Garderen, D. (2010). Creating optimal opportunities to learn mathematics: Blending co-teaching structures with research-based practices. *Teaching Exceptional Children, 42*(3), 14–21.

The authors discuss six different co-teaching structures. These structures are one teach/
one observe, team teaching, alternative teaching, parallel teaching, station teaching, and
one teach/one drift. They contend that these structures blend well with research-based
mathematics instruction. The authors recommend these methods for students who struggle with or have disabilities in mathematics.

Skylar, A., Higgins, K., & Boone, R. (2007). Strategies for adapting WebQuests for students with learning disabilities. *Intervention in School and Clinic, 43*(1), 20–28.

This article focuses on ways to adapt WebQuests, which are frequently used to incorporate
computers into the classroom, for students who have disabilities. Adaptations include use
of graphic organizers, annotated lists for web sites, and templates. The authors define
a WebQuest, explain why WebQuests are appropriate, and discuss the benefits of using
them with students who have learning disabilities. A step-by-step guide to modifying Web-
Quests is provided.

Supon, V. (2008). High-stakes testing: Strategies by teachers and principals for student success. *Journal of Instructional Psychology, 35*(3), 306–308. Retrieved from Education Research Complete database.

This article by Supon focuses on testing strategies and study skills. Principals and teachers recommend strategies to prepare and motivate students for high-stakes testing. The steps recommended by teachers are more academically focused, whereas administrators focus more on motivational strategies. Steps suggested by teachers include using any technological items allowed during testing in regular instruction (e.g., calculators, rulers), highlighting texts, using study guides, and using graphic organizers. Ideas from administrators include mentoring programs, a "Hall of Fame," and giving motivational pencils and stickers for rewards.

Therrien, W.J., Hughes, C., Cory, K., & Mokhtari, K. (2009). Effectiveness of a test-taking strategy on achievement in essay test for students with learning disabilities. *Journal of Learning Disabilities, 42*(1), 14–23. doi:10.1177/0022219408326218

This article highlights the importance of students becoming competent writers. A study was conducted to see whether an essay-writing strategy would effectively improve achievement scores for students with reading and writing disabilities. A six-step essay-writing strategy was used with a test group of seventh- and eighth-grade students. Results revealed that students in the test group significantly outperformed those in the control group.

ASSESSMENT

Aylward, G. (2010). Visual formative assessments: The use of images to quickly assess and record student learning. *Science Scope, 33*(6), 41–45.

Aylward describes the use of visual formative assessments in a middle school science class as a quick and effective way to assess students. After lessons or units, the students establish a visual response grid that is teacher guided. The drawing responses are to be quick and simple, to make the grid more efficient to assess. With a quick assessment and simple rubric, the teacher can easily determine who would benefit from reteaching.

Demski, J. (2009). Assess. Instruct. Repeat. *The Journal, 36*(5), 1–7.

This article deals with the response to intervention as a strategy for identifying and assisting at-risk students without assigning them to special needs services. It refers to the necessity of a consistent and constant assessment practice, both in and out of the classroom. The linking of instruction and assessment is the core point of the article. Placing students into certain tiers and monitoring their progress allows students to progress through each tier until they are learning more with less assistance.

Garrison, C., & Ehringhaus, M. (n.d.). *Formative and summative assessments in the classroom.* Retrieved January 16, 2011, from http://www.nmsa.org/Publications/WebExclusive/Assessment/tabid/1120/Default.aspx

The article defines the difference between formative and summative assessment and the uses for each type of assessment. The authors observe that the classroom needs to be a balance of each type of assessment with correlating strategies. Assessment is a tool used within the classroom. Balancing assessment types creates a clearer picture of the strengths and concerns of each student, along with the instruction of the concepts.

Harris, M. (2009). Implementing portfolio assessment. *Young Children, 64*, 82–85.

Portfolio assessment is an effective way of showing a student's progress over time. For a portfolio to be considered a complete assessment, it must contain samples of student work over time, the teacher's written observations, anecdotal records, a checklist of traits and/ or behaviors, rating scales, and interviews with the student and his or her family. Portfolio assessment is an easy way for parents and other educators to view firsthand how a student's work has changed over time. In addition, children take more pride in their own accomplishments when they can see improvements.

Jackson, C., & Larkin, M. (2002). RUBRIC: Teaching students to use grading rubrics. *Teaching Exceptional Children, 35*(1), 40. Retrieved from Education Research Complete database.

This article discusses the benefits and the importance of using a rubric when assessing student work. The authors state that students often have no idea why they received the grade that they did. Using rubrics and teaching students how to use them allows students to focus on what the teacher wants, allows them to understand where a grade came from, and opens communication for self-assessment and peer assessment.

Kleinert, H., Green, P., Hurte, M., Clayton, J., & Oetinger, C. (2002). Creating and using meaningful alternate assessments. *Teaching Exceptional Children, 34*(4), 40–47.

This assessment article focuses on students taking control of managing and evaluating their own learning. The authors provide helpful strategies for integrating alternate assessments into the ongoing assessments. The tactics described take work away from the teachers so they can focus on meeting academic objectives. When children take control of helping to assess their own work, they are enhancing their learning because they are helping in their own education. A performance-based assessment is the primary alternate assessment discussed.

Parrish, P.R., & Stodden, R.A. (2009). Aligning assessment and instruction with state standards for children with significant disabilities. *Teaching Exceptional Children, 41*(4), 46–56.

This article discusses how a teacher can align the assessments used in the classroom to state standards. There are many examples and ideas for how to set up the classroom. Making alignment charts and student portfolios are two successful ideas, according to the article.

Risko, V.J., & Walker-Dalhouse, D. (2010). Making the most of assessments to inform instruction. *The Reading Teacher, 63*(5), 420–422.

The authors contend that using benchmark goal assessments given periodically throughout the year to gauge and adjust instruction is not effective. They suggest that formative assessments be given frequently throughout the year based on the classroom curriculum. Research has shown that students made gains when teachers used formative assessment to guide their instruction, as opposed to benchmark assessments for forming instructional decisions.

Stahl, K.A., & Bravo, M.A. (2010). Contemporary classroom vocabulary assessment for content areas. *Reading Teacher, 63*(7), 566–578. doi:10.1598/RT.63.7.4

This article is presented to help teachers feel confident in developing vocabulary assessments that are effective and useful in the classroom. Typically vocabulary is assessed at the end of a unit by way of a multiple-choice or fill-in-the-blank test. These types of assessment do not indicate whether the student knows the meaning of the words. The article provides techniques that teachers can use to check for understanding and vocabulary growth with their students.

CLASSROOM MANAGEMENT

Anderson, C., & Spaulding, S. (2007). Using positive behavior support to design effective classrooms. *Beyond Behavior, 16*(3), 27–31.

Universal strategies for using positive behavior supports are shared in this article. Tactics can be implemented for all students to help reduce a range of behavior problems. Teachers are encouraged to take a proactive, consistent approach when using positive behavior supports. Three areas are emphasized in the article: defining and teaching the expected behavior and rules, acknowledging students showing the behavior, and responding to problems with a consistent and fair approach. The article shares means of implementing this approach into a classroom setting.

Beaty-O'Ferrall, M., Green, A., & Hanna, F. (2010). Classroom management strategies for difficult students: Promoting change through relationships. *Middle School Journal, 41*(4), 4–11. Retrieved from Education Research Complete database.

This article offers suggestions and strategies for middle school educators to promote positive personal relationships with their students. The greater the opportunity for middle school educators to build positive relationships, the more likely it is that effective classroom learning will take place. Some of the biggest challenges educators of young adolescents face are centered around being prepared to deal with their developing bodies, knowledge, and life skills.

Boniecki, K., & Moore, S. (2003). Breaking the silence: Using a token economy to reinforce classroom participation. *Teaching of Psychology, 30*(3), 224.

In this article, the authors describe the introduction of a token economy to a large classroom. Students earned tokens for participation. Once they earned the tokens, they were able to exchange them for extra credit. The authors' data revealed students were participating more during the token economy. After the token economy was removed, the students did not participate as much, and results showed that they declined back to their baseline performance.

Cook, M. (2005). The disruptive or ADHD child: What to do when kids won't sit still and be quiet. *Focus on Exceptional Children, 37*(7), 1–8. Retrieved from Education Research Complete database.

This article discusses using behavioral strategies in a classroom, especially for children with attention-deficit/hyperactivity disorder, oppositional defiant disorder, and conduct disorder. Behavioral strategies that work well with these students and should be taught include anger management and problem-solving techniques. Behavioral contracts are also discussed and should include the identified behavior and rewards offered to that student.

Gable, R., Hendrickson, J.M., & Hester, P.P. (2009), Forty years later—The value of praise, ignoring, and rules for preschoolers at risk for behavior disorders. *Education and Treatment of Children, 32*(4), 513–535.

Research shows that children who have behavior problems will have a difficult time with the educational aspect of the classroom. This article discusses the three most researched behavioral techniques, which are praise, ignoring, and classroom rules. The article takes a look at each of the three strategies and discusses the positives and negatives of each approach. Used appropriately, these strategies can be extremely effective.

Haydon, T., Borders, C., Embury, D., & Clarke, L. (2009). Using effective instructional delivery as a classwide management tool. *Beyond Behavior, 18*(2), 12–17.

Almost every educator has had at least one student who, no matter what the teacher tried, continued to disrupt the classroom. This article offers several behavioral strategies to use for just that student. Linking that one student into part of the classroom learning experience often gives that student ownership over his or her own learning and behavior. If the entire class is taught appropriate response techniques, such as choral responding, wait time, errorless learning, and the use of response cards, the student who engages in disruptive behavior also learns about self-control in a way that does not draw attention to the student's unfavorable verbal interruptions.

Jolivette, K., Gallagher, P., Morrier, M., & Lambert, R. (2008). Preventing problem behaviors in young children with disabilities. *Exceptionality, 16*(2), 78–92. doi:10.1080/09362830801981195

In the article, the authors discuss different types of prevention strategies for children who have behavior problems. They discuss promoting healthy, effective parenting strategies; providing interventions; and addressing the needs of families. They also state that interventions should be implemented early in a child's life. Children should also be given choices to increase compliance.

Kraft, M. (2010). From ringmaster to conductor: 10 simple techniques can turn an unruly class into a productive one. *Kappan, 91*(7), 41–47. Retrieved from ERIC database.

This article gives teachers different techniques to use in the classroom to encourage learning rather than having to manage inappropriate behaviors. It states that this teacher-as-conductor approach can replace the chaos of a mismanaged classroom. It is suggested that teachers using a relevant curriculum and challenging lesson plan that incorporate project-based learning have the best behaved students. The article also states that selecting two or three essential rules for maintaining order in the classroom and enforcing them minimizes students' confusion about what is expected of them.

Malmgren, K.W., Trezek, B.J., & Paul, P.V. (2005). Models of classroom management as applied to the secondary classroom. *The Clearing House, 79*(1), 36–39. Retrieved from Academic OneFile database.

Classroom management can be difficult and is often cited as a reason teachers leave the profession. This article describes three models of behavior management: assertive discipline, logical consequences, and teacher effectiveness training. Examples of how to use each model are provided. The assertive discipline model emphasizes reward and consequences and "catching students being good." The logical consequences model focuses on meeting students' needs for acceptance while using consequences to shape behavior. The teacher effectiveness training model emphasizes the importance of giving control of classroom behavior over to the students by teaching them self-control and management strategies.

Partin, T.C.M., Robertson, R.E., Maggin, D.M., Oliver, R.M., & Wehby, J.H. (2010). Using teacher praise and opportunities to respond to promote appropriate student behavior. *Preventing School Failure, 54*(3), 172–178. doi:10.1080/10459880903493179

This article addresses the fact that two teacher-centered strategies have been found to decrease inappropriate student behavior and increase appropriate student behavior. The strategies are the delivery of teacher praise as positive reinforcement for students' appropriate behavior and the provision of high rates of opportunities for students to respond correctly to academic questions, tasks, or demands. The authors present suggestions for teachers on how to use praise and opportunities to respond effectively in urban classroom settings.

Index

Tables and figures are indicated by *t* and *f,* respectively.

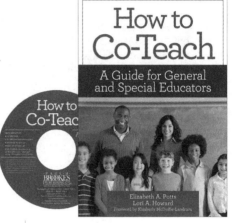